MAINTAINING PROFESSIONAL COMPETENCE

Sherry L. Willis
Samuel S. Dubin
Editors

MAINTAINING PROFESSIONAL COMPETENCE

*Approaches to
Career Enhancement,
Vitality, and Success
Throughout a Work Life*

 Jossey-Bass Publishers
San Francisco • Oxford • 1990

MAINTAINING PROFESSIONAL COMPETENCE
Approaches to Career Enhancement, Vitality, and Success Throughout a Work Life
by Sherry L. Willis and Samuel S. Dubin, Editors

Copyright © 1990 by: Jossey-Bass Inc., Publishers
350 Sansome Street
San Francisco, California 94104
&
Jossey-Bass Limited
Headington Hill Hall
Oxford OX3 0BW

Library of Congress Cataloging-in-Publication Data

Willis, Sherry L.
  Maintaining professional competence : approaches to career
enhancement, vitality, and success throughout a worklife / Sherry L.
Willis, Samuel S. Dubin, Editors.
    p. cm. — (The Jossey-Bass higher education series) (The
Jossey-Bass management series)
    ISBN 1-55542-227-6
    1. Career development. 2. Professions. 3. Performance.
I. Dubin, Samuel Sanford, date. II. Title. III. Series.
IV. Series: The Jossey-Bass management series.
HF5549.5.C35W55 1990
650.14 — dc20   89-77573
                                                                    CIP

Manufactured in the United States of America

JACKET DESIGN BY WILLI BAUM

FIRST EDITION

Code 9021

A joint publication of
The Jossey-Bass
Higher Education Series
and
The Jossey-Bass
Management Series

Consulting Editor
Adult and Continuing Education

Alan Knox
University of Wisconsin, Madison

Contents

ix

Contents

Preface

There is a growing recognition, in both the public and private sectors, that professionals need to continue to develop and maintain their professional competence throughout their work life. Because of the current knowledge explosion and rapid rate of technological change, midcareer professionals must spend more time in maintaining and enhancing their professional competence, or they will face the threat of obsolescence. In addition, increased foreign competition has forced American companies to invest more heavily in research and development activities, requiring competent, up-to-date employees.

Maintenance of professional competence is a rapidly evolving area of study. The literature is diverse, however, and not easily accessible. Much of the conceptual and empirical work has been discipline specific and published in specialty journals or as internal reports.

Maintaining Professional Competence contributes to the study of the maintenance of professional competence in three areas. First, it gives a cross-disciplinary review and discussion of several contemporary approaches from fields such as engineering, medicine, economics, and psychology. It provides a multi-

disciplinary perspective on procedures for assessing professional competence, as well as approaches to maintaining it.

Second, several chapters present models or conceptual
frameworks for maintaining professional competence. Although they focus on different aspects, each model highlights
the reciprocal relationship between personal characteristics of
the individual and features of the work environment, both of
which continue to develop and change throughout a work life.
Our focus is on competence in midcareer and senior-level professionals, rather than entry-level personnel, and we emphasize
a developmental, rather than a remedial, view of competence.
Maintaining professional competence is seen as a lifelong en-
deavor that involves continual enhancement throughout one's
career, in contrast with the "catch-up," "after the fact" perspective
of a remedial approach.

Third, several chapters in this volume suggest emergent
directions and needs within the field. The contributors, leading
authorities within their respective disciplines, are well qualified
to outline future trends and directions.

Audience for the Book

The primary audience for this volume are those in academia, in
industry, and in professional societies who assist professionals
in maintaining professional competence. Within academia, this
audience is researchers and educators in fields such as higher
education, adult education, continuing education, industrial
and educational psychology, business and management, organizational behavior, health care service provision, and instructional technology. The substantive level of the material is suitable for graduate seminars, training courses, and continuing
education workshops.

Within industry, the topic of maintaining competence is
of concern to professionals in personnel and human resource
management, executive development programs, midcareer retraining, and supervisory personnel. This book will serve as a
resource for planning groups and those who organize con-

ferences and workshops that are concerned with human resource management and development.

Many professional organizations and societies provide the primary mechanisms and resources for their membership to maintain professional competence. This book will be useful to organizational staff members who design and implement professional development and continuing education activities. Finally, the book should be of interest to professionals in government and military services who have instructional and supervisory roles.

Organization of the Book

Maintaining Professional Competence is organized in three major parts. Part One provides a general introduction and discusses issues related to the maintenance of professional competence at the levels of the individual, the work organization, and society. Chapters in this part present several models that focus on the reciprocal interaction between personal and environmental influences.

Part Two focuses on defining and measuring professional competence. Its chapters deal with delineating the professional's role and the knowledge base and skills required to function competently as a professional. Models for conceptualizing competence as a unitary versus multidimensional construct are considered, and procedures for validly assessing the current level of competence are discussed.

Part Three presents three approaches to maintaining professional competence: creating a work environment that fosters competence, training in specific skills considered deficient in midcareer professionals, and self-directed updating via electronic information systems.

It is important to note here that the literature on this subject is in its infancy. At present, the study of professional competence is confined to specific disciplines; most researchers have examined the issues with respect to a single profession. As a result, most of the chapters in this volume view competence through the lens of a single field (engineering, medicine, management). There has been little attempt to study professional competence across different professions.

Although the editors have encouraged consistency in use of certain terms, terminology does vary across chapters. This is a reflection of the current evolution of the field, the multidisciplinary approaches, and the multifaceted nature of the phenomena. In the absence of integrative studies, general definitions or models are lacking. The efforts of many contributors to extend their findings beyond their own profession suggest that generalizing current competence models may someday be possible. At present, however, much of the material in this book must be considered preliminary and speculative. It is intended to be provocative and creative, rather than confirmatory.

Acknowledgments

We would like to thank our colleagues and graduate students at The Pennsylvania State University for the many ways they have contributed to our study of professional competence and to our own professional development. Sherry L. Willis expresses appreciation to the National Institute on Aging for providing the initial funding for her research in this area; this book is an outgrowth of that support. The editorial and production staff at Jossey-Bass have our gratitude for their patience, encouragement, and help. Finally, we would like to acknowledge the love, support, and confidence in our own professional competence shown by our respective spouses, K. Warner Schaie and Lydia S. Dubin.

State College, Pennsylvania   Sherry L. Willis
January 1990   Samuel S. Dubin

The Contributors

Richard D. Arvey is the Carlson Professor of Industrial Relations in the Industrial Relations Center at the University of Minnesota. He has been a member of psychology faculties of the University of Tennessee and the University of Houston as well as a visiting professor at the University of California, Berkeley. He is the author of *Fairness in Selecting Employees*, which has been widely cited as a standard in employee selection. Arvey's primary research interests include the selection and placement of employees, discrimination and bias in selection, job analysis and classification, motivation and job satisfaction, work redesign, and aversive control systems in employment. He is a fellow of the division of industrial and organizational psychology of the American Psychological Association, serves on the editorial boards of the *Journal of Applied Psychology* and *Personnel Psychology*, and has served in several professional offices.

Alain Y. Dessaint is a research anthropologist and most recently worked as associate editor of *Psychological Abstracts*. He has been the director of public programs and research for the Southern Maryland Regional Library, and has also taught an-

thropology at American University in Washington, D.C., the
University of Maryland, the University of Hawaii, and the University of Pittsburgh.

Samuel S. Dubin is professor of psychology, emeritus, at
The Pennsylvania State University. He is a diplomate in
industrial-organizational psychology and fellow in the American Psychological Association.

Dubin's books include *Professional Obsolescence* (1972) and
(with others) *Professional and Technical Obsolescence of Older Engineers* (1974). He has directed six major studies of continuing
education needs of different professional groups: engineers,
managers, natural resource managers and scientists, managers
of cities and boroughs, and supervisory personnel in hospitals.
He has authored thirty-six articles and received two grants from
the National Science Foundation. He has taught at Penn State
and the University of Illinois, and has been a project director in
planning studies in continuing education and consultant to the
National Science Foundation. He has conducted numerous
workshops in the United States and abroad. He served as a
consultant to the International Labor Organization in Geneva,
Switzerland, and spent a year (1974–1975) as a consultant to the
Management Institute in Tehran, Iran.

James L. Farr is professor of psychology at The Pennsylvania State University. From 1986 to 1989, he was editor of *The
Industrial-Organizational Psychologist* and is now an editorial
board member of the *Journal of Occupational Psychology, Organizational Behavior and Human Decision Processes*, and *The Test Validity
Yearbook*. He is the coauthor (with F. J. Landy) of *The Measurement
of Work Performance* (1983) and coeditor (with M. A. West) of
Innovation and Creativity at Work (1990).

John A. Fossum is professor of industrial relations, chair
of the graduate faculty in industrial relations, and director of
the Industrial Relations Center at the University of Minnesota.
He has been on the business faculties of the University of Wyo-
ming and the University of Michigan and visited at the Univer-

sity of California, Los Angeles. He is the author of *Labor Relations: Development, Structure, Process* (4th ed., 1989) and a coauthor (with H. G. Heneman, III, D. P. Schwab, and L. Dyer) of *Personnel/Human Resource Management* (4th ed., 1989). He has been an officer and active member of the Academy of Management and the Industrial Relations Research Association and is consulting editor for the *Academy of Management Journal*. His current research is primarily involved with compensation theory and practice.

Arnold P. Goldstein joined the clinical psychology section of Syracuse University's psychology department in 1963, and both taught there and directed its psychotherapy center until 1980. In 1981, he founded the Center for Research on Aggression, which he currently directs, and in 1985 moved to Syracuse University's division of special education. Goldstein has a career-long interest in difficult-to-reach clients. Since 1980, his main research and psychoeducational focus have been school violence, incarcerated juvenile offenders, and child-abusing parents. He developed Skillstreaming, Aggression Replacement Training, and the Prepare Curriculum, psychoeducational programs designed to teach prosocial behaviors to chronically antisocial persons.

Lois Granick is the director of PsycINFO, a department within the American Psychological Association, and executive editor of *Psychological Abstracts*. An information scientist, with experience in both library and legal information systems prior to assuming her current position in 1974, she is an active participant in national and international organizations and projects that are concerned with information generation and transfer. These include the National Federation of Abstracting and Information Services, the Information Industry Association, the International Council for Scientific and Technical Information, and the American Society for Information Science.

Harold G. Kaufman is director of the Organizational Behavior Program as well as the Research Program in Science,

Technology and Human Resources in the division of management at Polytechnic University in Brooklyn, New York. In 1980, he received the Oustanding Paper Award for significant contributions to the literature from the Continuing Professional Development Division of the American Society for Engineering Education (ASEE). He served on the National Research Council's Panel on Continuing Education (1984–1985) and on the Engineering Manpower Commission's Engineering Utilization Study (1985–1986). His books include *Obsolescence and Professional Career Development* (1974), *Career Management: A Guide to Combating Obsolescence* (1975), and *Professionals in Search of Work* (1982).

Carole W. Keefe is coordinator for the clinical curriculum and community programs, Office of the Associate Dean, and assistant professor in the Office of Medical Education Research and Development, College of Human Medicine, Michigan State University.

Jack L. Maatsch is professor of medical education and director, Office of Medical Education Research and Development (OMERAD), College of Human Medicine, Michigan State University. His research activities have been in the use of simulation methodology in medical instruction and in the evaluation of clinical competency for purposes of medical specialty certification and recertification of continuing competency.

Donald E. Melnick is senior vice-president and director of research and development at the National Board of Medical Examiners. He is also adjunct assistant professor of medicine at the University of Pennsylvania.

Carolyn L. Middlebrooks works in the area of organizational effectiveness at Amoco Corporation and is a doctoral candidate in industrial/organizational psychology at The Pennsylvania State University. Her primary research interests are in employee involvement, reward and recognition systems, organizational development, and professional obsolescence.

Donald Britton Miller is a management consultant who specializes in the design and implementation of work environments that improve the professional's effectiveness and "psychic income." He received the 1978 Distinguished Service Award from the Society for Engineering Education, the 1983 Human Relations Award from the Society for Advancement of Management, and is the 1988 Saratoga, California, Citizen of the Year. Two of his significant books are *Personal Vitality* (1977) and *Managing Professionals in R&D* (1986).

Donna S. Queeney is director of planning studies and affiliate associate professor of education policy studies at The Pennsylvania State University. She is editor of the *Journal of Continuing Higher Education* and author of over thirty publications and book chapters on continuing professional education, adult learners, assessment, and program evaluation. She is also a frequent speaker on these topics.

Mary Ann Reinhart is associate executive director for evaluation and research of the American Board of Emergency Medicine. She was assistant professor in the Office of Medical Education Research and Development at Michigan State University during the conduct of the research reported in this book.

Wayne D. Smutz is head of the Office of Continuing Professional Education and associate director of planning studies at The Pennsylvania State University. His research and publications have focused on various aspects of continuing professional education, including the role of boundary-spanners in interinstitutional collaboration, higher education's contribution to professional development, self-assessment of professionals, and the preparation of professionals to be effective lifelong learners.

Robert P. Sprafkin is chief of the Syracuse, New York, Veterans' Administration Medical Center Day Treatment Center and director of its psychology training program. He is adjunct professor of psychology at Syracuse University and clinical associate professor of psychology at the State University of New York Health Science Center at Syracuse.

Joanne L. Tosti-Vasey is the research coordinator for Data Base, where she does program evaluation research on drug and alcohol abuse prevention.

Gary R. VandenBos is executive director for publications and communications with the American Psychological Association (APA), and he previously served as the director of national policy studies for APA. He is the coauthor (with B. Karon) of *Psychotherapy with Schizophrenics: The Treatment of Choice* (1981), associate editor of the *American Psychologist*, and editor of the "Psychology Update" column in *Hospital & Community Psychiatry*.

James C. Votruba is professor of higher and adult education at Michigan State University, where he is also assistant provost for lifelong education and director of a $10.2-million W. K. Kellogg Foundation lifelong education grant. Prior to his arrival at Michigan State University in 1989, Votruba served as dean of the school of education and human development at State University of New York, Binghamton.

Sherry L. Willis is professor of human development in the College of Health and Human Development at The Pennsylvania State University. Willis is principal investigator on the Adult Development and Enrichment Project, a short-term longitudinal study of cognitive functioning in later adulthood. She is on the editorial board of *Developmental Psychology* and is coauthor (with K. W. Schaie) of *Adult Development and Aging* (1986).

MAINTAINING PROFESSIONAL COMPETENCE

Part One

COMPETENCE
VERSUS OBSOLESCENCE:
UNDERSTANDING THE CHALLENGE
FACING TODAY'S PROFESSIONALS

There is a growing awareness, in both the public and private sectors, of the need for professionals to continue to develop and maintain their professional competence across the work life. The changing age structure of the American population has important implications for the study of professional competence. The median age of the population will continue to increase as baby-boom cohorts pass through middle to old age. In 2050, the median age will be 41.6 years. As a result, professionals in our society are, on average, middle-aged, and the median age of professionals will continue to increase into the next century. Also, because the average life expectancy has increased from 40 years in 1900 to approximately 72 years in the 1980s, an individual's average work life has been prolonged from 21 to 37 years. Today, midcareer professionals are confronted with the need to spend time to maintain and enhance their professional competence, or they will face the threat of professional obsolescence.

The challenge of maintaining professional competence throughout one's career is compounded by the current knowledge explosion and the rapid rate of technological change.

1

Approximately 1,500 scientific articles are published every day. This explosion makes it likely that the knowledge base and skills involved in many specializations will be significantly redefined or expanded during the work life of professionals. These re-orientations or expansions necessitate continued education of professionals in the field. Although the rapidity with which technological information becomes outdated varies by discipline, it is apparent that continual enhancement of professional competence is necessary in virtually all professions.

In the private sector, the competence of midcareer professionals is essential if companies are to develop innovative technologies and products. Because of increased foreign competition, American industries are now restructuring and investing more heavily in research and development efforts, which depend on highly competent personnel.

The Study of Professional Competence

Maintenance of professional competence is a rapidly evolving area of study. The literature, however, is very diverse and not easily accessible. Much of the conceptual and empirical work has been discipline specific, and it has been published in specialty journals, not widely accessible to the general research community. Also, many of the current programs of professional development have been produced by professional organizations or regulatory agencies and have been published only in the form of internal reports.

Although most writing about professional development has been restricted to a single profession, in recent years there have been some comparative analyses. Since Houle's landmark book, *Continuing Learning in the Professions* (1980), there has been an increasing number of comprehensive analyses of continuing education and updating in various professional fields (Cervero, 1988; Cervero and Azzaretto, 1989; Cervero and Scanlan, 1985; Green, Grosswald, Suter, and Walthall, 1984; Nowlen, 1987; and Schön, 1987).

Definition of Concepts and Terms

There is considerable diversity in the terminology used in the study of professional competence. This comes from the early developmental status of the field and also the multifaceted nature of the phenomenon being studied. In addition, the work to date has been discipline specific, with concepts and terminology reflecting the perspective of a given discipline. Thus, the chapters in this volume include a variety of terms. As an aid for the reader, general definitions for key terms are presented below.

Professional competence involves the ability to function effectively in the tasks considered essential within a given profession. Professional competence involves two broad domains. First, there are *proficiencies* specific to the profession or discipline: (1) the discipline-specific knowledge base; (2) technical skills considered essential in the profession; and (3) ability to solve the types of problems encountered within the profession. Second, the concept of professional competence represents *general characteristics* of the individual that facilitate the individual's development and maintenance of professional competence: intellectual ability, personality traits, motivation, attitudes, and values.

Professional competence is reflected in the *performance* of the professional. It is through performance in their particular professional domains that professionals demonstrate their level of competence. Management or supervisory personnel *assess* level of competence by observing the professional's performance. Assessment procedures associated with licensure or recertification involve obtaining a sample of the professional's behavior (performance) via tests, simulation tasks, and the like; a behavior sample is considered to represent the professional's level of competence.

It is important to differentiate between level of competence and level of productivity. It is assumed that there is a positive correlation between them, but competence cannot be assessed solely in terms of productivity. Competence is necessary for high levels of productivity, but by itself is not sufficient.

An individual may be highly competent but, because of personal or environmental factors, not productive.

This book focuses on a *developmental*, rather than a remedial, approach toward professional competence, emphasizing the continued enhancement of competence throughout the career. The developmental approach aims to prevent a decline in competence by considering personal and work environment factors that foster competence. In contrast, a remedial perspective focuses on "catch-up" procedures that are introduced after professional competence has begun to decline.

An important outcome of the maintenance of competence is *professional vitality*, as discussed in Chapters Nine and Ten. Vitality involves the ability to meet successfully the challenges of tomorrow. As a result of maintaining professional competence, professionals and their organizations are better positioned to anticipate and prepare for future challenges in their fields.

One outcome of the *failure* to maintain professional competence is professional obsolescence, defined by Dubin as the discrepancy between a person's stock of knowledge, skills, and abilities, and that person's capability to perform the required tasks of the professional (see Chapter One). The obsolete professional has inadequate command of the knowledge, skills, and problem-solving abilities considered current in the field. While skilled labor and blue-collar workers may be rendered obsolete as a function of technological change and management's ineffectual response to this change, obsolescence has received most attention within the professions. Obsolescence has been of greatest concern in fields such as engineering and computer science, where technological change has been particularly rapid, but it is a threat in all professions.

It is important to note that no professional is ever completely obsolete or totally up to date. Furthermore, competence and obsolescence are not simply polar opposites. While obsolescence may contribute to professional incompetence in some cases, lack of competence may reflect other factors, such as health or work environment. Moreover, as we will see, the antecedents of competence and obsolescence differ. While certain personal characteristics or conditions in the immediate work environment may be salient in facilitating the maintenance of competence, their absence does not necessarily lead to obsolescence.

Professional updating involves information-seeking and educational activities, both formal and informal, directed toward the enhancement of professional competence. The definition and nature of updating differs for a developmental versus a remedial approach to competence. Within a developmental approach, updating is a continual process, beginning immediately after professionals receive their terminal degree and continuing throughout their career. In contrast, in a remedial perspective, updating has an after-the-fact approach, involving procedures to compensate for obsolescence that has already occurred.

Maintenance of competence is largely self-directed. The professional determines what information or proficiency areas to focus on, and then determines the best mechanisms and procedures for acquiring them. In some professions, the updating process is being increasingly formalized and directed by other sources, such as professional organizations or regulatory agencies.

Overview of Chapters in Part One

Models regarding professional competence and professional obsolescence are presented by Dubin (Chapter One) and Fossum and Arvey (Chapter Two). Both models focus on the *interaction* between person and environmental influences.

In Chapter One, Dubin presents a model of the factors associated with the maintenance of professional competence. A "person × environment" interactional model is presented. Maintenance of professional competence reflects an interaction of personal characteristics of the professional and features of the work environment. The most salient person variable in Dubin's model is motivation. Five features of the professional's immediate work environment that can facilitate or limit maintenance of professional competence are presented. It is important to note that these work environment factors are psychological in nature; that is, the model focuses on the professional's *perception* of them (see also Chapter Eight).

While Dubin's model focuses on the immediate work environment, the model presented by Fossum and Arvey examines at a meta-level how the marketplace and organizations relate to professional competence. They believe that changes in the person (such as obsolescence) occur as job requirements change, and job changes, in turn, occur as new technologies and structural revisions occur in the marketplace or the organization. The individual's response to job change is influenced by variables such as motivation, personal characteristics, organizational conditions, and external factors.

The models presented in Chapters One and Two deal primarily with the environmental dimension. Chapter Three is concerned with the other dimension in the interactional model: the person. Willis concentrates on two personal variables: cognitive ability and motivation. She suggests that the study of professional competence must give more careful consideration to adult development, particularly the developmental changes that occur in middle age, since maintenance of competence is of particular concern to the midcareer professional. Just as the market and organizations undergo change over time, so the individual continues to develop and change throughout adulthood. The literature reviewed by Willis suggests a reciprocal relationship between individual characteristics and job demands. Cognitive and motivational characteristics influence the professional's response to job demands; subsequent job demands then affect the professional's future level of cognitive ability and motivation.

References

Cervero, R. M. *Effective Continuing Education for Professionals.* San Francisco: Jossey-Bass, 1988.

Cervero, R. M., Azzaretto, J. F., and Associates. *Visions for the Future of Continuing Professional Education.* Athens: Georgia Center for Continuing Education, 1989.

Cervero, R. M., and Scanlan, C. L. (eds.). *Problems and Prospects in Continuing Professional Education.* New Directions for Continuing Education, no. 27. San Francisco: Jossey-Bass, 1985.

Green, J. S., Grosswald, S. J., Suter, E., And Walthall, D. B. (eds.) *Continuing Education for the Health Professions: Developing, Managing, and Evaluating Programs for Maximum Impact on Patient Care.* San Francisco: Jossey-Bass, 1984.

Nowlen, P. M. *A New Approach to Continuing Education for Business and the Professions.* New York: Macmillan, 1987.

Houle, C. O. *Continuing Learning in the Professions.* San Francisco: Jossey-Bass, 1980.

Schön, D. A. *Educating the Reflective Practitioner: Toward a New Design for Teaching and Learning in the Professions.* San Francisco: Jossey-Bass, 1987.

1

Samuel S. Dubin

Maintaining
Competence Through
Updating

Several recent conditions have catapulted into prominence the issues of professional obsolescence and updating. For one thing, new knowledges have increased the requirements for greater expertise in all professionals. New facts, theories, and concepts are being introduced daily. Second, technological changes and innovations, especially in computer and microelectronic fields, have significantly changed skill requirements in all professions. Also, knowledge is becoming increasingly complex, especially interdisciplinary aspects. At the same time, the "half life" of knowledge is growing increasingly shorter. A person's stock of knowledge has a usefulness for a finite period of time; it becomes outdated and must constantly be replaced by new knowledge. For example, at Hewlett-Packard, professionals can become obsolete in about three years because of the exponential rate of change in electronics instrumentation (Miljus and Smith, 1987). Meanwhile, the public is demanding that professionals be accountable for their actions. The increased complaints and growing number of malpractice suits are symptoms of incompetence and obsolescence. Finally, international competition in business and industry along with deregulation have exposed weaknesses in American industry; market share has been lost (automobile, computer chips, machine tools), and smokestack industries have closed because of obsolete manufacturing processes.

What Is Obsolescence?

Technical obsolescence can be defined as the discrepancy between a professional's body of knowledge, skills, and abilities and the individual's capability to perform the required tasks at hand as well as those planned for the future. In a work situation, a person's proficiencies should match the requirements of the job; professionals' stock of knowledge, skills, and capabilities should be equal to the demands of their profession. The degree of obsolescence can be judged by the discrepancy between the individual's level of proficiency and the current state-of-the-art standards in the field.

Unfortunately, obsolescence is almost inevitable unless positive efforts are made to counteract it. Without continuous updating, technical proficiency will decline. People will carry on their work with increasing outdated techniques and hypotheses, ignorant of new data, techniques, and principles.

Fossum, Arvey, Paradise, and Robbins (1986) base their definition of skill obsolescence on psychological and economic definitions of job requirements as human capital theory: obsolescence is present when the "person" requirements of the job—tasks, duties, and responsibilities—become incongruent with the stock of knowledge, skills, and abilities currently possessed by the individual, presuming they were previously congruent. Technical obsolescence is characterized by inadequate knowledge of current technology, which results from the failure to maintain knowledge of current developments (Dubin, Shelton, and McConnell, 1973; Farr, Dubin and others, 1980b).

Kaufman added another dimension in his definition: "Obsolescence is the degree to which professionals lack the up-to-date knowledge and skills necessary to maintain effective performance in either current or future work. Thus it is possible to differentiate job obsolescence—pertaining to one's current job assignment—from professional obsolescence—the capability to perform in new and different jobs in one's profession" (1978, p. 22). Professional obsolescence implies a lack of competence on a higher level, that of originality and innovation.

Finally, obsolescence is a complex process of many dimensions. It occurs in any profession (Dubin, 1977). One may be obsolescent in one aspect of work but fully proficient in other aspects. Obsolescence usually does not develop overnight, but it can be either a sudden or a gradual longitudinal process. Its onset may arise at any age; it may be present in any age group. The condition is not static; it is not a fatal disease. Fortunately, it can be halted and reversed. Overcoming or staving off obsolescence is not an easy matter. It requires some fundamental changes in habits, strong personal motivation, and supportive conditions in the workplace.

Behavioral Example of Technical Obsolescence in Engineers

Dubin (1978) asked engineering managers to identify behaviors or incompetencies that they perceived as demonstrating technical obsolescence. A sample of their replies illustrates the range of responses:

- The individual is not aware of the latest concepts, approaches, and innovations in his field.
- The person's input is no longer competitive.
- He is not familiar with the latest tools and equipment for his work.
- He does not comprehend the technical literature in his field.
- He is unable to apply his concepts to his area of specialization.
- Colleagues fail to consult him on technical matters.
- He experiences decreased respect and credibility among colleagues.
- There is a low tendency to be selected for key assignments.
- He participates less in decision making on the job.

Measuring Obsolescence

Obsolescence was defined as a mismatch between the knowledge, skills, and abilities and the requirements to perform the necessary tasks at hand. Each profession has its own set of knowledge, skills, and abilities, and they can change rapidly, especially in the technical and scientific areas.

To arrive at a more precise method of measuring engineering performance, we developed a set of behavior-anchored scales (BAS) to evaluate technical job performance of engineers (Farr, Dubin, and others, 1980b). The objective was to provide a reliable and valid method for measuring technical competence at high, medium, and low levels of performance. The BAS method is based on consensus agreement on what behaviors characterize these three performance levels. In other words, 60 percent of the respondents had to agree that the item correctly characterized the competency indicated.

Eleven factors were identified through a succession of interviews with different engineering groups. Each factor represents an important area of competency of the technical performance of engineers. Figure 1.1 illustrates the high, medium, and low performance behaviors of one factor, technical communication. The competencies listed are general in nature so that they can be applied to a variety of engineering disciplines.

Each factor has a vertical scale with rankings from 1 to 9. To the right of the scale are performance examples that engineers agreed relate to this factor, grouped into three general performance levels: more than adequate, adequate, and less than adequate. The evaluator then places in the numbered column a mark that best represents his judgment of the typical performance on this factor.

The scales are useful feedback devices for managers to provide performance information to subordinates. The behavioral nature of the scale serves as understandable and specific guides for performance improvement and career development plans.

The BAS is a useful way for professionals to identify behaviors that characterize performance. The written descrip-

Figure 1.1. Sample Behavior-Anchored Scale.

Factor A. *Technical Communication*—the ability to transmit written and oral information related to technical projects and assignments.

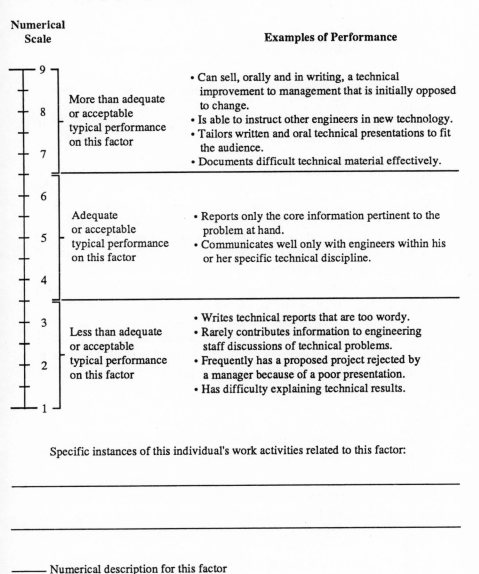

Numerical
Scale

Examples of Performance

Numerical Scale		Examples of Performance
9 8 7	More than adequate or acceptable typical performance on this factor	• Can sell, orally and in writing, a technical improvement to management that is initially opposed to change. • Is able to instruct other engineers in new technology. • Tailors written and oral technical presentations to fit the audience. • Documents difficult technical material effectively.
6 5 4	Adequate or acceptable typical performance on this factor	• Reports only the core information pertinent to the problem at hand. • Communicates well only with engineers within his or her specific technical discipline.
3 2 1	Less than adequate or acceptable typical performance on this factor	• Writes technical reports that are too wordy. • Rarely contributes information to engineering staff discussions of technical problems. • Frequently has a proposed project rejected by a manager because of a poor presentation. • Has difficulty explaining technical results.

Specific instances of this individual's work activities related to this factor:

_____

_____

—— Numerical description for this factor

tion at different parts of the BAS scale enable raters to agree on the scoring of the behaviors. When agreement between raters occurs, *reliability* is increased. When the ratings of the behaviors agree with the criterion, the *validity* of the scale is increased.

Conditions That Make Updating Necessary

Growth Rate of Knowledge and Information. The phenomenal growth rate of new knowledge and information constantly makes obsolete a portion of the knowledge base held by people in professional occupations, especially those in scientific or technical fields.

The data base at the Institute of Scientific Information (ISI) is growing by nearly a million items a year (Hinkle, 1985). This presents a massive information-processing challenge. The ISI processes 7,000 different journals. Each week 2,500 issues are received with 4,200 articles and 38,000 references to be processed. Two million papers are published each year in 80,000 different sources. Kelly (1984) estimates that research and development (R & D) professionals read about 200 of these articles per year. For every person who reads a scientific paper, 20 read the summary only and 500 read the title and stop there. President Baker of Rockefeller University points out (1983) that the volume of information has reached a level where it is frequently dealt with by ignoring it. A university professor of biophysics, a conscientious teacher as well as an outstanding researcher, says that he cannot use his same lecture notes from one year to the next because research findings are changing constantly. Since textbooks are rapidly out of date, he uses current journal articles instead.

The Doubling Phenomenon. Scientific and technical information is increasing at a rate of 13 percent per year, or doubling every 5.5 to 7 years (Naisbett, 1982). The doubling of knowledge and the availability of data bases make it imperative that professionals have training in techniques of information retrieval. The greater the ability to retrieve reliable current information, the more likely the professional will be to keep updated and maintain competency.

Baker cautions that heads of laboratories and corporate management must organize this vast knowledge base so that it becomes closer to R & D units and more accessible to the individual scientist or engineer who would be a prime user. A 1982 study by King, Griffiths, Rodera, and Weiderkekr estimated that R & D programs saved about $13 million annually (the dollar value of time and equipment) when professionals read the literature—$1,590 for each formal article and $1,280 for each technical report read. This type of evidence demonstrates the cost effectiveness of updating.

Complexity of Knowledge. The acquisition of new knowledge is rendered especially difficult in these times by the complexity of much of the new information. The difficulty can be attributed in large measure to the overlapping of boundaries between fields and the interaction of multiple factors in one field upon another. Boundaries interweave and interactions become more intricate, as in these currently paired fields: engineering and physics, physics and chemistry, biology and chemistry, medicine and engineering, physics and biology, psychology and computers.

To operate across fields in this manner requires the cooperation of highly qualified professionals with a wide base of knowledge. Interdisciplinary research is achieving many new and creative solutions to problems precisely because traditional boundaries are being dissolved (National Science Foundation, 1982). Solid-state physics and cellular biology have merged to create flow cytometry for analyzing cell components. Robotics and psychology are combining to analyze vision. The innovative use of instrumentation, using lasers and computers to analyze the nature of the cell, is resulting in an explosion of biological knowledge. Michael S. Brown and Joseph L. Goldstein, winners of the 1985 Nobel Prize in physiology, exemplify the synthesis of medicine and basic research methods.

Dr. Candice Pert, chief of brain biochemistry at the National Institutes of Health, commented, "I think the source of a lot of excitement in the new sciences is the merging of disciplines to produce an incredible explosion of knowledge. This growing interrelationship of scientific fields indicates a need for broadly educated scientists familiar with cross disciplines" (*New York Times*, 1983).

The increasing complexity of problems faced by industries has required the hiring of large numbers of Ph.D.s. The greater sophistication of modern industrial technology requires their specific expertise plus their ability to carry out independent R & D activity. With greater versatility the Ph.D. can cope with a wider range of activities and will enable the company to upgrade the quality of its R & D work. This emphasizes the importance of hiring professionals who are up to date in their own and allied fields.

The "Half Life" of Knowledge. The stock of a person's knowledge has a shelf life; it is useful for a finite period of time. A portion of it, at least, will become inactive and outdated by the existence of new knowledge. To designate the process of decay of knowledge, the concept of half life has been borrowed from the field of nuclear physics. The half life expresses the length of time that half the knowledge acquired at a given point (say at graduation from college) remains relevant to the work task. A half life of five years means that after five years a given body of acquired knowledge is only 50 percent applicable. However, the 50 percent that will be discarded is not predictable.

This concept can be used to determine the rate of change of knowledge in a specific field and to put a quantitative value on it. The half life can suggest to professionals how fast their information must be updated to be current. Therefore, it has a direct application in their career development, and in managerial policy decisions for keeping employees up to date.

In engineering the half life estimate is five to seven years; in computers, one to two years; software systems, one to two years; management, five to eight years; internal medicine, three to five years; physics, eight years; molecular biology, 20 percent per year; gene technology, three to four years; biotechnology, five to six years; accounting, five years; economics, eight years;

sports physiology, eight years; organizational behavior, five to six years; finance, seven years. (Many of these estimates came from personal interviews with faculty members and experts in their fields. No claim is made for exactness; they are educated estimates.)

The half-life idea can also be applied to a product. The half life of a high-technology product may be only two years, yet it may take four years to develop. Success or failure of a new product can turn on the difference of a few weeks in product introduction time. More than half of Hewlett-Packard's products were invented in the past five years. At the Siemens Corporation, new products accounted for 43 percent of sales in the past five years, 73 percent in the past ten years. In the pharmaceutical industry a product can be obsolete in six months. Such a rapid pace of change places a heavy burden for company growth on R & D productivity.

Technological Change and Innovation. The generation of new knowledge has been accompanied by a parallel growth of innovation in science and technology. Engineers by a large majority named innovations in technology as the prime contributor to obsolescence (Truxal, 1984). It is estimated that more technical changes will occur in the next ten to twenty years than have occurred in all of history—a continuous threat to our knowledge base. Robots, automation, microcomputers, optical scanners, and microchips are revolutionizing the way people will work henceforth.

Technological change may be described as an advance in technical knowledge, concepts, or ideas. It may be a change in technique, an alternation of a product or a piece of equipment, or new applications of existing technology. It can occur as a result of a new invention, but it does not necessarily rely on new scientific principles.

Technological innovation, on the other hand, is the purposeful transformation of new concepts into designs, products, or systems that have economic value or social significance. Over the past fifty years technological innovation has been the most important contributor to growth and productivity, surpassing the contributions of capital and labor (New York Stock Exchange, 1982).

An engineer of the 1960s would not recognize what his counterparts are doing today in computerized modeling, simulation, and analysis (Haddad, 1985); the engineer of today will have a lot of updating to do to be successful in the 1990s. Four years of undergraduate education is no longer adequate to equip a professional for a productive long-term career. Lifelong learning now becomes the requirement.

Global Competition. Finally, the hegemony of the United States in many sectors of the world economy has been challenged by international competition. Other nations have made substantial and increasing investment in research and development, have invented many innovative management techniques (just-in-time delivery, quality circles), and have made maximal use of their human resources through increased training and assignment of responsibilities. Fortunately, U.S. companies have introduced remedial measures: restructuring the company; building modern, semiautomated plants; using new managerial approaches and increased R&D funding to develop new and better products; reducing the lag time between the R&D lab and the marketplace; and, most important, better training of human resources.

Significance of the Obsolescence Problem

Rapid changes are occurring in every technical, scientific, and professional field. New findings are being introduced daily. To maintain professional status in one's chosen occupation, a person must stay on top of new developments or else become "topped out," obsolete.

The key issue is the professional's failure to advance at the same rate as the state of the art in the field. The fast pace of technological change today has greatly shortened the time allotted to keep current. Hans Jenny, manager of technical information service at RCA, pointed out (1983) that technical professionals are confronted today with fierce worldwide competition. To succeed they must innovate to stay ahead; they must use advanced technologies and facilities; they must update their knowledge to the state of the art. They must be aware of their competitors' technological achievements and leapfrog them. Operating with yesterday's techniques and methods is not good enough.

Bloch, director of the National Science Foundation, noted (1984) that technical obsolescence is a special concern in high-technology industries where the process of change is rapid. These changes automatically accelerate the obsolescence of the individual's data base, the tools at one's disposal, and the techniques and approaches used in the profession. The National Science Board task committee, in its 1986 report, emphasized that the most striking and pervasive change of the 1980s is the shift to a global economy. The only way the United States can continue to stay ahead of other countries is to keep new ideas flowing through research, to have the best technically trained and most innovative, adaptable work force of any nation. A conference of forty-five engineering deans and faculty from engineering schools convened at the Massachusetts Institute of Technology in 1986 concluded that the rate of innovation in techniques and basic ideas in electrical engineering is so rapid that new subjects are added to the curriculum every four to five years.

The rapidity of technological change and innovation has resulted in a shift of responsibility. A decade ago, technical obsolescence was regarded as the individual's problem and responsibility. Today, the emphasis and much of the responsibility have shifted to management. For example, IBM now requires every professional to take forty hours of course work a year, in addition to courses required for the technical specialty. At RCA, engineers were asked, "How important is keeping abreast of new technology in your present job?" Three quarters of the engineers (76 percent) rated keeping up to date on the two highest points of a competence scale, "extremely important" and "quite important." Interestingly, both supervisors and managers rated it even higher — 81 and 83 percent, respectively (Jenny and Underwood, 1977). A recent study on the utilization of engineers (American Association of Engineering Societies, 1986) showed that 87 percent of engineers considered avoiding obsolescence as very important professionally, but 48 percent indicated that this responsibility should be shared by the employer.

Results from a survey in Massachusetts (Leventman and Pierce, 1986) showed that a significant number of technologists were thirty-five or older: 49 percent in R & D companies, 38 percent in large computer companies, and 41 percent in smaller technology companies. If the half life of engineering knowledge in the fast-paced electronic field is five years — some argue three years — these companies will not be able to compete effectively unless their professionals are exerting great efforts to update themselves. The report noted that the degree of participation in educational programs was low even though companies paid for the tuition. This suggests that other factors are influencing updating.

The Prevalence of Technological Obsolescence. We can deduce a fair estimate of the extent of the obsolescence problem from a variety of published opinions and research findings. An early study by Roney (1966) concluded that one in fifteen scientists showed symptoms of job obsolescence. In Ritti's (1971) investigation, 41 percent of engineers admitted that they were "only fairly well" or "not at all well" up to date. The National Science Board (1976) reported that technological obsolescence was one of the twenty-five critical scientific issues facing the country, in the opinion of seventy-eight presidents and directors of major technological industries.

Knowledge obsolescence can be measured, as Lindsay, Morrison, and Kelly (1974) illustrated. These researchers conducted a well-designed study of high school physical education teachers. This study is presented in some detail because it provided a systematic procedure for assessing educational needs of a defined group of practitioners and for translating the identified needs into knowledge areas that can form the basis for an updating program.

The stimulus for the study was an increasing number of lawsuits involving high school athletes. Shin splints were treated improperly, and a number of heat stroke deaths occurred in high school football players. Many coaches were unaware of the correct procedures for treating an unconscious player or the proper technique for reducing strains in the groin muscle. Coaches were not up to date on proper eating habits.

To correct these deficiencies, a group of experts was assembled to determine the key areas of knowledge required by high school physical educators. Five key areas were identified: adaptive physical education, athletic training and conditioning, curriculum, exercise physiology, and methodology. Experts in each area described the technical nature of the subject, the potential harm to students from incorrectly treating an injury, and legal liabilities. Experts then established a minimum passing score for each area. A test, Inventory of Recent Knowledge in Physical Education, was administered to a carefully selected sample population. The findings showed that more than three fourths of the physical education teachers would be expected to fall below the passing scores on each of the five areas. (This method measured knowledge obsolescence only, not the coaches' actual performance in the field.)

The unique feature of the procedure is that the level of difficulty of the item is determined by the number of respondents who correctly answer the item. This provided a basis for setting up an educational program stressing information on the most difficult items. Professor Karl Stoedefalke of the Pennsylvania State University set up a two-day workshop on heart and circulatory systems response to exercise to deal with the exercise physiology area.

A second study that measured knowledge obsolescence using self-assessment tests was developed by the American Psychiatric Association (Carmichael, Templeton, Small, and Kelly, 1974). The findings showed a negative relationship between psychiatric knowledge and years since residency training. Today many different specialties in medicine use self-assessment objective tests to determine and measure knowledge deficiencies. Dubin and Cohen (1970) found that scores on a test of quantitative skills in industrial engineers decreased as the number of years since graduation increased.

Estimates of physician impairment, as measured by inability to deliver competent patient care, ranged from 5 percent to 15 percent of the 500,968 medical doctors in the United States (Feinstein, 1985). Causes of impairment included "deficiency in medical skills in addition to the well-known chemical dependency and alcoholism." A gubernatorial panel has proposed that a physician's competency to practice medicine in the state of New York be reviewed every six years ("Cuomo Plan," 1987).

Cost of Technical Obsolescence. Professionals who become obsolescent are a threat to their own growth as well as a costly liability to their organization. At worst, they detract from the organization's quality and its ability to meet competition successfully. Poor product and poor service breed consumer resistance and mistrust.

The management of an organization also may become obsolescent, complacent, and rigid, attempting to solve problems with outmoded theories and techniques. It is common knowledge that many U.S. industries (automobiles, cameras, electronic products, steel, textiles, and so on) suffered a decline in market share in the 1960s and 1970s. This can be attributed largely to the loss of the technological innovation advantages and mismanagement of domestic firms relative to foreign competitors. This has cost the United States billions of dollars in lost jobs and bankrupt industries, and in inestimable social costs to individuals and communities, as manifested by the rise in alcoholism, divorce, and family disruptions.

It has been estimated that each $1 billion of trade deficit results in the loss of 24,000 jobs. In the semiconductor industry from 1981 to 1986, approximately 65,000 jobs were lost because of steep price cutting and manufacturing efficiencies by foreign producers. In the U.S. steel industry, employment dropped from 700,000 in 1979 to 140,000 in 1985. Granted that foreign steel benefited greatly from low wage scales and government subsidies, a more critical factor was technological: approximately 80 percent of Japanese steel is made by the very efficient continuous rolling process; only 25 percent of American steel is produced that way. U.S. steel companies are now introducing the continuous rolling process to make themselves more competitive.

The machine tool industry is another example; American

firms failed to invest adequately in research and development, and lost out to foreign counterparts. In the electronics field more than a thousand U.S. firms manufactured consumer products before the Japanese entered the market with a better product at a lower price. Smith (1984) explains this loss as the result of management's concentration on profits rather than on developing advanced product technologies to meet the competition.

The key point is that technical obsolescence and poor management have resulted in the loss of a competitive edge and this culminated in lost jobs and trade deficits (Abernathy, 1982). Fortunately the restructuring of American companies is now taking place at an accelerated pace. Technical obsolescence can be corrected and reversed. General Electric retrained a group of engineers in digital circuit design and found a cost differential saving of 2.6:1 compared to hiring and training new engineers (Zukowski, 1983).

Up to this point we have examined the issues around technical obsolescence. The next section deals with human components for keeping up to date.

Keeping Up to Date

For professionals keeping up to date means making use of theories, points of view, techniques, and practices that are in the forefront of their field *and* allied or adjacent fields. It means being familiar with the problems other professionals in the same field are working on and the approaches they are using (National Science Foundation, 1969). Professionals who are up to date can use recently developed techniques to solve assigned problems. They do not overlook significant facts or implications arising from the work, they know how to translate theory into practice.

Keeping up to date takes a systematic approach, not just the occasional reading of a journal or book. It requires both individual motivation and stimulation from the work environment. A few years ago, individuals themselves were held responsible for keeping current in their profession. Today, under the stress of competition, organizations like Bell Labs, IBM, Hewlett-Packard, Honeywell, General Electric, and a host of others are assuming much of the responsibility of keeping their employees up to date.

Hans Jenny at RCA stressed the very real practicality: "If you are technically current you are ready to carry out an engineering assignment in today's highly competitive environment. No more, no less. . . You must apply the latest, most competitive engineering tools to your present assignment and be knowledgeable enough to work into a new product field should your old one become obsolete"(1983, p. 1).

We have just described some of the qualities that pertain to the updating process. Unfortunately, they do not identify potential changes in motivation or work environment that may be the critical operative factors in keeping up to date. To compensate for these deficiencies, the Dubin model has been designed.

The Dubin Model of Updating

Research on both obsolescence and updating has been descriptive (surveys, questionnaires, ratings), for the most part, without a strong conceptual and experimental foundation. A model provides a framework for an experimental approach in which conditions can be systematically identified, analyzed and acted upon. The Dubin model is an example of this methodology. It provided the conceptual basis for a large research project on updating of engineers, funded by the National Science Foundation that my colleagues and I conducted in 1977.

The Dubin model (see Figure 1.2) hypothesizes six factors that define and govern updating—individual motivation (explained by the expectancy theory) and five factors derived from the work environment: the job or work assignment, supervisory attitudes and behaviors, organizational climate, peer–colleague interactions, and management policies and practices. The model shows graphically that keeping current is a joint function of both motivation and the work-situation contexts. It also suggests that the combination permits specific predictions about professional updating. The goal of professional updating is to improve performance and competency. It can mean attaining the state-of-the-art level of knowledge, becoming more profi-

Figure 1.2. The Dubin Model of Technical Updating.

$$P(U) = M + WE$$

Where

$P(U)$ = Probability of updating

M = Individual motivation

WE = Work environment

The model can be represented graphically:

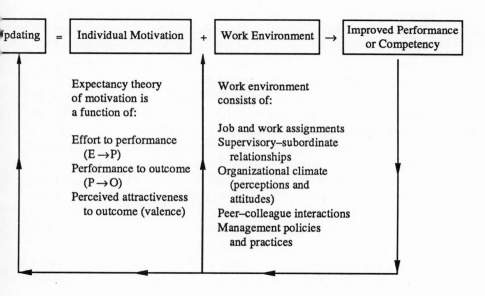

cient in skills and techniques, or raising personal esteem through being recognized as an authority by peers.

Motivating Individuals

Motivation can best be understood as a system of rewards and outcomes. Expectancy theory uses three kinds of information to predict an individual's motivation: expectancy beliefs, instrumentality beliefs, and valence of outcome. The theory suggests that people make rational choices based on expected payoffs. Expectancy refers to the perceived connection between effort (putting in hours of study, taking a course) and outcome (job performance). Instrumentality refers to the belief that attaining some outcome (level of performance, updating, or state of knowledge) will influence rewards. Applying instrumentality beliefs to updating, the individual who believes that keeping up to date will influence work-related outcomes (salary increase, promotion, recognition) will engage in updating activities. Valence refers to the value a person places on available rewards and outcomes. The theory recognizes individual differences in choice of rewards and goals (Vroom, 1964; Porter and Lawer, 1968). These differences can be critical, especially in workplace applications. For managers, expectancy theory provides a conceptual basis for understanding the motivations for keeping up to date and for improving performance.

Expectancies can be divided into two types: effort to performance and performance to outcome (Steers, 1981). Effort to performance ($E{\rightarrow}P$) represents an individual's belief that a given effort will lead to a certain accomplishment. (Will greater effort and time spent reading professional journals keep me current?) A number of conditions influence effort: a person's ability, the difficulty of the task, degree of self-confidence, level of self-esteem, or past experiences.

Performance to outcome ($P{\rightarrow}O$) is the belief that level of performance determines outcome; that if a person gives his best in a given situation, then certain outcomes will follow. (Will putting in longer hours result in a pay raise or recognition? What is the probability that if I increase my effort, rewards will follow?) The $P{\rightarrow}O$ is influenced by past experience, attractiveness of various outcomes, management policies and practices, and perceptions of conditions in the organization.

Motivational Facilitators. In our research study,* (Farr, Dubin, and others, 1980b), engineers rated thirty-one items on a scale,

* Special thanks to James L. Farr, E. Emory Enscore, Stephen W. Kozlowski, and Jeanette Cleveland for their collaboration on NSF grant: The Relationships Among Motivation, the Work Environment, and Updating in Engineers (1980).

with 1 (low) and 7 (high). The top nine reward and outcome items (greater than + 5 on scale) were rated as providing the greatest stimulus for keeping up to date:

1. Feeling of accomplishment resulting from work assignment
2. Opportunity for advancement based on quality of work performance
3. Opportunity to exercise personal initiative in assignment
4. Being assigned challenging work
5. Recognition for accomplishments and technical success
6. Salary and merit increases
7. Desire for excellence in work assignment
8. Opportunity to be creative and innovative
9. Having major responsibility for a project

The findings strongly support the idea that managers should have a solid intellectual comprehension of motivation and how it can be used to stimulate engineers to keep current. Managers and supervisors must be not only technically competent but also skilled in various ways of motivating subordinates: giving feedback on work accomplishments, making opportunities for use of personal initiative, designing a challenging job, giving recognition, stressing excellence, providing opportunities for creativity and innovation, and delegating responsibility.

Applying Expectancy Theory. Motivation deals with energizing and directing behavior through rewards and outcomes (Steers, 1981). The manager who understands both E→P and P→O is able to improve the performance of subordinates by using the following techniques:

1. *Clarify expectancy to performance relationships* (E→P). Let employees know they will be given training to improve skills, coaching to improve performance, and supervisory support to achieve required level of performance. Allow employees to participate in decision making. Give time off to take courses. Give guidance on appropriate readings and on specific goals to achieve.

2. *Clarify performance to outcomes* (P→O). Let the employee know which rewards can be expected for high performance. This is called arranging for performance–reward contingencies. One of a manager's most important tasks is to design reward systems that are based on actual performance and fit the specific individual. Let employees know what they can expect for high levels of performance. Do not assume that each employee has an accurate perception of reward contingencies. Make sure employees are qualified with appropriate skills and abilities.

3. *Match rewards to the individual employee's desires.* Try to understand each employee's personal reward preferences, and design reward systems accordingly, if the organization permits this flexibility.

4. *Clarify role expectations.* Discuss with employees what is expected of them. Clarifying objectives and standards and providing feedback will reduce random behavior and will increase task-relevant behaviors. Role perception is an essential feature of expectancy theory; it is the individual's definition of successful performance. Much effort is wasted if employees are not certain what is considered a successful performance. For example, many engineers believe that performing well technically is sufficient for promotion to supervisory level. However, most organizations now require "people" skills in managerial positions. Managers frequently overlook the fact that employees' perceptions of the task are different from theirs. Consequently they misunderstand subordinates' behavior, and employees are not rewarded when they think they should be. Agreements between manager and subordinate about work performance can help clarify role perceptions.

Work Environment and Updating

The work environment is where the action takes place. The total psychological work environment usually consists of the job, a manager or supervisor, peers to interact with, management and its policies, and the organizational climate (the individual's perception of management's philosophy). The *feeling* of the workplace has a powerful impact on the psychological health of the individual (Miller, 1986). The work environment can stimulate professionals to achieve the state of the art—or turn them off.

The five factors discussed below represent the top behaviors that stimulate updating. These are the ones that engineers themselves rated highest, and the ones that managers should use.

Keeping professionals current is highly important in today's competitive environment. It is essential for the survival of an organization—any organization. The significance of these findings is that they provide managers and supervisors with direct work-related recommendations. The findings, although formulated on the engineering profession, can mostly be generalized to other professionals.

Job Challenge and Work Assignments. The activities and work assignments that engineers rated highest as facilitators and motivators are:

- Job assignments are challenges that stretch the engineer's technical knowledge to the limit.
- Work assignments include state-of-the-art technology and advanced instrumentation.
- The engineer is given the responsibility to implement new ideas.
- Job rotation exposes the engineer to new technical disciplines.
- The engineer participates in technical decisions relevant to assignments.
- The engineer is allowed to see a project through from initial design to implementation.
- Assignments are made in the area of the engineer's personal interest.
- Job allows free time to explore new, advanced ideas.
- Job assignments require the evaluation of alternate solutions to technical problems.

Job challenge is generally the most important single facilitator in keeping up to date. The person working at a challenging work assignment is the most likely to consult a recent journal article or a knowledgeable colleague for updated information. When Margulies and Raia (1967) asked R & D scientists, "What was the most fruitful learning experience you have had over the past year or two?" the most frequent response (42 percent) was, "on-the-job problem solving." This was defined as being assigned "interesting tasks," "broadening tasks," and "writing proposals which force me to dip into the literature and become current on everything connected with the project."

What makes a job challenging? Pelz and Andrews (1966) cited a number of job conditions that offer challenge: encountering approaches different from one's own, facing an unfamiliar problem, having flaws in your solution pointed out, being exposed to other people's ideas and criticism, doing a diversity of tasks, encountering conditions that disrupt ongoing patterns of work, disagreement with colleagues in an intellectual dispute, and perception of a problem coupled with a belief that a solution can be found. The awareness that a problem exists is the essence of job challenge.

In a study of MBA graduates, Jelenek (1977) found that they crave intellectual challenge more than money. When asked what was the single thing they most wanted in their careers, 23 percent chose intellectual challenge, 20 percent wanted money, 14 percent preferred independence at work, and 11 percent chose security. Jelenek also found that job challenge was a high-priority factor in many of the professions: MBAs and engineers ranked intellectual challenge first, lawyers ranked it second, and physicians ranked it third.

Among middle managers in groups undergoing management development training, Bradford and Cohen (1984) reported that only 10 to 20 percent felt that their skills were fully used. When asked what challenged them most to use their skills, they gave these responses: the job itself if challenging, designing a new solution to fit a unique situation, tasks that are soft and ambiguous with unclear or inexact scope of difficulty, multiple tasks requiring simultaneous accomplishment, tasks that require working near the boundaries of personal competence, being given sole responsibility to do the job.

Supervisory Behaviors. The supervisory behaviors rated by engineers as most stimulating them to keep up to date are:

- The supervisor gives recognition and credit for good technical work.
- The supervisor bases salary and promotion recommendations on technical performance.
- The supervisor matches the engineer's need for professional development with opportunities to attend courses and technical meetings.
- Independent and innovative thinking are encouraged by the supervisor.
- The supervisor solicits ideas from the engineers on technical problems.
- The supervisor provides continuing education seminars on technological problems.
- The supervisor's performance reviews point out the engineer's strengths and weaknesses and offer suggestions for improvement.

Farr, Enscore, Steiner, and Kozlowski (1984) looked into the question, Do engineers who believe that more favorable outcomes result when one is technically up to date receive more positive performance evaluations from their supervisors? They found significant but small correlations: Engineers who believed that being more updated technically would result in rewards (opportunities for advancement, opportunities to use personal initiative in assignments) were evaluated more favorably by their supervisors in overall performance. Engineers who believed that remaining at the same technical level and not making an effort to update would lessen their opportunity for promotion and assignments on the forefront of technology, increase their likelihood for receiving negative feedback, and decrease their job security, generally received higher ratings from their supervisors. Smaller correlations were obtained between supervisory evaluation of overall performance and being technically updated and such rewards as challenging work assignments, salary increase, recognition for accomplishment, and feeling of achievement.

This study confirms that technical updating is recognized by supervisors and positively influences their performance evaluations. Kaufman's earlier study (1974) suggested that supervisors motivate engineers to update when they themselves are perceived to be technically competent and participatory, emphasize technical competence and innovation, and provide rewards and recognition. Kaufman stressed that it was the recognized competence of the supervisor that encourages subordinates to keep up to date.

Supervisory behaviors that advocate technical competence and practice participatory decision making, autonomy, goal clarity, recognition, and rewards should provide a firm basis for updating behaviors of subordinates. If organizational policies are favorable, if concerns for updating are clarified at the supervisory level, and if updating can be expected to lead to desired outcomes, then appropriate updating should follow.

Organizational Climate. The organizational facilitators top-rated by engineers are these:

- The organization is dedicated to staying at the cutting edge of technology.
- Innovation is enthusiastically received within the organization.
- Organizational rewards are given to engineers with technical competence.
- The organization expects continuing technical excellence and competence.
- The organization is a leader in technical development.
- The organization has a progressive atmosphere.
- The organization attempts to be better technically than its competition.

The organizational climate of a workplace is a cluster of perceptions about the organization's operating practices and principles held by those who work there. Perception in this case means interpretation. The worker perceives the way the organization operates, the way company policies are translated into day-to-day work tasks, communication patterns, degree of participation in decision making, demand for excellence, reward systems, attitude toward mistakes, security, goal setting, and professional development. If workers interpret these climate elements as positive, they are encouraged to engage in updating.

Each organization has its own unique climate, and that climate has considerable influence on workers' motivation, behavior, and attitudes. A particular climate may be effective in one organization and not at all in another. A high-tech firm may allow risk taking, revolving task assignments, task uncertainty, decentralization, entrepreneurial initiative, and generally freewheeling modus operandi. A bureaucratic type of organization, on the other hand, will require a more static work climate, maintain structured approaches to problems, and adhere to standardized procedures.

The advantage of defining and analyzing the climate of any organization is that it can then be measured and used as a diagnostic tool. Instruments such as questionnaires can reveal how employees perceive management's practices, procedures, strengths, and weaknesses; identify present and potential problems; detect where change is needed; and assess whether the organization's climate will promote the organization's goals.

There is a distinction between organizational climate and organizational culture, although the terms are frequently used interchangeably. Climate deals with perceptions about management policies and practices; organizational culture can be described as shared values and beliefs. Culture pertains to more abstract values, whereas climate deals with the real world of work, which can be defined, measured, and manipulated to attain specific ends.

Peer-Colleague Interactions. The peer-colleague interactions rated highest by engineers as facilitating updating are:

- Peers are able to provide reliable information about current technical developments.
- Peers usually draw one's attention to useful new journal articles and technical papers.
- Peers are able to suggest new approaches to technical problems based on their own experiences.
- Peers are willing to act as sounding boards for new ideas.

Peers play a very prominent role in professional updating. The best sources of information for engineers are colleagues within the organization. Communication among peers is also important because it creates a competitive atmosphere, which spurs updating activity.

At Bell Labs scientists repeatedly cited the benefits of being able to bounce ideas off one another at a moment's notice. Ernest Ambler, technical director of the National Bureau of Standards, has noted that person-to-person communication among researchers is the most timely method for obtaining scientific information. At RCA, engineers ranked informal discussion with colleagues second, after technically challenging work, as a method for keeping current. At General Motors, scientists and engineers from staff and manufacturing departments have frequent contacts, which provide cross fertilization of ideas, promote creativity, and provide intellectual stimulation. In addition to preventing duplication of effort, these contacts constitute valuable pathways for sharing ideas and learning new techniques.

At Procter & Gamble, Techlinberg (1981) found that half of all critical technical communications were informal and unplanned. To take advantage of this natural inclination of colleagues, he set up nooks along the corridors with chairs and blackboards to encourage impromptu conversations and informal exchanges of ideas. Productive new ideas began to surface from the interaction of various disciplines and project teams.

Management Policies and Practices. The highest-rated management policies and practices are these:

- Management has an appraisal system that ties financial gain to technical competence.
- Management provides in-house technical seminars.
- Management provides its engineers with current technical equipment and facilities.
- Management has a systematic rotational program to give its engineers diversified job assignments during the first years of employment.
- Management maintains a current technical library.

The most important facilitator for updating in an organization is a clear management policy that the appraisal system must link financial gain to technical competence. To motivate employees to undertake further education, organizations must show that such a direct relationship exists. In addition to financial rewards, management should openly express its support of various updating efforts such as in-house seminars, state-of-the-art equipment and facilities, and a well-stocked current library.

Miller (1977) believes that management must have an explicit policy of rewarding updating if it expects personnel to keep up to date. He puts the responsibility for keeping professionals current squarely on management's shoulders by insisting that organizations provide other incentives for updating, such as challenging projects and goals, planning ahead for technical change, and ensuring that present talent is continually developed to meet future challenges.

In a similar vein, Kaufman (1974) argued that if management hopes to motivate personnel to update, organizations must reward self-development, allow technical professionals to influence decision making that affects them, and assure that dual career ladders provide professionals with status comparable to management.

Behavioral Examples of Up-to-Date Engineers

Dubin (1978) asked a sample of engineering managers to list behaviors that characterize an up-to-date engineer. Their responses:

- Keeps current with advanced technologies in own and related fields
- Demonstrates innovative solutions to solving problems
- Seeks challenging assignments that are stimulating and involve advanced technologies
- Accepts tough assignments and takes risks on unfamiliar assignments
- Continuously improves proficiency and work performance
- Is recognized as an expert by peers and associates
- Has active peer–colleague interactions
- Takes a critical approach to problem solving and product development
- Uses performance feedback and evaluation effectively

Redesigning the Work Environment to Stimulate Updating

In these rapidly changing times the work environment plays a vital role in supporting the talent and in updating the knowledge and skills of the people who work within it. Managers and supervisors can initiate rewards and outcomes that will spur new learning and updating. Their guidelines should be the highest-rated items of the six factors described earlier.

Many companies have accelerated their training programs for managers and supervisors, to make use of these facilitators for raising employees' achievement levels. These organizations — large, medium, and small — recognize that human capital is the prime source of innovation, quality, and production gains.

Farr, Dubin and others (1980b) examined the relationship between motivation and work environment for engineers. Farr, Enscore, Steiner, and Kozlowski (1984) carried the question further by examining the relationships among the work environment factors, work-related rewards and outcomes, and updating. Significant positive correlations were found between the work environment factors and four rewards and outcomes: recognition for accomplishment, opportunities for advancement, salary increase, and challenging work assignments.

Engineers believed that the likelihood of receiving recognition for their accomplishments would increase if they were more up to date, provided the following cluster of work-environment conditions existed: good supervisory feedback and communication, organizational policies that encourage updating, challenging work assignments, an organizational climate stressing technical performance, and a technical company orientation.

Engineers believed that being technically up to date would enhance their opportunity for advancement when these work environment conditions were present: good supervisory feedback and communication, organizational policies encouraging updating, technical expertise among peers, and challenging work assignments.

They believed that being technically up to date would increase the likelihood of a salary increase when the following work environment factors were present: good supervisory feedback and communication, organizational policies that encouraged updating, technical support within the organization, challenging work assignments, an overall organizational climate favoring technical performance, and the technological orientation of the company.

They believed that being more technically up to date would lead to more challenging work assignments when the work environment provided good supervisory feedback and communication, or overall organizational climate favoring technical performance, and work assignments of a challenging nature.

The opportunity to exercise personal initiative was perceived as a consequence of being technically up to date when there was organizational support for being technically current.

These findings show the close relationship between work environment and updating. Professionals will engage in updating activities when they perceive a link between specific conditions of the work environment and rewards and outcomes. Organizations that wish to encourage updating—and that must surely mean *all* organizations—are therefore advised to redesign their work environment and review their reward systems.

Summary and Conclusion

This chapter deals with two issues: (1) keeping professionals up to date using the model that stresses motivation and the work environment and (2) conditions that lead to technical obsolescence. The Dubin model provides a conceptual understanding of the multiple components that contribute to updating and improved performance. The model is concerned with the human, not the technological, aspects of updating. Both engineers and managers have emphasized the importance of the human components; this does not minimize the essential contribution of advanced technology (computers).

The updating model is the key contribution of the chapter. Educators, managers, and professionals need to recognize that keeping up to date is a complex issue with multiple determinants. The chapter spells out the specific dimensions that underlie individual motivation and each of the five environmental factors.

The findings on individual motivation demonstrate that multiple intrinsic rewards and outcomes stimulate engineers to keep up to date: a feeling of accomplishment, opportunity for advancement, a challenging environment. Similarly, each of the five work-environment factors has multiple stimulants to updating. Job activities and work assignments include such facilitators as challenging assignments that stretch the engineers' technical knowledge, responsibility to implement new ideas, or participation in decision making. Supervisory behavior contributes to updating by providing recognition and credit for good technical work, encouraging independent and innovative thinking, and soliciting ideas. The organization climate stimulates updating when the organization is at the cutting edge of technology or when innovation is enthusiastically received. Peer–colleague interactions facilitate updating when peers suggest new approaches to technical problems or provide reliable information on new developments. Finally, management policies and practices facilitate updating when the performance appraisal system ties financial gain to technical competence, when the company provides current technical equipment and facilities, and the company uses a rotation program to give diversified assignments.

Up-to-date professionals provide an organization with a competitive edge. The Japanese have learned the importance of this lesson. Japanese companies ensure that all employees receive the best training, and they also invest heavily in research and development to assure a constant stream of technological innovations.

Conditions that make updating necessary are the rapid growth and complexity of knowledge, the half life of knowledge, and the fast pace of technological change and innovation. Both the significance and cost of technical obsolescence are described. Specific actions are proposed that managers can undertake to stimulate updating.

Knowledge is a driving force on both the national and international scene. Continually acquiring new knowledge, and applying it, are vital if we are to maintain strategic leadership in global competition. In my judgment, keeping up to date will become an increasingly critical issue for all professionals, and particularly for faculty, technicians, scientific personnel, physicians, managers, and members of Congress.

References

Abernathy, W. J. "The Competitive Decline in U.S. Industries— The Management Factor." In H. Fusfeld and R. N. Langlois (eds.), *Understanding R & D Productivity*. Elmsford, N. Y.: Pergamon Press, 1982.

American Association of Engineering Societies. *Towards the Effective Utilization of American Engineers*. Washington: American Association of Engineering Societies, 1986.

Baker, W. O. "R & D Complexity and Competitiveness." *Research and Development: Key Issues for Management*. New York: Conference Board, 1983.

Bloch, E. "Countering Obsolescence in the Workplace." *Research Management*, 1984 (Nov./Dec.), p. 6.

Bradford, D. L., and Cohen, A. R. *Managing for Excellence: The*

Guide for Developing High Performance in Contemporary Organizations. New York: Wiley, 1984.

Carmichael, H. T., Templeton, B., Small, M., and Kelly, P. R. "Results of a 1972 APA Self-assessment Program." *American Journal of Psychiatry*, 1974 (June), pp.131–136.

"Cuomo Plan for Physician: Reviews Gain Support." *New York Times*, June 28, 1987.

Dubin, S. S. "Obsolescence or Lifelong Learning." *American Psychologist*, 1972, *27*, 486–498.

Dubin, S. S. "The Updating Process." *Continuing Education in Science and Engineering*. 1977 (Dec.), 165–186.

Dubin, S. S. Personal correspondence, 1978.

Dubin, S. S., and Cohen, D. *Quantitative Competence of Industrial Engineers*. University Park: Pennsylvania State University, 1970.

Dubin, S. S., Shelton, H., and McConnell, J. *Maintaining Professional and Technical Competence of the Older Engineer: Engineering and Psychological Aspects*. Washington: American Society for Engineering Education, 1973.

Farr, J. L., Enscore, E. E., Steiner, D. D., and Kozlowski, S.W. J. *Factors That Influence the Technical Updating of Engineers*. A final report prepared for National Science Foundation, Grant #SED78-21941. Washington: National Science Foundation, 1984.

Farr, J. L., Enscore, E. E. and others. *Behavior Anchored Scales: A Method for Identifying Continuing Education Needs of Engineers*. Washington: National Science Foundation, 1980a.

Farr, J. L., Dubin, S. S. and others. *Relationships Among Individual Motivation, Work Environment, and Updating in Engineers*. A final report prepared for National Science Foundation, Grant #SED78-21940. Washington: National Science Foundation, 1980b.

Feinstein, R. J. "The Ethics of Professional Regulation." *The New England Journal of Medicine*, March 21, 1985, pp. 801–804.

Fossum, J. A., Arvey, R. D., Paradise, C. A., and Robbins, N. E. "Modeling the Skills Obsolescence Process: A Psychological and Economic Integration." *Academy of Managerial Review*, 1986, *11*, 362–374.

Haddad, J. A. "The Changing Nature of the Engineering Community." In *Keeping Pace with Change: The Challenge for Engineers.* Boston; College of Engineering, Northeastern University, 1985.

Hinkle, I. M. *Automation in Producing Division of Chemical Information.* Chicago: American Chemical Society, 1985.

Jelenek, M. "MBAs Look at the World." *Career Management.* 1977, pp. 16–20.

Jenny, H. "Technical Currency—It's Money in the Bank." *RCA Engineer,* July/Aug., 1983, pp. 1–6.

Jenny, H., and Underwood, W. H. *Engineering Information Survey Results.* Cherry Hill, N.J. RCA Corporation, 1977.

Kaufman, H. *Obsolescence and Professional Career Development.* New York: AMACOM, 1974.

Kaufman, H. "Technical Obsolescence: An Empirical Analysis of Its Causes and How Professionals Can Cope with It." *Proceedings of the 86th Annual Conference of the American Society of Engineering Education,* Washington, D.C., 1978.

Kelly, K. "Information as a Communicable Disease." *Current Contents: Social and Behavioral Science,* Oct. 29, 1984, pp. 4–6.

Leventman, P. G., and Pierce, G. "Assessment of Lifelong Learning Programs: Needs for Engineers and Scientists in Massachusetts High Technology Companies." In *Keeping Pace with Change: The Challenge for Engineers.* Boston: College of Engineering, Northeastern University, 1986.

Lindsay, C., Morrison, J., and Kelly, E. J. "Professional Obsolescence: Implications for Continuing Education." *Adult Education,* 1974, *25,* 3–22.

Margulies, N., and Raia, A. P. "Scientists, Engineers and Technological Obsolescence." California Management Review, Winter 1967, pp. 43–47.

Miljus, R. C., and Smith, R. L. "Key Human Resources Issues for Management in High Tech Firms." In A. Kleingartner and C. S. Anderson (eds.), *Human Resources Management in High Tech Firms.* Lexington, Mass.: Lexington Books, 1987.

Miller, D. B., "How to Improve the Performance and Productivity of the Knowledge Worker." *Organizational Dynamics,* 1977, *5,* 62–80.

Miller, D. B. *Managing Professionals in Research and Development: A*

Guide for Improving Productivity and Organizational Effectiveness. San Francisco: Jossey-Bass, 1986.

Naisbett, J. *Megatrends: Ten New Directions Transforming Our Lives.* New York: Warner Books, 1982.

National Science Board. *Science at the Bicentennial: A Report from the Research Community.* Washington, D.C.: National Science Board, 1976.

National Science Board. *Human Resource Practices for Implementing Advanced Manufacturing Technology.* Washington: National Science Board, 1986a.

National Science Board. *Task Committee on Undergraduate Education and Engineering.* Washington: National Science Board, 1986b.

National Science Foundation. *Continuing Education for R and D Careers.* Washington: National Science Foundation, 1969.

National Science Foundation. *Emerging Issues in Science and Technology.* Washington: National Science Foundation, 1982.

New York Stock Exchange. *People and Productivity: A Challenge to Corporate America.* New York: The New York Stock Exchange Office of Economic Research, 1982.

Pelz, D. C., and Andrews, F. M. *Scientists in Organizations.* Ann Arbor: Institute of Social Research, University of Michigan, 1966.

Porter, L. W., and Lawer, E. E. *Managerial Attitudes and Performance.* Homewood, Ill.: Irwin, 1968.

Ritti, R. R. *The Engineer in the Industrial Corporation.* New York: Columbia University Press, 1971.

Roney, J. G. Paper presented at conference on Occupational Obsolescence. Menlo Park, Calif.: Stanford Research Institute, 1966.

Smith, L. F. *The Competitive Environment: New Concepts.* New York: Conference Board, 1984.

Steers, R. M. *Introduction to Organizational Behavior.* San Francisco: Goodyear, 1981.

Techlinberg, H. "Using Social Scientists in Research and Development." *Research Management,* Nov. 1981, pp. 24–27.

Truxal, C. "EE Careers: New Directions but Old Issues." In *Beyond*

1984: Technology and the Individual, IEEE Spectrum, June 1984, pp. 53–58.

Vroom, V. H. *Work and Motivation.* New York: Wiley, 1964.

Zukowski, R. W. *Managing Technological Careers.* Paper presented at IEEE Career Conference, 1983.

2

John A. Fossum
Richard D. Arvey

Marketplace
and Organizational Factors
That Contribute to Obsolescence

Professional obsolescence is a recurring theme in both the popular and scholarly literature. In response to growing concerns about this issue, we published a survey of the literature and suggested a model of the process by which job-related proficiencies become obsolete (Fossum, Arvey, Paradise, and Robbins, 1986). In that review, we proposed that professional obsolescence takes place at the individual job level and suggested that it occurs when "the person requirements of a job which are demanded by its tasks, duties, and responsibilities become incongruent with the stock of knowledge, skills, and abilities currently possessed by the individual; given that the knowledge, skills, and abilities were previously congruent with job demands" (p. 364).

We also suggested that expectancy theory (Campbell and Pritchard, 1976; Vroom, 1964) and human capital theory (Becker, 1975; Schultz, 1961; Thurow, 1970) are useful heuristics to help explain individual decisions and behavior associated with job-related proficiencies.

In preparing our review, we found relatively few papers that either defined or directly measured professional obsoles-

Figure 2.1. Factors Involved in Skills Obsolescence.

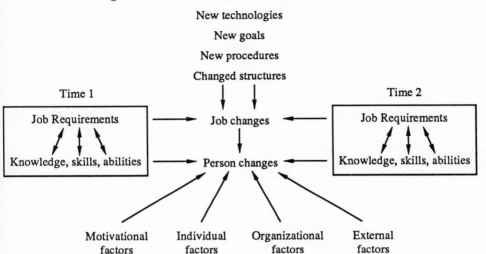

cence. Those that did tended to be occupationally specific (Arvey and Neel, 1976; Dalton and Thompson, 1971; Kaufman, 1972; 1973; 1978; Kopelman, 1977). We also did not find professional obsolescence expressed in individually or organizationally relevant terms.

We introduced a model of professional obsolescence (contained in Figure 2.1) that identified several factors which might influence changes in a person's job-related proficiencies (knowledge, skills, and abilities), including motivational, individual, organizational, and other external factors. We also suggested that task, duty, and responsibility changes in the job could result from the introduction of new technologies, goals, or procedures, or from changing structures within the organization. Further, we indicated that job changes were more likely to influence person changes than the reverse. The greater the gap between the rate or trajectory of job changes and the rate of changes in a person's knowledge, skills, and abilities, the more obsolescence could be expected to occur.

In Figure 2.1, it is important to recognize that the proposed direction of causality is from the job to the individual; this means that the individual is required to adapt to changes in job requirements. Also, job changes can be quite rapid, while personal response is limited by the configuration of abilities, aptitudes, and the rate at which the individual can learn.

In this chapter we further elucidate the factors and variables that we believe contribute to professional obsolescence. These ideas should be considered preliminary and speculative. Little empirical data exist to confirm these hunches and hypotheses. This chapter is intended to be provocative and creative, rather than confirmatory.

The Origin of Job Changes

Economists see employers' demand for labor as derived from consumers' demands for goods and services. Goods and services are produced by transforming raw materials through the application of capital (production technologies) and labor. The demand for labor (and the specific way tasks, duties, and responsibilities are configured) depends ultimately on the overall level of consumer demand and the specific goods and services consumers prefer. The mix of specific goods preferred will change as their characteristics and relative prices change. The mix of goods produced also depends on the relative prices of raw materials and production equipment (see Ehrenberg and Smith, 1985).

Changes in Overall Consumer Demand. The decisions consumers make about their levels of purchases directly influence producers' uses of inputs (labor, capital, and raw materials). During growth phases of the economic cycle, employers hire more employees, and if they believe that the increase in demand will last, they may invest in more plants and equipment. When recessions occur, producers may or may not sell plants and equipment, but they almost always reduce employment.

At such times, if the employer has a choice, employees with a wider variety of job skills are retained, to cover more of the production process at a lower volume of output. The employer is unlikely to shut down completely until the value of sales is exceeded by the costs of labor and raw materials. Thus, the scope of job-related skills becomes an important employer consideration during economic downturns. During upturns, the employer is concerned about the rate at which added employees can acquire knowledge, skills, and abilities. Tradeoffs may be made in the scope of duties, given the employees' aptitudes and learning rates.

Changes in Prices of Production Factors. Employers choose production methods that result in the lowest costs. Production factors include machinery and equipment, plant, transportation, job designs, and materials necessary to produce the organization's products and services. If the price of equipment relative to labor decreases, or if one type of labor can be substituted for another at a lower wage, then the employer would be expected to make a change in labor structure,

When prices for particular types of production equipment drop, it is not immediately apparent what the effects will be on employment. Consider, for example, the introduction of optical scanning of universal product codes at retail checkout registers. Retailers have installed these for a variety of reasons including real-time tracking of inventory levels and reduced checker-training requirements. As the price of scanners drops, more scanners will be purchased and the use of employees to manually enter product code and price data will diminish. But at the same time that an employer changes its relative use of scanning equipment and key-entry employees due to the equipment price change, it also experiences an increase in its real income because its overall costs dropped. It may increase its number of checkout personnel to most efficiently use the amount of equipment that will enable it to make the most profits.

The overall effect for employees depends on the rate of substitution of equipment for labor as compared to the motivation of the employer to add more of that type of labor in order to be able to produce or serve the market at a higher level. In other words, increased profits may come from both increased efficiency and the expansion that increased efficiency may allow.

If the net effect is a reduction in employment, then skills obsolescence will occur.

Technological Change. Changes in technology frequently capture
processes that were previously accomplished by employees. For
example, numerical control equipment allows machining activities to be performed in programmed modules without significant human interaction. Computer hardware and operating
software enable automatic storage and retrieval of information
with no human intervention. These changes can lead to sudden
reconfigurations of task, duties, and responsibilities.

As technologies evolve, workers will recognize both a
market effect and an employer effect. First, as organizations in
general begin to use new technologies, the demand for certain
job-skill configurations will decrease; people with those job
skills will experience lower relative wages or increased periods
of unemployment. Second, as a particular employer substitutes
a new production technology, there is an immediate mismatch
between much of the individual employees' knowledge, skills,
and abilities and the new tasks associated with the technology.

The organization bringing in the new technology must
then evaluate its current employees, determining whether there
are available replacements in the external market, the current
employees' aptitudes for learning the job skills, the length of
time necessary for retraining, and its costs.

Organizational Change. Human capital theory divides job proficiencies (knowledge, skills, and abilities) into two different categories: general human capital and specific human capital. General human capital is represented by job proficiencies that many
different organizations use to accomplish work. Examples
might include Fortran programming, arc welding, typing, and
the like. Specific human capital is represented by job proficiencies that are of benefit only to one specific organization. It might
include things like knowledge of company policies and procedures, set-up skills to manufacture a specific product, and
information about how one job relates to others in the
organization.

General human capital becomes obsolete when no employer requires it in its firm's production function. General human capital is embodied in the individual and the costs of obtaining it are generally borne by the employee, since an employer would lose its investment if the employee decided to quit. Employees would probably be attracted by higher pay rates from other employers for a given set of knowledge, skills, and abilities since they would earn a higher return for their investment.

Specific human capital becomes obsolete when the firm reorganizes, changes its product lines, or makes other similar decisions unique to the organization. The individual usually does not personally invest in acquiring specific human capital since it has no market value. The employer, on other hand, may provide it (and may pay an employee a premium to avoid turnover) after there is evidence that the employee is likely to remain with the organization. Reorganization frequently makes some specific human capital obsolete. The organization should consider the benefits of new structuring against the costs of acquiring new specific human capital.

Technological changes are likely to have major effects on general human capital job proficiencies; organizational changes influence specific human capital job proficiencies. Both technological and organizational changes are likely to have relatively abrupt effects on the match between job proficiencies and job tasks. In a technological change, we could say that the old tasks are used through the end of the week that the old equipment is in place and a new set is required the following Monday.

On the other hand, changes in product demand are likely to take place more slowly; consumers must know something about new products before they can have an effect on employers' needs for certain job proficiencies. People involved in product development probably have a relatively extended period during which job tasks, duties, and responsibilities and general human capital job proficiencies remain congruent.

Market, Organizational, and Individual Levels of Professional Obsolescence

As Figure 2-1 indicated, "person" change is the dependent variable in the professional obsolescence model. Once learned, job proficiencies are embodied in the individual. We can assume that changes in the environment at the market and organizational level act as stimuli to which the individual responds. In both expectancy and human capital theories, the individual is expected to respond to stimuli that will lead to personal gain, often increased income.

In a strict sense, employers do not suffer from professional obsolescence since they purchase job proficiencies rather than possess them. Only employees can have obsolete knowledge, skills, and abilities. Employers find, rather, an incongruence between their present job designs and the stocks of job proficiencies available among present and potential employees.

Market Level. In the labor market, professional obsolescence occurs on an occupational level. It does not necessarily result from a mismatch between job responsibilities and job proficiencies, but from a relative reduction in the numbers of workers demanded by employers as compared to the supply. Those working in the occupation recognize these reductions in the form of relatively lower wage levels. These reductions are likely to take place gradually, as the public's demand for products and services that require their job proficiencies declines, or firms gradually replace production methods with general innovations.

Since these changes involve all employers within an industry or all employers who use a particular production method, individuals within occupations would be expected, under usual conditions, to develop their own general human capital job proficiencies to avoid obsolescence. There are, however, certain factors that reduce the motivation to change. Consider steel production, for example. There are presently a large number of unemployed steel production employees in an essentially obsolete occupation. As the steel industry began an employment decline in the 1970s, many workers did not acquire new job proficiencies. There may be many reasons for this. First, pay (a valent outcome) was very high in steel production. Second, employment was a function of both demand for steel and seniority. As the demand for steel began to decline, most steel workers with general human capital job proficiencies were unaffected since seniority clauses insulated them from employment cutbacks. Third, as the decline began to accelerate and more senior workers were affected, many did not see major benefits from retooling for a lower-paying job given their likely remaining work years.

Organizational Level. Before beginning to explore professional obsolescence at the organizational level, we must draw a distinction between an occupation and a job. In the market, configurations of general human capital job proficiencies demanded by many employers can be conceived of as occupations. Within an organization, the addition of particular specific human capital job proficiencies creates a job unique to the employer. Changes in job responsibilities that are unique to the organization create incongruencies with an existing stock of specific human capital job proficiencies. The organization should be able to predict likely professional obsolescence since it knows the requirements of its new job designs. Employees will become aware of professional obsolescence as relative opportunities for advancement begin to decline or salary increases cease. In extreme cases, where the bulk of an employee's knowledge, skills, and abilities are specific to the firm, that person may suffer a layoff in the face of redefined tasks.

At the organizational level, professional obsolescence occurs primarily in jobs with a high content of specific human capital job proficiencies. This is not to say that obsolete employees do not exist in jobs with general human capital proficiencies, but for this to occur, the organization or the professional must have failed to recognize a change in the configuration of proficiencies within the occupations where these jobs are located. Perhaps the best recent example of this type of professional obsolescence is the large number of middle managers who lost their jobs during recent reorganizations.

Individual Level. Individual-level obsolescence is primarily a function of changes in individual ability levels or job performance requirements. If there have been no changes in market or organizational factors, then the knowledge and skills necessary to perform the job have not changed. However, ability levels for these knowledge and skill areas may decline for a number of reasons, which we will detail in the next section. A given individual's ability levels may also not have changed, but the average ability level in the labor market to perform required tasks may have improved enough that a particular employee is no longer comparably effective in a job. Individual-level obsolescence is frequently demonstrated by an inability to perform at acceptable levels. However, poor performance, in itself, is not evidence of obsolescence, but may rather be related to a perceived low relationship between job performance and rewards.

The Origins of Person Changes

Employment performance takes place within a set of tasks, duties, and responsibilities. As we have seen, changes in tasks, duties, and responsibilities precede changes in job proficiencies (knowledge, skills, and abilities) except in those few situations where the particular proficiencies create products that will eventually lead to changes in job responsibilities in other areas of the economy. One might say, however, that even R & D job responsibilities are broadly defined.

Performance is seen as a multiplicative function of ability and motivation (Dunnette, 1976). Competent job performance requires job proficiencies that are congruent with current job responsibilities. Acquiring job proficiencies requires both aptitudes and motivation. From a human capital perspective, aptitudes represent economic ability (Thurow, 1970). Motivational influences include the valences of outcomes, the perception that valent outcomes will follow from the acquisition of proficiencies, and the perception that personal effort will enable one to acquire certain proficiencies. Job-change information must be available to the individual to act as a stimulus for considering whether the effort to acquire new skills will be productive.

Influences on Present Abilities. Present job proficiencies are a function of aptitudes and motivation during previous periods.

Given the information available in the labor market and previous experiences they had with applying their aptitudes, employees make choices about acquiring additional job proficiencies, given the expected outcomes associated. Other things
equal, people might be expected to acquire job proficiencies
that could be learned more rapidly, given their aptitudes. Employers might be expected to offer greater economic rewards for
job proficiencies that yield a larger return. This means that the
present stock of job proficiencies should have been acquired
because they led, other things equal, to more rewarding outcomes, had stronger acquisition-to-outcome expectancies, and
were perceived to be more easily acquired than other sets.

Unless the organization is ignorant about the market in
which it operates, it hires people who possess the requisite
general human capital job proficiencies for its jobs. Without
these proficiencies the individual would not be hired. Thus,
through the act of hiring, the employer has determined that the
employee's proficiencies are not obsolete for its purposes.

Before joining the organization, the individual knows
more about the acquisition-to-outcome relationship for general
human capital job proficiencies than the performance-to-
outcome relationship for performance in a job. Given their
capabilities, we would expect people to choose to acquire general human capital that would yield the greatest expected rewards during their working lifetimes. Among the factors that
people would have to estimate in making this choice is the level
of performance organizations might be expected to require for
different jobs. They would also be concerned with the period of
time during which the general human capital would remain
current. Individuals would not be expected to develop job proficiencies for occupations in which they believed that they could
not achieve required performance levels.

The choice of which skills to acquire would depend both
on pay rates and their perceived durability. A baccalaureate
preparation in elementary education returns a lower starting
salary than an engineering degree. But, there is less need for
retooling. Some evidence exists that occupations with durable

skills earn less in the short run (McDowell, 1982), but have longer periods of return after they have been acquired.

Individual development decisions also reflect perceptions about the likely future need for various general human capital configurations. Jobs with lower vacancy rates would be associated with lower acquisition-to-outcome expectancies. Lower acquisition-to-outcome relationships would also be perceived by individuals whose expected remaining work life would not allow them to recapture as great an amount of outcomes as would be possible over the useful life of the proficiencies. Finally, lower acquisition-to-outcome relationships would also be perceived by individuals who were currently earning more than others who might consider acquiring the same job proficiencies, since they would have to forego more income to learn them (thus putting forth more effort).

Employees would also be expected to consider the effort-to-acquisition relationship for acquiring the proficiencies demanded by potential jobs. These relationships might be influenced by the employee's knowledge of his or her aptitudes and the speed with which employers will demand that employees achieve an acceptable level of performance. To an extent, the employer's communications to the employee contain information about the steepness of the necessary learning curve and the height of the necessary performance asymptote. Employers can be expected to increase wages for certain duties as the profit levels from their output are greater than others if there is not an adequate current supply within the organization (for specific human capital) or in the external labor market (for general human capital). Other things equal, wages will have to be increased more to attract employees into jobs in which the tasks will change quickly since retooling will be necessary and the long-run acquisition-to-outcome perception will decrease. Thus, the employer may need to guarantee retraining to attract employees to these types of positions.

Age. Age has several influences on employees and job proficiencies. First, some aptitudes, particularly physical, decline with age. Aptitudes establish an upper limit on ability levels. To the extent that jobs require a constant level of skill application, individuals may fall short of desired performance levels over time. Where job-related aptitudes have declined, skill acquisition may not be possible. The obverse may also obtain, however, when maturity enables a person to consolidate previous job proficiencies into a new, higher-level skill.

As individuals approach their desired retirement age, the returns on investments in acquiring additional job proficiencies decrease. Unless all the returns are obtained by the time of retirement, the older the individual is, the less the expected return, even if valence is constant. This helps to explain the popularity of early-retirement options when appropriately structured by employers.

Other things equal, employers with older employees should expect greater obsolescence because employees may not perceive they will recoup their investment in new job proficiencies before their retirement. Organizations with a history of frequent retraining should have employees whose perceived returns should all be realizable within an expected working life. Early-retirement options, however, cut the alternative returns to the efforts of retraining by the retirement benefits.

Briefly, this analysis suggests that age influences effort-to-performance perceptions where aptitudes decline or improve; performance-to-outcome relationships decrease as the perceived opportunities to realize investments in training are shortened by impending retirement; and motivation may also change as certain outcomes change in valence.

Changing Valences. If outcomes that employees associate with skill acquisition change in value, then the motivation to acquire new skills will be affected. For blue-collar workers, if collective bargaining agreements are examined, evidence suggests that more senior employees prefer jobs with less adverse working conditions. There is also evidence for blue-collar employees that while turnover is associated with repetitive jobs, when age is introduced the relationship reverses (Bartel, 1981), suggesting that older employees may not be interested in using as wide a repertoire of job proficiencies as younger employees.

However, among professional employees, Arvey and Neel (1976) showed that a sample of older engineers demonstrated relatively high values for making use of abilities, accomplishments, and security whereas the three least important outcomes were receiving praise, supervising others, and advancement. No comparisons were made, however, with the values or job duties of younger engineers.

The valence associated with increased real income may also change over time as family responsibilities and expenditures vary.

Diagnosing Professional Obsolescence

While professional obsolescence is a phenomenon of individual labor supply, its impact influences markets, organizations, and individuals. Thus, measures can be made at each of these levels to help employers and individuals recognize current and likely future areas of obsolescence. Even though professional obsolescence is a labor-supply phenomenon, at the market and organizational level it is originally caused by a change in the demand for certain job proficiencies.

Market-Level. Market-level diagnosis, by definition, can involve only occupations for which general human capital job proficiencies are required, since specific human capital job proficiencies are not in the market. On a periodic basis, comparisons may be made between proficiency requirements reflected in job definitions published in the *Dictionary of Occupational Titles* and job proficiencies reflected in educational attainment (Rumberger, 1981). Other demand-side projections may be made in publications such as *Occupational Outlook* published by the Department of Labor.

To make more short-run projections, we can examine the relative growth (or shrinkage) rates of employment in industries published monthly by the Bureau of Labor Statistics. Since changes in job responsibilities reflect changes in demand and since we assume that demand changes are stimuli that influence future labor-supply behavior by employees, these changes indicate likely future areas of obsolescence.

Changes in relative wage rates also indicate possible imbalances between demand and supply of individuals with particular job proficiencies. Where wages are increasing more rapidly for one occupation than others, it means that there are inadequate stocks of general human capital job proficiencies in the economy. These skills would definitely not be obsolete. In situations where relative wage levels are falling, the demand for these proficiencies in relation to the supply is falling. Supplies of job proficiencies are likely to change in response to wage rates and are likely to be more fixed in the short run than demand would be.

Exogenous shocks, such as changes in production technology, would have major effects on occupational skills. Consider, for example, the effects of word-processing hardware and software on secretarial job proficiencies, advanced imaging technologies on the radiological occupations, and numerical control equipment on the machining trades. These would be associated with occupational professional obsolescence while simultaneous growth in the industries formerly employing these skills would continue, or even increase, if productivity was improving.

Obsolescence may also occur ultimately in situations where the match between job requirements and job proficiencies is relatively unchanging, although this would be a long-run phenomenon. Consider a situation in which consumer demand for a particular product or service is declining. Steel mill outputs would be a good recent example. While the job requirements have not changed greatly, relative wages have fallen and unemployment has increased. Employees with steelmaking skills have very little opportunity as the numbers of jobs requiring these proficiencies decline. These skills are largely obsolete on a market-level basis (but may not be within the organization that continues to use them).

Organizational Level. Organizational-level diagnosis becomes more difficult. Professional obsolescence at the organizational level may occur within an industry or within a company. The production and transmission of goods and services require general human capital job proficiencies. However, some of these proficiencies do not become general human capital until the market determines the value of a new product or service.

Within an industry, if production technologies are relatively similar, differences in performance between firms *may* be an indicator of professional obsolescence. To determine whether this is the case, a diagnostician must first determine that the job tasks are similar, and that the reward systems associated with acquiring job proficiencies are similar. If so, performance differences might be apparent in the rate and quality of new products and services introduced into the market.

A firm that continually lags competitors in the marketplace will find a shorter life cycle for its products and will often be faced with an imitative or cloning strategy that results in relatively lower profit margins per unit of output. The firm may *believe* that its problems are related to professional obsolescence (assuming it is not purposely following an initiative strategy), but its problem may rather be obsolescent jobs (mismatches between firm and market tasks, duties, and responsibilities).

Within the organization, obsolescence may occur as the result of a rapid change in production methods. This causes major changes in tasks, duties, and responsibilities that require some time for adapted job proficiencies to match. Organizational changes such as restructuring business units and changing objectives also result in reapportioning or creating new job tasks. If they no longer match job proficiencies, professional obsolescence becomes either a momentary or a permanent problem.

Some organizations are following labor market strategies that can potentially make them more vulnerable to general human capital professional obsolescence. Locating a plant in an area where there are few employers desiring similar skills may confer a monopsonistic (single employer) advantage in the labor market, but may also require the employer to make investments in general human capital job proficiencies. Employers who design job progressions that are markedly different from the labor market also encounter this risk. Skill-based pay plans (Lawler, 1982) are sometimes used to reduce this possibility where job proficiencies are specific to a given firm or are in short supply in the area labor market. However, they would not be an attractive alternative for an employer where the job proficiencies are general human capital in its relevant labor market because the employer would have to offer a competitive wage to hire new employees, and would risk losing those it trained if it did not at least meet the market as they acquired general human capital job proficiencies. Thus, we would expect skill-based pay to be used most often when the employer is a single purchaser of labor in a given market or needs to motivate strongly the acquisition of specific human capital job proficiencies. Where the job proficiencies are general human capital, the employer would be likely to hire inexperienced employees at a discount from the going wage and then gradually increase rates as they are trained and become more comparable to the market proficiency level.

Individual Level. Individual-level diagnosis should be relatively straightforward. We noted earlier that tasks, duties, and responsibilities serve as stimuli for acquisition of job proficiencies. (Of course, some individuals may have skills unused by a current job that could be immediately applied to a new job.) We also noted that while professional obsolescence is a labor supply problem, it has particular relevance for the employer when the obsolete job proficiencies are specific human capital.

At the individual level, professional obsolescence could be diagnosed through the use of achievement tests, maximum ability measures, observational techniques in job analysis, or carefully prepared performance appraisal instruments. The information gathered must relate to the *potential* to perform the required tasks rather than their actual performance or the output that they might enable. These would all be organizationally relevant measures.

From the individual's perspective, professional obsolescence might be reflected in an inability to obtain employment at previous earning levels, lower levels of outputs as tasks change, or a narrowing of job responsibilities.

Preventing Professional Obsolescence

Performance is a function of ability and motivation. Tasks, duties, and responsibilities serve as stimuli to acquire job-relevant proficiencies, but acquisition-related rewards are necessary to maintain skill-acquiring behaviors. There are five issues that organizations, in particular, should consider in preventing professional obsolescence.

1. Aptitude levels of employees create upper limits on the speed, depth, and breadth at which job proficiencies can be acquired.
2. Reward systems influence persistence in acquisition of job proficiencies. If, for example, acquisition of job proficiencies has primary instrumentality for future promotions, not present job rewards, then older employees might be less likely to exhibit acquisition behavior.
3. If an organization desires to operate differently from competitors, then it must expect to invest more heavily in development of job proficiencies since employees will find them to be specific human capital in their labor markets.
4. To avoid the occurrence of professional obsolescence with the introduction of a new technology, companies must diagnose the degree of relearning necessary and start retraining in time so that breadth and depth requirements are met within the employees' aptitudes.
5. We have argued that the decision to acquire new job proficiencies requires that the individual respond to changed task, duty, and responsibility stimuli. Where the lead time to acquire job proficiencies is relatively long, individuals need information that the tasks, duties, and responsibilities will change in the future if they are to be ready at the change. Further, they need information that changes their motivational levels for acquisition of job proficiencies. This means that pay for new job proficiency configurations must increase (raising the valence of outcomes) and that information about the relationship between occupational attainment and pay-level improvements be readily available.

Training programs best matching aptitudes to new job proficiencies need to be developed to enhance effort to performance perceptions as well.

Summary

Professional obsolescence occurs when tasks, duties, and responsibilities required change in magnitudes or directions beyond the job proficiencies of employees who perform them. These changes occur when new production technologies are introduced or demand for goods and services changes. Decreases in demand for certain goods and services lead ultimately to occupational professional obsolescence. Changes in technology make the employment of certain skills uneconomical.

Technological change reduces the demand for certain skills. For employees to retain their economic value (and pay), new job proficiencies need to be acquired and some current proficiencies allowed to erode. Changes in organizational design also require learning new skills. These, however, are valuable only to the present employer. Thus, an employee must make a choice with regard to the likely reward stream from learning employer-specific proficiencies and skills that have a broader application in the labor market.

Individual obsolescence may occur through the erosion of an individual's job proficiencies or through the enhancements in the general level of job proficiency in the labor market for a given occupation. Obsolescence may result from decreases or changes in aptitude levels that reduce abilities in some skill areas, or it may result from changes in motivation to retain or acquire certain skills given the interests of the individual, perceptions about the likelihood of acquiring a certain skill, or beliefs about the skills' usefulness for obtaining employment-related rewards.

Professional obsolescence may be diagnosed on a market-level basis by identifying decreases in employment levels for certain occupations and changes in the manner in which jobs are described. At the organizational level, lower performance relative to other organizations in the industry with comparable technologies may signal obsolescence. At the individual level, obsolescence can be identified through achievement tests, performance appraisals, and other available measures.

Professional obsolescence is an individual-level phenomenon resulting from a variety of factors that change a person's capabilities and interests in maintaining job proficiency. A variety of methods can be used to identify demand and supply changes in skills and to enhance individuals' motivation to acquire and enhance job-related proficiencies.

References

Arvey, R. D., and Neel, C. W. "Motivation and Obsolescence in Engineers." *Industrial Gerontology*, 1976, *3*, 113–120.

Bartel, A. "Wages, Nonwage Job Characteristics, and Labor Mobility." *Industrial and Labor Relations Review*, 1981, *34*, 578–589.

Becker, G. S. *Human Capital*. (2nd ed.) New York: National Bureau of Economic Research, 1975.

Campbell, J. P., and Pritchard, R. D. "Motivation Theory in Industrial and Organizational Psychology." In M. D. Dunnette (ed.), *Handbook of Industrial and Organizational Psychology*. Skokie, Ill.: Rand McNally, 1976.

Dalton, G. W., and Thompson, P. H. "Accelerating Obsolescence of Older Engineers." *Harvard Business Review*, 1971, *49* (5), 57–67.

Dunnette, M. D. "Aptitudes, Abilities, and Skills." In M. D. Dunnette (ed.), *Handbook of Industrial and Organizational Psychology*. Skokie, Ill.: Rand McNally, 1976.

Ehrenberg, R. G., and Smith, R. S. *Modern Labor Economics*. Glenview, Ill.: Scott, Foresman, 1985.

Fossum, J. A., Arvey, R. D., Paradise, C. A., and Robbins, N. E. "Modeling the Skills Obsolescence Process: A Psychological and Economic Integration." *Academy of Management Review*, 1986, *11*, 362–374.

Kaufman, H. G. "Relations of Ability and Interest to Currency of Professional Knowledge Among Engineers." *Journal of Applied Psychology*, 1972, *56*, 495–499.

Kaufman, H. G. "A Critical Incident Study of Personal Characteristics Associated with Technical Obsolescence Among Engineers." *Studies of Personnel Psychology*, 1973, *5*, 63–67.

Kaufman, H. G. "Continuing Education and Job Performance: A Longitudinal Study." *Journal of Applied Psychology*, 1978, *63*, 248–251.

Kopelman, R. E. "Psychological Stages of Careers in Engineering: An Expectancy Theory Taxonomy." *Journal of Vocational Behavior*, 1977, *10*, 270–286.

Lawler, E. E. *Pay and Organization Development*. Reading, Mass.: Addison-Wesley, 1982.

McDowell, J. M. "Obsolescence of Knowledge and Career Publication Profiles: Some Evidence of Differences Among Fields in Costs of Interrupted Careers." *American Economic Review*, 1982, *72*, 752–768.

Rumberger, R. W. "The Changing Skill Requirements of Jobs in the U.S. Economy." *Industrial and Labor Relations Review*, 1981, *34*, 578–590.

Schultz, T. W. "Investment in Human Capital." *American Economic Review*, 1961, *51*, 1–17.

Thurow, L. C. *Investment in Human Capital*. Belmont, Calif.: Wadsworth, 1970.

Vroom, V. H. *Work and Motivation*. New York: Wiley, 1964.

3

Sherry L. Willis
Joanne L. Tosti-Vasey

How Adult Development, Intelligence, and Motivation Affect Competence

Chapters One and Two have discussed professional competence and its loss through obsolescence as an interaction between personal and environmental dimensions, with special attention to environmental issues. Chapter One focused on factors in the professional's immediate work environment that are associated with updating. Chapter Two discussed skills obsolescence from a macro-environmental perspective, considering marketplace and organizational factors.

In this chapter, we will consider issues related to the person variables in the interactional model, mental ability and motivation. These two issues are important to maintaining professional competence, and since maintaining competence is of particular concern to midcareer professionals, we will give special attention to developmental changes in cognitive ability and motivation occurring by middle age. Moreover, we will consider generational differences in cognitive ability and motivation. The midcareer professional's skills and abilities are often compared to those of younger, more recently trained professionals; it is necessary, then, to examine the research literature on generational (that is, cohort) differences in mental ability and motivation.

Adult Cognitive Ability

How a professional performs in the workplace is, of course, a product of many factors, of which cognitive ability is only one. Professional competence involves other personal variables, such as interpersonal skills, motivation, and prior education and training. While level of cognitive ability alone does not assure professional competence, it is a necessary condition; it is important, therefore, to consider how cognitive abilities relate to professional competence at various career stages.

One of the dominant approaches to the study of cognitive functioning in adulthood has been the psychometric ability approach, where intelligence is seen as involving a number of different mental abilities (Botwinick, 1977). Although the specific abilities studied vary among the different psychometric models, many are commonly recognized: verbal, mathematical, spatial, inductive reasoning, memory, and perceptual speed abilities (Thurstone and Thurstone, 1941).

Mental ability is a theoretical construct that cannot be directly observed. Individuals' level of ability functioning is assessed by observing their behavior (performance) on tests or measures shown to represent a given ability. An individual may demonstrate a high level on one ability, but average or below-average performance levels on others. These individual differences in ability level are important, since particular abilities appear to be associated with achieving competence in various professions. For example, high levels of spatial ability are critical for pilots and engineers (Hills, 1957), while verbal competence is necessary for journalists.

Abilities and Professional Competence

How do mental abilities contribute to the acquisition and maintenance of competence in a given profession? Think of abilities as mental building blocks used by an individual in developing the knowledge base and proficiencies required by a profession (Willis and Schaie, 1986). The tasks performed by a professional are complex and typically involve multiple abilities. For example, computer programming involves inductive reasoning, mathematical abilities, and spatial abilities; if the programmer writes the documentation for a program, verbal abilities are also required. A manager developing a budget needs mathematical ability; however, making budgetary projections also involves other abilities, such as inductive reasoning, the ability to see patterns of logical relationships, and the ability to use these patterns in predicting future trends.

Schaie's stage model of cognitive development (1977–1978) is useful in considering how cognitive abilities relate to professional competence at various stages — career entry, mid-career, and late career. Schaie argues that acquiring basic mental abilities (verbal, mathematical, reasoning) required for effective functioning in our society is a major developmental task of childhood and adolescence. Much of the acquisition process occurs as a function of schooling. Then, beginning in young adulthood, there is a shift from acquiring abilities to applying them to adult roles and responsibilities. In early adulthood, many individuals are particularly concerned with achieving a work role and a family role. Thus, much of the young adult's cognitive efforts are applied to developing job-related knowledge and proficiencies.

In middle age, many individuals find that their professional and familial responsibilities expand. They may assume supervisory and mentoring responsibilities, such that intellectual abilities are directed not only to their own career development, but also to that of subordinates and colleagues. Some professionals assume more extensive responsibilities at the executive level, involving the management of work groups, departments, or entire organizations. These responsibilities require applying cognitive abilities and skills to increasingly complex problems and situations. The executive must be able to think hierarchically and consider a problem from multiple levels of the organization.

Midcareer professionals are also required to apply their cognitive abilities to the maintenance of their own professional competence, as well as to the training of apprentices and subordinates. Thus, many of the basic mental abilities and skills acquired in childhood are used throughout adulthood. These basic abilities are applied to increasingly complex problems and tasks at work. As one's career progresses, these abilities are used first in developing complex job proficiencies in one's professional specialties, and then in modifying these proficiencies as new information and technologies become available.

Developmental Changes in Abilities

It is important to consider how intellectual abilities change from early to middle adulthood, and the implications of these changes for maintaining professional competence. Findings from a number of longitudinal studies (Bray and Howard, 1983a; Schaie, 1983; Siegler, 1983) indicate that reliable decline on most of the abilities is not observed until the early sixties. In a twenty-one-year study of managers at AT&T, Bray and Howard (1983a) found no normative decline in intellectual performance from the early to the midcareer phase. Moreover, some longitudinal studies have found that for abilities that are routinely employed in daily living, such as verbal skills, peak performance levels are reached only in midlife, on average (Schaie, 1983). The ability to make quick and accurate perceptual discriminations is one of the few abilities to exhibit significant age-related decline beginning in early middle age. However, there is some evidence that the average magnitude of decline in the speed at which behavior can be performed reaches a critical threshold for only a limited number of job demands (Schaie, 1986). There are, of course, wide individual differences in the rate and timing of decline. Some people show significant decline at a relatively early age, while for a few individuals no reliable decline on certain abilities is found even in old age.

It is well known that level of ability is a significant predictor of successful entry into a given profession (Hills, 1957). That is, individuals entering a field demonstrate, on average, a higher level of performance on certain abilities than for population norms. Moreover, ability level at early career stages is also a significant predictor of professional competence at *midcareer*. In their longitudinal study of AT&T managers, Bray and Howard found that intellectual ability at career entry predicted career achievement in midlife (Howard, 1984). Likewise, Kaufman (1972) found that cognitive ability at the beginning of engineers' careers significantly predicted both professional productivity and professional updatedness in midcareer; early ability level was related to the number of patents disclosed and the number of articles published. Because there is considerable stability in level of cognitive ability across much of adulthood, individuals who were more able at career entry are also likely to be more able in midcareer. Also, high levels of cognitive functioning may be particularly advantageous at midcareer in facilitating the professional's ability to engage in updating activities that require the acquisition of new knowledge and proficiencies and adapt to technological advances.

Generational Differences

Although adults, as we have seen, do not show significant age-related cognitive decline until the sixties, the midcareer professional may still appear less competent in some areas than a younger colleague. There are generational differences in level of performance on many mental abilities. When different generations (such as, adults born in 1900 as opposed to those born in 1950) are compared at the same chronological age (for instance, age 25), significant generational differences are found. The nature of these generational differences varies for different abilities. There is a strong positive cohort trend for inductive-reasoning ability, with more recent cohorts showing higher levels of performance when assessed at the same chronological age. In contrast, there is a curvilinear cohort trend for numerical ability, with cohorts born in the 1920s performing at a higher level than either earlier or later generations.

As a result of positive cohort trends, the midcareer professional may appear at a disadvantage compared with younger colleagues even though the middle-aged professional has suffered no age-related decline in competence. As we saw in Chapter Two, the middle-aged professional may be disadvantaged when the level of ability demanded in a field increases as a result of new technologies; this is likely to occur when the abilities required are those exhibiting positive cohort trends. However, on the other hand, curvilinear or negative cohort trends can be advantageous to middle-aged or older professionals, since their ability level may be higher than that of more recent cohorts.

Creativity, Expertise, and Professional Competence

The relationship between cognitive functioning and professional competence has also been examined in terms of creativity and expertise. One index of creativity is the unique or significant contributions that professionals make to their field. Expertise refers to extensive and advanced knowledge and proficiencies in a profession.

Creativity. Recent research on age-related changes in creativity (Simonton, 1988) indicates that the *proportion* of significant contributions to total contributions made by a professional remains constant across the career. That is, the proportion of "hits" to total attempts does not differ significantly across age periods or career stages. This finding has been demonstrated across a variety of disciplines (Simonton, 1977; 1985). If quantity (total contributions) rather than quality (significant works) is considered, productivity has been found to peak in the forties and fifties for many fields that emphasize scholarship, including fields as diverse as medicine and history (Simonton, 1975). In fact, the first ten years in a professional's work life is the *least* productive decade of the entire career. Thus, many professionals in their sixties, who have been active throughout their career, can be expected to be somewhat more productive than in their twenties even though modest decline from peak productivity in midlife may have occurred.

Expertise. So we see that there is little normative decline in ability level in midlife. Are there other types of change in cognitive functioning that are relevant to maintaining professional competence? Here, recent research on expertise is of interest, since many experts are midcareer professionals. Differences between novices and experts in their understanding of a body of knowledge have been examined (Anderson, 1982; Brown, 1982). A major difference is the structure of their knowledge base. The novice's knowledge base tends to be fractionated, not well integrated, with few connections between various knowledge domains. The expert's knowledge base is highly organized and integrated. When the expert's knowledge system is diagrammed, the knowledge base is hierarchically organized, and there is a rich system of pathways and connections relating various parts of the knowledge base (see also Chapter Four). Moreover, experts have developed a repertoire of cognitive strategies specific to the knowledge domain. It is the richly integrated knowledge base of the expert and the availability of domain-specific strategies that enable the experts to solve problems in their field very quickly and efficiently.

How might the expertise that has been achieved by mid-career professionals affect their efforts to maintain professional competence? When professionals acquire new information via updating that can be integrated within their existing knowledge base, then experts would seem to be at a definite advantage. The richly connected structure of their existing knowledge base should facilitate identifying possible relationships between new and old knowledge and integrating the new information (Brown, 1982). Previously acquired domain-specific strategies should also "work" with the new data. Thus, in most updating endeavors, the expert should be at an advantage, unless there is some psychological commitment to previously held ideas that are no longer valid.

When updating involves acquiring information or skills that are novel or largely *unrelated* to the expert's domain of knowledge, then expertise may be of less advantage. Take, for example, the case of a distinguished physician, with no previous computer experience, who needs to acquire a certain level of computer literacy to take advantage of new advances in the medical field. In this case, the expert may be no more advantaged than less distinguished colleagues. Current evidence suggests that there is relatively little transfer across disparate domains of expertise (Chi, Glaser, and Rees, 1982). Expertise in one domain does not automatically lead to competence in another domain.

When a person seeks to acquire new knowledge or skill, largely unrelated to previously acquired competencies, basic mental abilities previously discussed are of particular importance. Since most midcareer professionals will have suffered little decline in these abilities, the cognitive aptitude for acquiring new knowledge and skills should be intact. Individuals functioning at a high level on the relevant basic abilities should be particularly advantaged. This position is supported by recent research that examined the relationship between basic abilities and middle-aged adults' proficiency in learning computer software for spreadsheet designs (Garfein, Schaie, and Willis, 1988); the adults studied had little or no previous computer literacy. Acquisition of computer skills was significantly related to the adults' level of inductive reasoning and spatial abilities.

Environmental Factors and Cognitive Ability

Complexity of the Work Environment. Since basic mental abilities continue to be important to maintenance of professional competence in midcareer, what environmental factors are related to the maintenance of these abilities? The reciprocal relationship between the work environment and intellectual functioning has been examined in a ten-year longitudinal study by Kohn and Schooler (1983). Three dimensions of the work environment were examined: routinization, closeness of supervision, and substantive complexity of work. Substantively complex work requires initiative and independent judgment, and often involves dealing with people or ideas. In contrast, less complex work is often repetitive (routinized), requires little independent judgment, and tends to be closely supervised. Kohn and Schooler found that men who had jobs that required independent decision making and working with complex environmental demands became more intellectually flexible across time, even when prior levels of intellectual flexibility were controlled for. The work we do influences our cognitive functioning, and vice versa.

Related findings have been reported for the older worker, when the relationship between timing of retirement and ability performance was examined. Schaie and associates examined the relationship between early and late retirement from substantively complex work and changes in inductive reasoning performance over the retirement period (Dutta, Schulenberg, and Lair, 1986). Older workers who were involved in substantively complex work and delayed retirement showed maintenance of reasoning ability. In contrast, early retirees from complex jobs suffered some loss in reasoning performance.

Active Lifestyle and Enriched Environment. In a similar vein, research findings indicate that an active, involved lifestyle — that is, living and working within an enriched, stimulating environment — fosters maintenance of both basic cognitive abilities and professional competence. Healthy individuals who were living very active lifestyles that included involvement in a number of different stimulating and challenging pursuits showed an increase in level of ability over the prior seven-year period (Gribbin, Schaie, and Parham, 1980). In contrast, individuals who reported increasing withdrawal or disengagement from previous activities and a rather passive life-style exhibited significant declines in functioning over the same time period. In particular, older women who had experienced family disruptions, such as death of a spouse, and had subsequently withdrawn from previous pursuits appeared to be vulnerable to cognitive decline. An enriched, challenging work environment also is important in maintaining professional knowledge and skills. Reinhart and Keefe (Chapter Five) report that an enriched work environment is a significant predictor of maintenance of professional competence for midcareer emergency room medical personnel.

Self-assessment of Cognitive Performance

For the most part, maintenance of professional competence is self-directed (see also Chapter Thirteen). The individual engages in a self-assessment of the current level of professional competence and then determines the knowledge and proficiencies to be enhanced and the procedure (workshop, self-directed readings, and so on). While this is not always the optimal procedure for maintaining professional competence, it is a very common approach. Therefore, it is important to examine how accurate professionals are in assessing their work-related competencies and in evaluating the success of their efforts to maintain competence (see Green, Grosswald, Suter, and Walthall, 1984).

There appears to be very little empirical data on accuracy of self-assessments in professional competence. However, there has been research on adults' competence to judge the level of their performance on various abilities, and to assess whether their abilities have declined over time. Several studies have shown that adults are fairly accurate in self-assessment; research of their performance on various abilities by Lachman (1983) and MaloneBeach (1987) found significant relationships between actual ability performance and self-assessment on the ability.

Likewise, adults appear to be sensitive to decline in their level of intellectual functioning (Willis, 1988). When asked to rate on a five-point scale whether their own level of ability performance had improved, remained stable, or declined over a seven-year period, adults who had suffered reliable ability decline rated themselves as having experienced greater decline than did individuals who had not declined. Finally, it appears that adults possess some self-knowledge of whether their performance has improved as a function of educational training. Adults who had demonstrated significant gain after a cognitive training intervention rated themselves as having improved more than adults who had not shown reliable improvement after training.

Motivation

Motivation is considered to be the most salient personal variable in models of professional competence that emphasize personal and environmental interactions (see Chapters One and Two).

Expectancy theory (see Chapters One and Eight) is based on the premise that the professional's level of motivation to engage in some activity (in this case, updating) is influenced by the individual's beliefs about whether a certain level of performance can be attained, and whether that level of performance will result in desired outcomes (Vroom, 1964). Expectancy theory has typically been concerned with the relationship between certain beliefs and expectancies and outcomes within a specific context; for example, the relationship between a professional's willingness to enroll in a continuing education class and beliefs about his or her ability to perform in the course, or expectancies about the relationship between taking the class and receiving a merit pay increase. In each case, the beliefs, expectancies, and outcomes are specific and are typically associated with a particular context (work context). In contrast, much of the research on personality in adulthood and old age has studied more general motivational factors that are less closely related to a specific context.

In this section, we briefly consider some of these other motivational dimensions. Our analysis of this literature will focus on three issues:

1. Are there changes with age in these motivational variables?
2. Are there generational differences in level for some motivational dimensions?
3. What motivational dimensions are significant predictors of professional productivity and competence?

On the first question, there has been considerable debate in the study of adult personality on whether and to what extent there is stability or change in personality and motivational dimensions across the adult years (McCrae and Costa, 1984; Neugarten, 1977). Do adults exhibit the same level of achievement motivation or desire for autonomy in young adulthood and middle age? Is the rank ordering of individuals on a personality trait stable from middle age into old age? There is evidence for *both* change and stability in personality dimensions related to the workplace.

With regard to the second question, it is important to examine cohort trends to determine whether some of the motivational differences observed between young and midcareer professionals reflect generational differences rather than age-related changes. For example, differences in level of achievement motivation between early and midcareer managers may be associated with age-related changes in motivation for middle-aged managers. On the other hand, perhaps the two generations had different levels of motivation even when compared at the same chronological age.

As to the third question, motivational variables as predictors of professional competence need to be studied in the context of what is known about normative age-related changes in these variables. Longitudinal data are useful in differentiating between variables that are good predictors of professional competence at all career stages, and those that become particularly useful at early or later stages. Predictor variables for which there is little normative change tend to be useful across career stages; those for which there is reliable normative change are likely to be more useful predictors at specific career stages.

Little research has examined directly the relationship between general motivational variables and efforts to maintain professional competence. Thus we will be examining, for the most part, the relationship between motivational variables and professional productivity and success. There is some evidence that maintenance of professional competence is related to professional productivity and success. For example, in our own research with college faculty, we have found that more up-to-date faculty also publish more (Willis and Tosti-Vasey, 1986). Nevertheless, we acknowledge the limitations in using productivity or success as an indirect index of remaining professionally competent.

Motivational Dimensions Showing Age-related Change and Generational Differences

Career Advancement Expectancies. When professionals are studied longitudinally, there is evidence that their expectations and motivation for career advancements decline on average. The AT&T study of managers (Bray and Howard, 1980, 1983b; Howard and Bray, 1988) found that managers' expectations about career advancement decreased, on average, within the first five years. Very early in their career, many managers developed more realistic expectations regarding the possibilities for advancement; they became increasingly aware that in a pyramid organization, such as AT&T, the possibility for continued advancement into upper levels of management becomes increasingly unlikely. There was a slight decline across time in motivation or expectation for advancement even among men reaching upper-management levels, although the decline was less steep than for the total sample.

In addition to age-related change, generational differences have been noted in motivation for advancement. Cohorts born in the 1950s and entering careers in the 1970s have lower expectations about career advancement than young professionals in the same fields who were born in the 1930s and entered the job market in the 1950s (Howard and Wilson, 1982; Howard and Bray, 1988). More recent cohorts had lower expectancies.

Work Involvement. Research findings on age changes in level of work involvement—the priority that people give to work within their lives—are somewhat mixed. Longitudinal studies have reported that level of work involvement declined on average slightly from early to midcareer. There was a decline in the self-reported importance and priority of work in the managers' lives (Bray and Howard, 1983a; Howard and Bray, 1980, 1988). While the trend was toward a decrease in work involvement, there were wide individual differences in trajectories, depending on career success. Men who attained only lower levels of management showed a drop in the importance of work within the first five years. Those who reached middle-management levels showed a stable level for the first career decade, with some decline thereafter. However, men who attained upper-management levels actually reported increased involvement in work across time. These findings are striking since there were no differences in level of work involvement at the beginning of their careers. Thus, work involvement became a significant predictor of career success only in midcareer.

In contrast to longitudinal findings that show a decline in work involvement with age, Rhodes' extensive review of cross-sectional studies (1983) found a positive, but modest, relationship between age and job involvement. This discrepancy in findings may be the result of cohort differences in work saliency. Age and cohort effects are confounded in the cross-sectional studies of work involvement (Yankelovich, 1981). More recent-born cohorts report lower levels of work involvement, on average, than earlier cohorts when assessed at the same chronological age (Howard and Wilson, 1982).

Desire for Autonomy. Several studies have reported that the desire for autonomy or independence in one's life and work increases with age (Bray and Howard, 1983a; Stevens and Truss, 1985; see also Chapter Nine). In fact, autonomy and independence in decision making have been found to be some of the most desired work environment characteristics. If we recall the findings of Kohn and Schooler (1983) that a complex work environment involving independent decision making was related to increased intellectual flexibility, the professional's desire for autonomy would seem to have important developmental implications. However, Bray and Howard did not find desire for autonomy to be a predictor of the managerial level attained (Howard, 1984). Desire for autonomy appears to be related to work satisfaction, but not to career success.

Dominance. Dominance, the disposition to take charge and exert leadership, increases from young to middle adulthood (Stevens and Truss, 1985). Bray and Howard found it a significant predictor of career success at all career stages. Men who scored high on a dominance scale were more likely to reach higher management levels (Howard, 1984). In our research, we have found tenured college faculty who scored higher on dominance were more likely to be up to date in their field (Willis and Tosti-Vasey, 1986).

Moreover, generational differences were found in the AT&T study. More recent cohorts of managers were less desirous of leadership roles than previous cohorts had been at comparable stages in their career (Howard and Wilson, 1982).

Nurturance and Affiliation. Longitudinal studies report some evidence for an age-related decrease in nurturance and affiliation needs from young to middle adulthood (Stevens and Truss, 1985). In midlife, there appears to be some decline in the disposition to seek out friendships or social relationships and also a decline in being nurturant or supportive of others.

Nurturance has shown significant relationships with career success and professional competence. Men who remained at lower management levels showed increases in nurturance across the AT&T study. In contrast, men reaching upper management levels showed a decrease (Howard, 1984). In our own research with tenured college faculty we found analogous trends; nurturance was related to greater professional obsolescence in the faculty member's field. The more up-to-date faculty member was less nurturant.

The issue of nurturance is important for its implications for professional mentoring, a role typically assumed by mid-career professionals. If nurturance is an important element in serving as a mentor, then the data, at first glance, might be interpreted as suggesting that competent, successful professionals are less disposed to mentoring activities. Such professionals do engage in mentoring, but closer scrutiny often indicates that they are very selective in choosing the recipients of their time and attention. Thus, while distinguished professionals may not be high on nurturance as a general personality trait, they do engage in mentoring in highly selected contexts.

In addition, significant cohort differences have been found for nurturance, with recent cohorts scoring higher than earlier cohorts (Howard and Wilson, 1982; Stevens and Truss, 1985). More recent generations give more emphasis to being supportive of others, in general. Some in the business domain have questioned whether nurturance and affiliation, as general personality characteristics, are compatible with an aggressive, competitive approach to free enterprise, and thus whether business practices will change as a function of generational differences in these personality dimensions (Howard and Wilson, 1982).

Behavioral Flexibility. Longitudinal data indicate normative increases in behavioral rigidity with age. As individuals age they become less flexible in their approach to tasks and less willing to consider alternative viewpoints (Schaie, 1983). However, there are wide individual differences. Studies have shown that behavioral flexibility is an important predictor of later ability performance and of career success. First, adults who exhibit flexible styles in midlife are more likely to perform at high ability levels in their sixties (Schaie, 1983). In a similar vein, behavioral flexibility in midlife has been shown to be a significant predictor of attaining higher levels of management (Howard, 1984). Upper-level managers were found to be more flexible and willing to consider alternative viewpoints.

Motivational Dimensions Showing Stability

Inner Work Standards. Although expectations and desires about career advancement decrease significantly across the career, it does not follow that the professional becomes less committed to maintaining certain work standards or "doing a good job." Inner work standards involve intrinsic motivation to maintain personal standards of excellence, unrelated to the implications for career advancement or supervisor approval. No age-related decline in inner work standards was found in the AT&T study of managers; even those who experienced little career advancement remained committed to performing their current job in a competent manner (Bray and Howard, 1983b; Howard and Bray, 1980). We too found that high inner work standards in college faculty were predictive of remaining professionally up to date (Willis and Tosti-Vasey, 1986). Fortunately, there is also no evidence for cohort differences in inner work standards (Howard and Wilson, 1982).

Job Satisfaction. Both longitudinal and cross-sectional studies suggest no significant age differences in level of job satisfaction. Moreover, while those who are successful in their careers reported high job satisfaction, even managers who did not progress to advanced levels maintained stable levels of job satisfaction into midcareer (Bray and Howard, 1980). In a review of a number of cross-sectional studies, Rhodes (1983) also found little evidence for age differences in job satisfaction. In fact, the trend was toward a positive relationship among age, job satisfaction, and organizational commitment.

Summary

In this chapter, we have presented a selected review of the literature on developmental changes in cognition and motivation and the implications for the midcareer professional. The cognitive literature suggests a very positive view of midcareer professionals' intellectual abilities and their potential for maintaining professional competence. The tasks and responsibilities that the professional assumes become increasingly complex, and require many distinct mental abilities. Longitudinal research indicates that normative age-related decline on most of these abilities is not observed until the sixties. Indeed, some abilities, such as vocabulary, do not reach their peak until middle age. Thus, most midcareer professionals should have intact the mental abilities that are involved in acquiring new information and skills in order to maintain professional competence.

Moreover, findings on creativity indicate that a professional's total output peaks in midlife for many scholarly fields. However, the proportion of notable works to total works is constant across career stages. The research on expertise indicates that as professionals become more experienced in their specific domains, the structure of their knowledge base becomes increasingly organized and interrelated. This not only enables professionals to perform more efficiently, but also should facilitate their ability to integrate into the current knowledge base the new information acquired.

Finally, several characteristics of the professional's work

environment have been shown to enhance cognitive functioning. These include work complexity and environmental richness. Work that required independent decision making in complex tasks involving people and ideas was found to enhance intellectual flexibility.

Age-related changes have been found for several dimensions of motivation, while other dimensions, such as job satisfaction and inner work standards, appear to be stable. Age-related declines have been reported for work involvement, flexibility, and nurturance. Dominance and desire for autonomy have been found to increase from young to middle adulthood.

These changes in motivational dimensions must be differentiated from their significance as useful predictors of job productivity or success. Desire for career advancement and dominance have been found to be important early predictors of career success. In contrast, work involvement and flexibility became significant predictors only at later career stages. Although desire for autonomy increases with age and is perceived to be important to worker satisfaction, it is not a significant predictor of career success.

Finally, important cohort differences have been noted for variables such as work involvement, dominance, and nurturance; these generational differences must be carefully monitored as recent cohorts progress through advanced career stages.

In summary, research literature suggests that the professional has the intellectual potential to remain professionally competent and that important motivational predictors of productivity have been identified and must be given careful consideration in career development and enhancement programs.

References

Anderson, J. R. "Acquisition of Cognitive Skill." *Psychological Review*, 1982, *89*, 369–401.

Botwinick, J. "Intellectual Abilities." In J. E. Birren and K. W. Schaie (eds.), *Handbook of the Psychology of Aging*. New York: Van Nostrand Reinhold, 1977.

Bray, D. W., and Howard, A. "Career Success and Life Satisfactions of Middle-aged Managers." In L. A. Bond and J. C. Rosen (eds.), *Coping and Competence During Adulthood*. Hanover, N. H.: University Press of New England, 1980.

Bray, D. W., and Howard, A. "The AT&T Longitudinal Studies of Managers." In K. W. Schaie (ed.), *Longitudinal Studies of Adult Psychological Development*. New York: Guilford Press, 1983a.

Bray, D. W., and Howard, A. "Personality and the Assessment Center Method." In C. D. Spielberger and J. N. Butcher (eds.), *Advances in Personality Assessment*. Hillsdale, N.J.: Erlbaum, 1983b.

Brown, A. L. "Learning and Development: The Problem of Compatibility, Access, and Induction." *Human Development*, 1982, *25*, 89–115.

Chi, M.T.H., Glaser, R., and Rees, E. "Expertise in Problem Solving." In R. J. Sternberg (ed.), *Advances in the Psychology of Human Intelligence*. Vol. 7. Hillsdale, N.J.: Erlbaum, 1982.

Dutta, R., Schulenberg, J., and Lair, T. J. "The Effect of Job Characteristics on Cognitive Abilities and Intellectual Flexibility." Paper presented at the annual meeting of the Eastern Psychological Association, New York, Apr. 1986.

Garfein, A. J., Schaie, K. W., and Willis, S. L. "Microcomputer Proficiency in Later-middle-aged and Older Adults: Teaching Old Dogs New Tricks." *Social Behavior*, 1988, *3*, 131–148.

Green, J., Grosswald, S., Suter, E., and Walthall, D. (eds.). *Continuing Education for the Health Professions: Developing, Managing, and Evaluating Programs for Maximum Impact on Patient Care*. San Francisco: Jossey-Bass, 1984.

Gribbin, K., Schaie, K. W., and Parham, I. "Complexities of Life Style and Maintenance of Intellectual Abilities." *Journal of Social Issues*, 1980, *36*, 47–61.

Hills, J. "Factor Analyzed Abilities and Success in College Mathematics." *Educational Psychological Measurement*, 1957, *17*, 615–622.

Howard, A. "Cool at the Top: Personality Characteristics of Successful Executives." Paper presented at the annual meeting of the American Psychological Association, Montreal, Canada, Aug. 1984.

Howard, A., and Bray, D. "Continuities and Discontinuities Between Two Generations of Bell Managers." Paper presented at the annual meeting of the American Psychological Association, Montreal, Canada, Aug. 1980.

Howard, A., and Bray, D. *Managerial Lives in Transition: Advancing Age and Changing Times.* New York: Guilford Press, 1988.

Howard, A., and Wilson, J. A. "Leadership in a Declining Work Ethic." *California Management Review*, 1982, *24*, 33–46.

Kaufman, H. G. "Relations of Ability and Interest to Currency of Professional Knowledge Among Engineers." *Journal of Applied Psychology*, 1972, *56*, 495–499.

Kohn, M. L., and Schooler, C. *Work and Personality: An Inquiry into the Impact of Social Stratification.* Norwood, N.J.: Ablex, 1983.

Lachman, M. "Perceptions of Intellectual Aging: Antecedent or Consequent of Intellectual Functioning?" *Developmental Psychology*, 1983, *19*, 482–498.

McCrae, R. R., and Costa, P. T., Jr. *Emerging Lives, Enduring Dispositions: Personality in Adulthood.* Boston: Little, Brown, 1984.

MaloneBeach, E. "Cognitive Ability, Depression, and Performance Perception." Paper presented at the annual meeting of the American Psychological Association, New York, Aug. 1987.

Neugarten, B. L. "Personality and Aging." In J. E. Birren and K. W. Schaie (eds.), *Handbook of the Psychology of Aging.* New York: Van Nostrand Reinhold, 1977.

Rhodes, S. R. "Age-related Differences in Work Attitudes and Behavior: A Review and Conceptual Analysis." *Psychological Review*, 1983, *93*, 328–367.

Schaie, K. W. "Toward a Stage Theory of Adult Cognitive Development." *Aging and Human Development*, 1977–78, *8*, 129–138.

Schaie, K. W. "The Seattle Longitudinal Study: A Twenty-one Year Exploration of Psychometric Intelligence in Adulthood." In K. W. Schaie (ed.), *Longitudinal Studies of Adult Psychological Development.* New York: Guilford Press, 1983.

Schaie, K. W. "Relating Age Change and Behavior to Job Requirements." Paper presented at the annual meeting of the Gerontological Society of America, Chicago, Nov. 1986.

Siegler, I. "Psychological Aspects of the Duke Longitudinal Studies." In K. W. Schaie (ed.), *Longitudinal Studies of Adult Psychological Development*. New York: Guilford Press, 1983.

Simonton, D. K. "Age and Literary Creativity: A Cross-cultural and Transhistorical Survey." *Journal of Cross-Cultural Psychology*, 1975, *6*, 259–277.

Simonton, D. K. "Creative Productivity, Age, and Stress: A Biographical Time-series Analysis of Ten Classical Composers." *Journal of Personality and Social Psychology*, 1977, *35*, 791–804.

Simonton, D. K. "Quality, Quantity, and Age: The Careers of Ten Distinguished Psychologists." *International Journal of Aging and Human Development*, 1985, *21*, 241–254.

Simonton, D. K. "Does Creativity Decline in the Later Years? Definition, Data, and Theory." In M. Perlmutter (ed.), *Late Life Potential*. Washington: Gerontological Society of America, 1988.

Stevens, D. P., and Truss, C. V. "Stability and Change in Adult Personality over Twelve and Twenty Years." *Developmental Psychology*, 1985, *21*, 568–584.

Thurstone, L. L., and Thurstone, T. G. "Factorial Studies of Intelligence." *Psychometric Monographs*, 1941, no. 2.

Vroom, V. H. *Work and Motivation*. New York: Wiley, 1964.

Willis, S. L. "Contributions of Cognitive Training Research to Understanding Late Life Potential." In M. Perlmutter (ed.), *Late Life Potential*. Washington: Gerontological Society of America, 1988.

Willis, S. L., and Schaie, K. W. "Practical Intelligence in Later Adulthood." In R. J. Sternberg and R. Wagner (eds.), *Practical Intelligence: Origins of Competence in the Everyday World*. New York: Cambridge University Press, 1986.

Willis, S. L., and Tosti-Vasey, J. "Professional Obsolescence Among Senior College Faculty." Paper presented at the annual meeting of the American Educational Research Association, San Francisco, Apr. 1986.

Yankelovich, D. *New Rules: Searching for Self-fulfillment in a World Turned Upside Down*. New York: Random House, 1981.

Part Two

APPROACHES
TO SPECIFYING,
MEASURING, AND ASSESSING
PROFESSIONAL COMPETENCE

In the beginning of Chapter Six, Melnick draws an important analogy between the practice of medicine and the process of maintaining professional competence. In both cases, the first step is to define and assess the state of the individual's health. Medical science has defined a model of the functional capacities of an optimally healthy human being, and has developed diagnostic tools for assessing the current level of functioning of a given individual in terms of these health criteria. In medical procedures, diagnosis and assessment always precede treatment or intervention, and the particular treatment prescribed is based on the diagnostic workup. Similarly, there is need for conceptual models of professional competence (a "healthy," optimally functioning professional) and tools for measuring and assessing that competence. Ideally, procedures for maintaining professional competence are derived from previously determined competence models. Just as physicians recommend regular medical checkups, the assessment of professional competence should be a continual, ongoing process across the work life.

Medical science is increasingly emphasizing prevention

and the maintenance of health, rather than the remedial treatment of illness. Likewise, this volume takes a developmental
perspective to the maintenance of professional competence,
focusing on prevention, rather than remedial, "catch-up" interventions. The physician employs different criteria for defining
what is healthy in an adolescent versus a middle-aged individual; likewise, criteria for professional competence will differ
for entry-level versus midcareer professionals.

While diagnosis and assessment have traditionally been
the responsibility of the physician, health professionals are
increasingly emphasizing that patients themselves need to be
knowledgeable about biological functioning, and to monitor
their own level of functioning. The assessment of professional
competence is also the shared responsibility of the professional
and in some disciplines regulatory agencies or professional
organizations. Traditionally, professionals have had the primary
responsibility for monitoring their level of competence. This
raises the question of whether individual practitioners are sufficiently informed about the knowledge base and skills required
for competent performance in their profession, can accurately
assess their own strengths and deficiencies, and can prescribe
appropriate professional activities for enhancing competence,
based on this self-assessment.

Definition and Measurement of Professional Competence

In the history of scientific inquiry (Kuhn, 1970), definition and
description of a phenomenon are prerequisites to subsequent
steps. These subsequent steps include measurement and assessment of the phenomena, causal explanations, and intervention
or enhancement.

The four chapters in this part focus on issues of definition
and measurement. At present, the study of professional competence is confined to specific disciplines or professions. Definitions and models of professional competence are discipline
specific. There has been little attempt to define or study professional competence across different professions, the work of
Queeney and Smutz within the Practice Audit Model being a

notable exception. Although a few general models of professional competence and development have been developed in recent years, much empirical testing and refinement are needed (Cervero, 1988; Cervero, Azzaretto and Associates, 1989; Cervero and Scanlan, 1985; Green, Grosswald, Suter, and Walthall, 1984; Houle, 1980; Nowlen, 1988; and Schön, 1987). Many of the authors in this volume have suggested generalizations from their finds that extend beyond their own profession, suggesting that some generalizability of current competence models is possible. We believe that the time is ripe for cross-disciplinary research on professional competence, and that such research would help various professions clarify their current definitions and approaches to the study of competence.

Role Delineation. The first step in assessment is to define professional competence as it applies to a given profession. Several professions have developed a role delineation, a hierarchical description of a professional's activities organized into major domains of tasks and responsibilities. Although no individual professional may perform all the tasks specified, a role delineation serves to define the scope of tasks involved in the practice of a given profession (see Chapters Four and Seven). In many professions, there is a long history of attempts to specify such a role delineation. In Chapter Four, Maatsch briefly describes the debates over the past twenty years, related to this topic within medicine.

Queeney and Smutz (Chapter Seven) describe a collaborative, team approach to role delineation involving university-based researchers and staff from professional associations and regulatory agencies. University faculty provide information on new knowledge base required within a discipline; professional associations represent the concerns of the practicing professional and are involved in continuing education activities; regulatory agencies often function in an assessment and licensing role. Using a role delineation as the basis for defining and assessing professional competence is an important issue, since it is based on the assumption that competence should be defined and measured by what the up-to-date professional knows and does in actual practice, rather than in hypothetical terms. Queeney and Smutz, in particular, emphasize assessment of competence within the context of actual professional practice.

Professional Knowledge Base and Skills. Once the activities and responsibilities of a professional are described, there is need to define the knowledge base and skills that are required to perform these activities. Professional competence has been defined in terms of a set of proficiencies, with factual knowledge and skills being major types. However, there has been and continues to be spirited debate over the major proficiencies (components) underlying the phenomenon of professional competence.

An implicit assumption in many of the chapters in this part is that the concern is with the competence of the practicing professional, rather than entry-level recruits in the field. This distinction is important, since much of the prior work on conceptualization and measurement of competence has been focused at the entry level (such as certification exams). Much less is known about midcareer competence, and the similarities and differences between entry-level and midcareer competence and their assessment require further investigation.

Entry-level certification exams within many professions have traditionally emphasized factual knowledge; paper-and-pencil multiple-choice or short-answer measures have often been used. However, it has been effectively argued that professional competence must also involve the *application* of knowledge and skills within the professional context. Maatsch has called this "clinical problem-solving ability." This problem-solving component is particularly relevant to maintenance of competence among midcareer professionals, since the emphasis is on how effectively they are performing in daily practice, and whether specific skills need improvement or updating. Likewise, the problem-solving component is especially salient in recertification assessment, as noted by Maatsch (Chapter Four), since recertification is concerned with assessing competence to continue to practice within the profession.

Unitary versus Multidimensional Models of Competence. There is need for further study of professional competence at both the theoretical and measurement levels, as discussed in Chapters Four and Six. Conceptual and empirical work on models of professional competence is needed both to provide direction for the education and training of professionals, and for the assessment and evaluation of practitioners at various stages in their career. Several issues are addressed in this section: (1) the utility of unidimensional versus multidimensional conceptualizations of competence; (2) the nature of the relationships among various components of competence; (3) developmental changes in the proficiencies (components) underlying competence and their interrelationships, at various career stages; and (4) the reciprocal relationship between conceptual and measurement models of competence.

Maatsch presents a multidimensional model of competence for professionals in emergency medicine (Chapter Four). While the instruments used to measure competence were specific to medicine, many of the issues discussed are applicable to other professions. Once the specific tasks and responsibilities performed by a competent professional are described, there is need to conceptualize these specific behaviors at a more abstract level, and to define broad domains of proficiencies underlying competence. There has been much debate about whether professional competence is best defined and measured as a unidimensional construct (a unitary, global phenomenon), or as a multidimensional construct involving multiple components (proficiencies). Chapter Four illustrates that both models are supported by the empirical data and are differentially useful in the study and assessment of competence.

Conceptualization of competence as a general, global (unidimensional) construct is supported by both casual observation and empirical studies. Professionals evaluated as competent on a global rating are typically also rated highly on the various proficiency dimensions. As reported in Maatsch's research, there are significant positive relationships among various competence dimensions (knowledge base, skills, clinical problem-solving ability). Since most current measurement models of competence focus primarily on the *cognitive* aspects of competence, the high intercorrelations among the various components may be partially attributable to the cognitive dimension. Given the positive relationship among various proficiency dimensions, a global assessment of competence will often be the best single predictor of competence. Lower intercorrelations would be expected among noncognitive proficiency areas, such as psychomotor skill or interpersonal skills. Both Maatsch and Queeney and Smutz (Chapters Four and Seven) have noted the importance of these noncognitive dimensions, and further research in conceptualization and measurement of these proficiency areas is needed.

A unitary versus multidimensional model of competence may be differentially useful, depending on the particular question asked. For example, a unitary model of competence may be most efficient if the question is one of prediction; a global measure of competence is the single best predictor of competence at a later career stage (see Chapter Five). A multidimensional approach to competence is useful in at least three respects. First, competence is expected to become more differentiated with professional experience, and thus needs to be conceptualized and assessed multidimensionally. That is, as individuals develop in their professions, their knowledge and skills become increasingly differentiated and specialized. The wide variety of experiences accrued by midcareer results in development of competence along various dimensions.

Second, a multidimensional approach to competence is particularly useful in targeting those knowledge areas and skills most in need of updating efforts. In this case, a global measure of competence is of little utility in diagnosing particular deficits. It is likely that the relative level of competence for midcareer professionals varies across competency domains. Because of a supportive work environment or deliberate updating activities, a midcareer professional may remain up to date on some dimensions but less competent on others.

Third, a multidimensional approach to competence is useful in examining how specific factors in the work environment support or limit particular areas of competence. A number of work environment factors have been identified as fostering the maintenance of professional competence (see Chapters One, Five, Eight, and Ten). However, there has been little research examining the relationships between particular dimensions of competence and specific environmental factors. For example, collaboration with peers may be particularly useful in maintaining an up-to-date knowledge base, while work assignments involving a variety of responsibilities may be more useful in maintaining clinical problem-solving skills.

The interrelationship among various components of competence varies across different stages of professional development. Maatsch suggests (Chapter Four) that the magnitude of the relationship between knowledge and performance components may increase across the professional career. These changes are important since they bear on determining the most effective measures of competence at various career stages and the predictive power of these factors across time.

Measurement at the Construct Level. Chapters Four and Six provide summaries of two of the most innovative approaches to the measurement of competence. Traditionally, competence has been defined by many distinct skills and abilities, each measured by a different test. Attempts at defining a parsimonious set of constructs underlying competence have had relatively little success. Since the different tests often involved different assessment methods (multiple choice, simulation exercises, oral exams), there was a confound between the construct and the method of assessment. The research described in Chapter Four represents an attempt to use the relatively new and powerful statistical procedures of confirmatory factor analysis to represent components of competence (knowledge, clinical problem solving) at the level of latent constructs and to examine issues such as the multidimensionality of competence, and the interrelationships among a parsimonious set of constructs representing different components of competence.

Tests and exercises represent only a sample of behaviors. However, it is the skill and ability domains represented by these behavioral samples that is of most interest in defining and measuring competence. Competence, as a latent construct, is not directly observable and can only be inferred from behavioral samples taken during observation or examination. Factor analytic techniques are useful in examining competence at the level of constructs, rather than in terms of a myriad of test scores.

Chapter Four illustrates the reciprocal relationship between articulation of theories of competence and the development of measurement models to assess competence. Theories of competence define what components (constructs) are believed to underlie competence. Through analytic procedures, such as confirmatory factor analyses, one can examine whether these constructs are represented in data, and what tests are related to a given construct. Findings from empirical studies can then be employed to support, disconfirm, or refine existing theories of competence.

Features of an Assessment Procedure. Chapter Six offers an in-depth description of one of the most innovative and advanced assessment procedures, the computer-based simulation model (CBX), under continuing development by the National Board of Medical Examiners. The CBX model measures four dimensions of competence: knowledge, clinical problem solving, interpersonal skills, and psychomotor (manipulative) skills. In describing the CBX model, Melnick outlines the important features of a diagnostic procedure to assess professional competence: (1) face validity, (2) interactive nature, (3) individualization, (4) reliable scoring procedures, (5) cost effectiveness, (6) time demands, (7) user friendliness, (8) potential for self-directed assessment, and (9) a coherent, integrated system.

The tasks and exercises in the assessment procedure should be representative of the professional activities typically encountered by the practitioner and must be presented in a context-valid manner (simulation, interactive nature). Ideally, the assessment system should have the capacity to be customized to match the profile of activities of an individual professional. Since the CBX system, as well as many other assessment systems, involve the use of computers, there is need to consider the user friendliness of the system and the initial "warm up" time required for the professional to become comfortable with computer simulation procedures. Both Melnick and Queeney and Smutz (Chapters Six and Seven) note two major limitations in existing assessment systems: the relative cost effectiveness, and the amount of examination time needed to obtain a reliable evaluation of a professional's competence.

Chapter Five represents an example of the type of empirical research that is needed to study maintenance of professional competence among midcareer practitioners. The study was grounded in well-defined conceptual and measurement models. The research examines individual differences in competence, and changes in competence over time. The salience of particular environmental variables in facilitating midcareer competence is considered. Physicians who worked in complex, enriched environments were more likely to maintain or enhance their level of professional competence.

Linking Assessment and Maintenance Approaches

While issues related to the measurement and assessment of professional competence are of such magnitude and importance to merit an entire volume, it is important to hold in perspective the end point. That is, the role of assessment is to provide direction for developing activities that will maintain and enhance professional competence. Returning to Melnick's analogy, the linkage between diagnosis and treatment is a critical aspect of the process, one that is often given limited consideration. The assessment of competence, and activities or programs for maintaining professional competence, have often been studied and monitored by different groups. For example, assessment of competence has typically been conducted and directed by a regulatory agency. In contrast, programs for maintaining professional competence have typically been offered by professional organizations or academic institutions.

As noted by Queeney and Smutz (Chapter Seven), a team approach, involving academics, professional organizations, and regulatory agencies, is needed to develop approaches that link assessment and updating activities. The Practice Audit Model presented in Chapter Seven provides one outstanding example of the interface between assessment and activities that enhance and maintain competence. The authors argue that traditional professional continuing education has focused too heavily on acquisition of new knowledge. While practitioners are frequently aware of their limitations with regard to new developments in their field, they are often not conscious of their deficiencies in everyday skills and practices; these everyday skills also need to be included in the assessment and enhancement phases.

References

Cervero, R. M. *Effective Continuing Education for Professionals.* San Francisco: Jossey-Bass, 1988.

Cervero, R. M., Azzaretto, J. F., and Associates. *Visions for the Future of Continuing Professional Education.* Athens: Georgia Center for Continuing Education, 1989.

Cervero, R. M., and Scanlan, C. L. (eds.). *Education: Problems and Prospects in Continuing Professional Education.* New Directions for Continuing Education, no. 27. San Francisco: Jossey-Bass, 1985.

Green, J. S., Grosswald, S. J., Suter, E., and Walthall, D. B. (eds.). *Continuing Education for the Health Professions: Developing, Managing, and Evaluating Programs for Maximum Impact on Patient Care.* San Francisco: Jossey-Bass, 1984.

Houle, C. O. *Continuing Learning in the Professions.* San Francisco: Jossey-Bass, 1980.

Kuhn, T. S. *Structure of Scientific Revolutions* (2d ed.). Chicago: University of Chicago Press, 1970.

Nowlen, P. M. *A New Approach to Continuing Education for Business and the Professions.* New York: Macmillan, 1988.

Schön, D. A. *Educating the Reflective Practitioner: Toward a New Design for Teaching and Learning in the Professions.* San Francisco: Jossey-Bass, 1987.

4

Jack L. Maatsch

Linking Theories of Competence to the Construct Validity of Performance Assessment Tests

This chapter summarizes a ten-year sustained research program to develop and evaluate a new specialty certification examination. The examination was developed by the Office of Medical Education Research and Development (OMERAD) and in collaboration with the American Board of Emergency Medicine (ABEM). With extensive collaborative support from ABEM and a multiyear grant from the National Center for Health Services Research (NCHSR), four major experimentally designed field tests were conducted sequentially. Each field test involved a variety of objective test formats and assessment methods that tested medical knowledge and clinical performance in emergency medicine. Groups of subjects in the various studies ranged in education and experience from fourth-year medical students, residents undergoing graduate education, through practicing physicians sitting for specialty certification board examinations, to a sample of boarded diplomates undergoing a

Note: The opinions expressed in this chapter do not necessarily reflect the position or policy of the National Center for Health Services Research or the American Board of Emergency Medicine, and no such endorsements should be inferred.

comprehensive competency assessment five years after specialty certification.

The large arrays of findings in the earlier studies were at first in conflict with rational expectations about physician competence. This situation provided both a challenge and an opportunity to formulate and then evaluate various informal theories of clinical competence. After repeated confirmatory factor analyses, a psychometric theory of clinical competence emerged that appears to best explain and predict the many empirical findings. The theory also appears to fit clinical performance as measured across a spectrum of education and experience. This chapter, then, provides a review of some conceptions of professional competence in medicine and a set of explanatory constructs that may be useful in understanding and interpreting professional performance evaluation data. It concludes with some implications of the theory for the measurement of clinical competence and for professional updating.

The Role of Theory

Applied behavioral sciences tend to evolve and mature because of a continuing need to better understand some socially significant set of complex human behaviors. This evolutionary process matures through a learning process involving the interaction of conceptualization, observation, and measurement. Somewhere in the maturation process, informal conceptualizations and later more formal theories begin to emerge that attempt to explain and predict the growing, and often conflicting, body of empirical knowledge.

The more rigorously defined formal theories require operational definitions of their component constructs that are anchored by observation and reliable measurement. The reverse requirement is also true. The interpretation of measurement data and the relationships between these data sets require a rationale that can be provided only by formal theories composed of a set of interrelated constructs. In other words, tests and other forms of measurement should have construct validity if the data are to be interpreted.

To progress from informal largely verbal conceptualizations to more quantitative formal theories, researchers often use factor analysis to identify a few latent constructs (factors) underlying a large array of measurement data and their interrelationships. The objective is to increase the explanatory power of a fewer number of constructs, thus simplifying the theory and the task of explanation. It is also possible to evaluate more informal theories with confirmatory factor analysis techniques. This is a process of theory building and evaluation, a process that requires a number of reliable measurement methods operationally defining component constructs or factor structures and their structural interrelationships. For theories of clinical competence, these measurement methods are objective tests and clinical performance assessment methods.

In turn, theories of competence serve as measurement models for the assessment of clinical competence. If we obtain data through several measurement methods and ask what do these data mean, how do they relate to other measures, and are we measuring the same proficiencies or something different, then we are asking questions about the construct validity of the measures. The answers to these questions are provided by the theory or measurement model. In essence, the theory development and evaluation process is inexorably intertwined with the continuing development and valid interpretation of tests and performance assessment methods.

In the medical profession, the need to measure a physician's clinical competence for educational purposes, for licensing, and for specialty certification is longstanding and socially important. More recently the need to measure physician competence in *re*licensure and *re*certification, to ensure continued competency and professional updating throughout a physician's career, has been recognized. In response to this need, the evaluation of physician competence has matured from the use of the oral and essay examination in the 1800s and earlier, to the gradual development of more objective methods of testing and performance assessment during the first half of this century. Development of a formal conceptualization of physician competence during this period was relatively dormant. In the last twenty years, however, interest in better understanding the nature of clinical competence has grown, along with methods of measuring it. The process has been one of postulating a new proficiency and then developing a new instrument to measure it.

Perplexing problems have arisen with the interpretations of the relationships among the different types of tests and performance assessments. Over time, literally hundreds of presumably different medical skills or specific proficiencies have appeared in the literature, each with its own definition, each with its unique method of measurement, and each with its own application setting and purpose. Most of these measures have been developed in relative isolation from other postulated proficiencies and their measures. Informal theories have begun to appear that are by and large attempts to propose fewer, more generalized definitions of skill, ability, or proficiency categories and thus to reduce the conceptual confusion. As we will see later, even these more generalized conceptualizations appear to shift over time at the whim of the authors rather than on the basis of empirical evidence.

This state of affairs led to this recent characterization:

> Clinical competence is a battered child: a child because it is a relatively new area of interest, with most of the research and development having been done in the past 10 to 15 years; battered because it has been mistreated by researchers, who cannot agree on what it is and how to measure it. Consider these examples of confusion about clinical competence:
>
> Ask any number of clinical educators or professional groups to define the term clinical competence and somewhat different responses will be obtained from each of them. Until recently, there has been little attempt to study what a clinician actually does, and it is even rarer to find performance assessment procedures which are systematically based on new insights into clinical methods.

Measures of clinical competence have been described in the literature which appear to have been adopted prematurely, without the benefit of step-by-step methodological development. In some cases, the measures are in the early "pilot project" stage or are simply untested ideas [Neufeld and Norman, 1985, p. 3].

The same authors define six different methodological approaches that have been used to advance knowledge about clinical competence and its measurement: (1) reflective/philosophical, (2) task analysis, (3) descriptive studies, (4) studies of diagnostic thinking, (5) consumer opinion, and (6) epidemiologic and quality of care.

This chapter presents my attempt to develop a seventh approach, namely a theory development and evaluation process. To help the battered child continue to mature, it is essential that we identify and define a fewer number of stable and measurable constructs. The structural relationship between these constructs or latent factors must be specified to form a theory of clinical competence. Eventually a more complete and formal measurement model must be developed.

Hypotheses generated by alternative theories need to be tested against the performance data produced by various measures taken concurrently. If they are found inaccurate or misleading, the theory should be revised appropriately or rejected. If we exercise this methodology of science, perhaps our battered child can reach adulthood. The social need for maturity in the field of measurement of professional competence is too important to permit an extended period of juvenile delinquency. To overextend the analogy still further, this chapter should be viewed as one modest attempt to help our battered child move through a painful period of adolescence. We begin with a selective review of some of the more important historical conceptualizations of clinical competence in medicine.

Overview of Selected Informal Theories

This section briefly summarizes different conceptualizations of clinical competence appearing in the medical education literature over the past twenty years. The review is, of necessity, selective. The various conceptualizations are, however, representative of the diversity of commonly held views prevailing in medicine today. They may be instructive for the assessment of competence in other professions. Before the review, it may be helpful to define a few technical terms and conceptions.

Standards for Educational and Psychological Testing (1985) defines evidence for test validity as content-related, construct-related, and criterion-related. In construct-related evidence, the construct of interest (the skill or ability) should be embedded in a conceptual framework, no matter how imperfect, in order to establish the validity of a test that purports to measure the construct. A conceptual framework, if formalized, is called a theory. Thus a theory of clinical competence is composed of a number of unique but interacting constructs identified as specific skills or abilities. Tests seek to measure one or more of those constructs. If they do, they have construct validity with respect to the ability postulated in a theory.

Each of these proposed skills is a construct individually attributed to the medical student, resident, or physician. Each is assumed to be learned, remembered, and forgotten over time if not exercised. All are assumed to be measurable at different levels of attainment within each of the professions. They are also presumed to be observable in performance and, if rated by a trained examiner, should provide a performance profile of the quality of care likely to be provided to future patients.

Many different objective test formats and performance rating methods purport to measure or rate these uniquely different abilities. The diversity of constructs and their many unique measures appear driven by educators' need to break a highly sophisticated and integrated problem-solving clinical interaction between physician and a broad spectrum of patients into simple, teachable, and hence measurable components, to avoid overwhelming the student. This need to decompose clinical competence into components is a necessary process for education and training purposes. However, a theory of clinical competence concerns professionals who have completed a significant part of the professional education process. From this point of view, it is fair to ask, does each of these educationally defined components remain unique, separately measurable, and necessary for predicting the quality of subsequent care? The prevailing assumption of medical educators is that they do.

Figure 4.1 summarizes the skills proposed in five significant publications over the past twenty years. A little study of the skills identified and their overlap clearly demonstrates the possibility of confusion and the need for conceptual clarification. If any trend is observable, it is a shift to fewer more general skill categories that compose clinical competence.

The work of Levine and McGuire and adaptations of their work by the Canadian College of Family Physicians influenced the initial design of the ABEM Certification Examination. A comparison of columns 2 and 3 illustrates the similarities and differences in the skills assumed as part of clinical competence. Later we will discuss the landmark research methodology applied by Levine and McGuire and its influence on the proposed theory of clinical competence.

The various formulations of general skills in Figure 4.1 should be expanded to include two more parsimonious conceptions of clinical competence that also anticipated and influenced our later research. In 1976, Senior reported a conceptual debate between himself and Robert Ebel, a nationally respected consultant to the CBX development project headed by Senior. The continuing development of computer-based exercises (CBX) is described in detail in Chapter Six.

In the final report of the CBX project, Senior reports the following discussions:

Is Competence Just a Special Kind of Knowledge?

There are dissenting views. Even among those who worked hard on committees of the CBX Project, there were some who doubted whether competence really was a definable entity. A thoughtful comment was offered in June 1975 by Dr. Robert Ebel, of the CBX Advisory Group:

Knowledge of what to do is a major element in *competence* to do, and hence in performance. Does a

Figure 4.1. A Selective Comparison of Hypothesized Skills and Abilities Composing Clinical Competence Over the Past Twenty Years.

Skill or Behaviors	NBME* 1965	ABOS* 1971	ABEM* 1978	Burg, Lloyd, and Templeton 1982	Neufeld and Norman 1985
Remembering medical knowledge (recognition, recall)	X	X	X	X	X
Acquiring clinical data (history taking)	X	X	X	X	X
Physical examination	X			X	X
Interpreting clinical data (using tests and procedures)	X	X	X	X	X
Problem solving, judgment, or diagnostic acumen	X	X	X	X	X
Implementing care (patient management)	X	X	X	X	X
Technical skills (psychomotor skills)		X		X	X
Interpersonal skills (doctor/patient)	X	X	X	X	X
Attitudes and work habits		X		X	

A   Combined as "surgical skills"
B   Combined as "attitudes"
C   Combined as "technical skills"
D   Combined as "problem-solving or judgment ability"
E   Combined as "clinical skills"
F   Combined as "problem solving and clinical judgment"

*NBME = National Board of Medical Examiners.
See Hubbard, Levit, Schumacher, and Schnable, 1965.

ABOS = American Board of Orthopedic Surgery.
See Levine and McGuire, 1970, 1971.

ABEM = American Board of Emergency Medicine.
See Maatsch, 1978, 1980.

computer-based examination test performance more directly than does the more conventional paper and pencil test? Words constitute the means of communication in both cases. An obvious difference between CBX and conventional tests is the sequential and response-dependent presentation of problem data in the CBX. This makes the test problems seem more realistic in CBX than in multiple-choice testing. But it creates difficult problems of scoring rationales. Whether it leads to the measurement of a different dimension of competence remains to be determined. The most plausible hypothesis to me is that it does not. I know of no good reason to expect that it should. . . . Research on CBX is innovative. It makes use of the modern magic computer technology, but it seems to me to lack a strong rational basis in psychometric theory.

The nub of the matter is struck by the statement that there is no applicable body of rational theory to apply for the measurement of competence. The use of known psychometric approaches that have been developed for measurement of knowledge has met with only limited success, . . .

The definition of competence, then, has been an incomplete concept. Despite this, considerable progress was made in the CBX Project by accepting the basic idea that competence is distinct from and somewhere in between knowledge and performance. Competence was taken to mean using knowledge to solve problems and was taken to be potentially useful as a predictor of later performance. The programs and systems to handle the simulated clinical interactions and to capture the decision of the examinees was therefore developed to produce the data to which a variety of scoring techniques could be applied. It was felt that a new body of rational theory should be developed for measurement of competence [Senior, 1976, p. 16].

Clearly the quoted argument is about how to conceptualize clinical competence. The issue is whether the CBX computer simulations are measuring a construct different from the knowledge construct measured by conventional paper-and-pencil tests. For our purposes, Ebel would appear to be arguing that the cognitive component of clinical competence is composed of a single construct—relevant clinical knowledge—and that clinical performance in simulated patient encounters is just another measure of that construct. We have identified this position as a single-factor theory of competence and call it Ebel's Theory in his memory. His theory has significantly different implications for the design and interpretation of measurement instruments as compared to the multi-construct conceptualizations identified earlier in Figure 4.1, and obviously it differs from Senior's position.

Senior holds that knowledge is different from the ability to apply clinical knowledge in clinical situations. He calls the second construct "competence." To avoid conflicting terms, this performance-based construct will be identified as "clinical problem solving." Thus Senior argues that "clinical problem solving" must be measured by methods other than objective knowledge tests. Elsewhere in the monograph, he observes that clinical knowledge is necessary but not sufficient for clinical problem solving. The two constructs are somewhat related—one makes possible the other—but they are different. This two-construct conceptualization is identified as Senior's Theory.

In summary, the literature provides a variety of informal theories ranging from one construct (Ebel's Theory), two related constructs (Senior's Theory), to the variety of multi-construct theories summarized in Figure 4.1. Which of these conceptualizations best fit the data? There are innumerable relationships observed in the many objective measures of the performance of physicians obtained by the different test formats and performance assessment methods. In an applied science, the answer should be contained in these empirical data and their interrelationships.

Empirical Research

I was provided the opportunity to evaluate informal theories of clinical competence in a series of interrelated research studies associated with the initial development of the certification and recertification examinations of the American Board of Emergency Medicine. The nature and findings of the four studies that led to the development of a more formal theory of clinical competence are summarized below. These findings are compared to the only comparable study, one undertaken seven years earlier by George Miller and associates Christine McGuire and Harold Levine for the American Board of Orthopedic Surgery.

Field Test Research. In 1978 a field test of the American Board of Emergency Medicine certification examination was undertaken following two years of test development and research planning. The field test was designed to establish the reliability, concurrent validity, and criterion-related validity of the test libraries before the examination was given for the first time in a newly recognized specialty board.

The libraries were organized into five different test and performance assessment formats. Three objective test formats were used: (1) multiple-choice items (MCQ), designed to measure relevant clinical knowledge; (2) pictorial multiple-choice items (PMCQ), designed to measure an ability to interpret clinical data presented visually by patients and by diagnostic technology; (3) patient management problems (PMP), a case simulation on paper designed to measure a clinical problem-solving ability. We tried to cover the waterfront of conventionally used objective tests.

The patient simulations used for performance assessments by examiners were organized into two formats. Simulated patient encounters (SPE) are highly structured role-playing interactions between examiner and candidate. The examiner plays all support personnel and the patient, and provides the results of diagnostic tests if ordered. The candidate, as the attending physician, verbally manages the "patient" by interacting with the examiner. The second format, simulated situation encounters (SSE), uses a role-playing format identical to the SPE but requires the candidate to manage three patients concurrently. The role-playing formats were designed to meet special circumstances of the practice of emergency medicine.

In both role-playing simulations, highly trained teams of examiners rate the candidate on seven skills: (1) appropriateness of data acquisition, (2) ability to interpret clinical data, (3) problem-solving ability, (4) patient management, (5) health care provided (outcome), (6) patient relationship, and (7) comprehension of pathophysiology. Examiners then provide an estimate of the overall clinical competence of the candidate based on the specific case they administered.

Representative samples of medical students, second-year residents in emergency medicine, and peer-nominated exemplar practicing emergency physicians — in a total of ninety-six subjects — participated in the two and a half-day field test. All tests and performance assessments except patient management problems (PMP) were found to be highly reliable, concurrently valid (highly correlated), and clearly discriminated among the criterion groups involved. PMPs were, at best, marginal with respect to these criteria (Maatsch 1980).

The First Administration: Confirmation of Field Test Results in the Real World of Certification. A second study, undertaken in 1980, involved several hundred candidates sitting for the first official administration of the specialty certification examination. All the test formats and test library items and cases that survived the field test were again used. They were separated into two parts. Part I comprised objective group-administered tests assessing clinical knowledge (MCQ), clinical data interpretation (PMCQ), and problem solving (PMP). Part II consisted of examiner-administered simulated patient and situation encounters. Analyses of data from the various tests and performance assessments confirmed all findings of the earlier field test analyses where direct comparisons could be made. The details of test development and the statistical analyses of these first two research studies were reported elsewhere (Maatsch, 1980; Maatsch, Munger, and Podgorny, 1982).

A Predictive Validity Study: Linking Test Scores to Actual Clinical Performances. The third major study, also funded by the National Center for Health Services Research, was conducted in 1981–82. It was a carefully designed two-year predictive validity study comparing Part I test scores and Part II performance assessments with actual on-site clinical performance of the physicians one and a half to two years after taking the certification examination. Clinical performance with real patients was measured retrospectively within a month of actual patient care by a new criterion measure I developed called chart-stimulated recall (CSR). Trained medical examiners, blind to previous certification test scores and performance ratings, selected a sample of six charts from thirty sequential patient records seen, and then conducted a structured interview based on the physician's recall of the case. Recall was stimulated by the medical chart, copies of which were before both the examiner and the physician. Ratings of the quality of care provided followed the interview about each patient.

A large representative sample of physicians practicing in hospital emergency departments throughout the country participated. Ratings of actual care of patients were comparable to those made during the structured role-play simulations of Part II of the certification examination. Interrater agreement and coefficients of generalizability for chart-stimulated recall measures were comparable to those observed in simulation exercises of Part II. In other words, the actual performance measured (criterion) was about as accurate as the Part II performance assessment tests involving simulated patients (predictor).

Part II mean overall ratings were found to predict with modest accuracy the overall quality of care as rated by the chart-stimulated recall method. Slightly lower correlations were observed for Part I written examinations. Subsequent regression analyses demonstrated that Part I objective tests and Part II performance assessments both contribute to the prediction of subsequent quality of care provided but that the Part II examination was about twice as powerful a predictor. The details of this research study are reported elsewhere (Maatsch, Huang, Downing, and Barker, 1982).

A Recertification Field Test: Continuing Competence Five Years Later. The fourth major study, the recertification field test, was begun in 1985. This three-year study was funded by the American Board of Emergency Medicine (ABEM) and involved the comprehensive testing and performance assessments of a stratified random sample of ABEM diplomates five years after they had successfully passed the certification examination. Several different test formats were added to the certification Part I objective test formats, namely a proctored open-book comprehensive multiple-choice test, a proctored closed-book medical content domain-specific multiple-choice test, and a take-home comprehensive multiple-choice test. A proctored closed-book comprehensive multiple-choice test modeled on the certification Part I examination, but shorter, served as a control. Under the direction of Professor Robert Bridgham, several variants of the chart-stimulated recall (CSR) method were also employed in this two-day field test. Included was the CSR face-to-face interview method used in the predictive validity study. A CSR evaluation was also conducted by telephone (no visual contact between examiner and physician). Finally, an independent chart audit without any contact was followed by reevaluation after limited telephone contact.

The primary purpose of this field test research was to further develop user-friendly methods of measuring clinical competence for purposes of conducting a recertification examination ten years after initial specialty certification. A second objective was to understand the potential improvement or loss in professional knowledge and skills of emergency physicians and the effect of experience variables occurring during the five-year interval on the gains or losses. This latter research is presented in more detail in Chapter Five. A final ancillary objective was to again evaluate findings and interpretations from the previous research studies.

Throughout the ten-year research program, I and other project members were continually confronted with a growing array of empirical findings produced by the variety of different statistical methods employed to analyze the data sets. Initially the results of many of the analyses disconfirmed expectations based on the then current multi-construct conceptions of clinical competence reviewed in Figure 4.1. Unfortunately, the original design of the certification examination had been based on these conceptualizations. We were perplexed. The tests and performance assessments were measuring clinical competence and its components with demonstrably high reliability. These tests and performance assessments were concurrently valid; that is, they were highly correlated but the performance data did not agree with our conceptions of clinical competence. We were experiencing the same problem that Levine and McGuire (1970) had confronted in testing their formulation of clinical competence.

After countless exploratory factor analyses, with different rotations and later confirmatory factor analysis and Linear Structural Relationships (LISREL) analyses, a somewhat different theory of clinical competence emerged from the data. The theory appeared to consistently predict (or explain) a large array of empirical relationships observed in the different studies involving different populations. Tentatively then, it appeared that a small set of uniquely organized but conventional constructs might have some generalizability within the medical profession. While the theory also may be applicable to other professions that involve a professional-client relationship, that remains to be evaluated.

Testing the Theories

Each of the studies in the research program described above offered an opportunity to test differential hypotheses drawn from the theories and to directly test the "fit" of the other proposed theories with the complex data set produced. From the initial field test study, a new theory was proposed that retrospectively fit the data after others in the literature were rejected. In subsequent studies, confirmation of the theory and reevaluation of the rejection of the others could and did occur — the theory development and evaluation process.

The Levine and McGuire Methodology and Findings. To illustrate the process and its complications, we will revisit the landmark study of Levine and McGuire (1970, 1971). This study was the first to use the theory evaluation approach to confirm rational definitions of clinical competence. The project team, under the direction of George Miller, M.D., at the Center for Educational Development, University of Illinois, in cooperation with the American Board of Orthopedic Surgery, rationally identified a number of skills and abilities essential to demonstrate clinical competence in that specialty. The skills and abilities are identified in Figure 4.1 under the column identified as ABOS 1971.

Specific test and performance assessment methods were designed to measure optimally each of those constructs in several ways. Thus, for example, multiple-choice items were designed to measure recall of factual knowledge and problem solving, patient management problems were designed specifically to measure problem solving, and several structured role-play simulations required the examiners to rate the candidate's problem-solving ability, recall of factual knowledge, interpretation of clinical data, and interpersonal skills and attitudes. Special oral examinations were also specifically designed to measure ability to interpret clinical data and interpersonal skills.

This design of a certification examination for measuring clinical competence and the evaluations that followed are classical and have heavily influenced the design of several other certification examinations such as the American Board of Otolaryngology and the one the Office of Medical Education Research and Development designed for ABEM several years later. Measuring multiple skills conceptions by different test formats remains a very conventional and widespread practice in medicine today, as illustrated in Figure 4.1.

Levine and McGuire's attempts to confirm their highly appealing rational conception of clinical competence also represent a landmark study of the process used for construct validation of a specialty certification examination. Of particular interest in this context is their use of factor analysis methodology to confirm the rational conceptual structure of clinical competence upon which their various test and performance assessments were based (Levine and McGuire 1970, 1971). In retrospect, it is unfortunate that they employed only a single method, a principal components method of factor analysis with rotation.

Their findings were also perplexing. They had designed tests and performance assessments to measure or rate the six abilities shown in Figure 4.1. However, five factors emerged that underlie their written and performance assessments. In their interpretation (Levine and McGuire, 1970), the most important was a general ability factor, defined by the ratings given by examiners in the oral examinations. The second most important was a knowledge factor, defined by the total scores on multiple-choice (MCQ) tests and some of the orals. The third factor was redefined as inductive reasoning rather than problem solving because of some unanticipated factor loadings. This factor was defined by the oral exam stressing interpretation of clinical data and some subscores on the PMPs but not, paradoxically, other subscores that were intended to measure problem solving. The fourth factor was identified as an ability to respond effectively. This new factor was defined by scores produced by the structured role-play simulations used in the oral examinations. It was a general oral examination factor. The fifth and least important factor, called decisiveness and efficiency in decision making, was defined by the other subscores of the paper-and-pencil patient management problems (PMP) not measuring the inductive reasoning factor.

The factor structure that emerged was based on empirical measures of physician knowledge and performance, and it did not fit the researchers' initial rational conceptions of clinical competence. Stated in another way, the construct validity of many of the tests and performance assessments were not confirmed within the measurement model they had proposed. The rational theory was suspect. A general ability factor appeared, a skill in interpretation of clinical data disappeared, and PMPs specifically designed by McGuire to measure problem solving loaded on two different factors. Finally, the oral performance examination, which involved examiner ratings of several of the proposed skills, identified two quite different factors. From their empirical evidence, we are left with a different conception that includes a general ability factor related to ratings in oral examinations, a knowledge factor, an inductive reasoning factor, a decisiveness factor, and a second general ability-to-respond factor again related to oral examination scores.

Development of the Theory. Our first factor analytic studies of the data produced by our initial field test were as perplexing as Levine and McGuire's study. After countless factor analytic studies, using different methods and rotations on parts of the data and the whole data set, a simple pattern of more general constructs finally appeared. As reported in 1978, a clinically relevant knowledge factor (K) was highly correlated with a clinical performance factor identified as problem solving (PS). The unexpectedly high correlation of these two factors was explained by the assumption of a third general competence factor (G) underlying both the K factor and the PS factor (Maatsch, 1978). Conceptually speaking, this three-factor structure is remarkably similar to both Ebel's Theory and Senior's Theory, although subtly different. In one sense, it combines the two positions that they debated in the passage quoted earlier in the chapter. It also confirms but redefines the more important factors that Levine and McGuire found.

Later Dr. Raywin Huang, the statistician and primary collaborator in this work, was able to employ LISREL, a maximum likelihood confirmatory factor analysis computer program developed by Joreskog and Sorbom (1978). With this program it is possible to specify a theory and test its fit of a complete data set. LISREL will probabilistically reject theories that do not fit. For theories that do fit, it is possible to determine which one best accounts for the relationships observed in the test scores and performance ratings. With LISREL it was possible to report rejection of several models but a failure to reject one model, namely the proposed two highly correlated factors model. This model fits the initial field test data, the subsequent first official administration of the certification examination, and a pooling of these two different subject groups (Maatsch, 1980; Maatsch, Munger, and Podgorny, 1982).

In these exploratory analyses, two paradoxical findings emerged. Using a total score (proficiency index), the paper-and-pencil patient management test (PMP) that Levine and McGuire had problems interpreting was found to load weakly on our clinical knowledge (K) factor, but it inefficiently measured the construct. In contrast, our theory was rejected if we assumed PMPs measured our clinical problem-solving (PS) construct, which was in fact measured by examiner ratings of clinical problem solving with simulated patient encounters. Ironically PMPs were designed as an economical paper-and-pencil group-administered substitute for the more expensive individually administered oral examinations seeking to rate problem-solving ability. In many ways our conflicting findings and theirs were similar.

Recent and yet unpublished LISREL analyses were performed on the same diplomate populations during the recertification field test. An even more diverse battery of different types of MCQ tests and performance assessments was employed. This test was conducted more than five years after the earlier field test and predictive validity research. We find again that two highly correlated constructs, the knowledge factor and the problem-solving factor, cannot be rejected; furthermore, they are even more highly correlated structurally (K = .85). While the two-factor theory fits the data better, apparently the several intervening years of clinical practice serves to further strengthen the correlation between the knowledge factor and the clinical problem-solving factor to a point where they can almost be interpreted as a single factor.

A Theory of Clinical Competence

A schematic model of the theory that appears to best fit our many data bases and other relevant literature is shown in Figure 4.2. The concept of three overlapping, highly correlated, yet subtly different constructs is emphasized. The Venn diagram illustrates the conception that medical knowledge (K) is different from but essential for clinical problem solving (PS)—the ability to cognitively apply cognitive knowledge in clinical situations—as Senior emphasized. It is proposed that because of the very high correlation between K and PS, both constructs overlap with a general competence factor (G) attributed to the individual. This construct incorporates individual differences in intelligence, motivation, personality, background education, and other personal factors not directly attributed to clinical knowledge (K) specifically measured or to the clinical problem-solving skill (PS) rated in the various performance assessment methods. Bright, highly motivated medical students and physicians with good educational backgrounds, those high on a G factor scale, tend to excel in all types of tests and performance assessments regardless of how or when competence is measured. When measures of knowledge and clinical problem solving are combined, they incorporate the effect of G and produce the single best estimate of the cognitive component of general clinical competence (GCC). The large overlap of the three circles suggests that Ebel's position was at least partially correct.

The model also illustrates the construct validity of various test formats. Objective tests measure knowledge and general competence; performance assessment methods measure problem solving and general competence. The more content-relevant and reliable the test, the more construct-valid it is within this theory. Objective tests should be composed of clinically relevant knowledge; if not, they will tend to measure general competence more than medical knowledge. Performance assessment orals should realistically simulate the ambiguity and uncertainty of clinical information that is based on actions taken and orders given by the physician. If they do not, oral examinations will tend to measure medical knowledge and general competence

Figure 4.2. General Clinical Competence (Cognitive Domain).

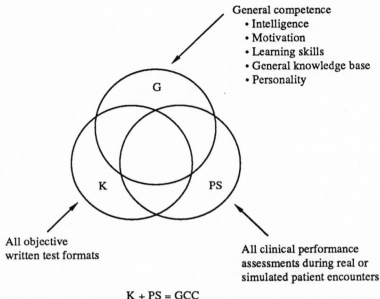

General competence
- Intelligence
- Motivation
- Learning skills
- General knowledge base
- Personality

G

K   PS

All objective
written test formats

All clinical performance
assessments during real or
simulated patient encounters

K + PS = GCC

more than clinical problem solving. That is, if oral examinations become conversational interactions between examiner
and physician about medical knowledge in general, then ratings
become influenced by the general competence of the individual
and the ability to discuss that knowledge. This hypothesis could
explain Levine and McGuire's weak "ability to respond" factor
produced by their oral examinations.

*On the Interpretation of Empirical Correlations and Structural
Relationships.* It is beyond the scope of this chapter to critically
evaluate medical evaluation research literature involving only
two or three test formats and limited samples of subjects. The
literature has numerous examples of such studies that report
low to moderate correlations between scores on two or three test
formats. Authors tend to optimistically conclude from this type
of data that the tests in question must be measuring the different
constructs they propose or else they would have correlated more

highly! However, there are many purely statistical reasons for low to moderate empirical correlations that must be ruled out before such interpretations are made. Unfortunately, the analyses necessary to identify and correct for potential sources of error or attenuation are not usually provided in such studies. In general, these small marginal pilot studies cannot provide the statistical basis for any logical inferences about the existence of two or more constructs. Neufeld and Norman are accurate in describing the field as a battered child.

Why Has Conceptual Confusion Occurred About the Nature of Clinical Competence? When attempting to interpret the conceptual meaning of a correlation between two sets of test scores in terms other than "variance accounted for," it is first necessary to consider and understand several purely statistical and methodological factors that can influence the observed correlation.

• *Reliability and error of measurement.* Assume we observe an empirical correlation of .40 between a content-valid multiple-choice test of clinically relevant medical knowledge and content-valid clinical performance assessment in the same specialty. The unreliability of a multiple-choice test measuring medical knowledge (K) and the unreliability of the performance assessment measuring problem solving (PS) will attenuate or lower the true underlying correlation because of errors in measurement. Statistical corrections can be made to correct for this type of attenuation. The correction provides an estimate of the true or structural (theoretical) correlation between the two constructs measured, assuming that the measures could be made perfectly reliable. Still other purely statistical sources of errors in measurement—small subject sample sizes, rater errors, item and case sample bias—may cause the observed correlation to be erroneously lower than an underlying true theoretical correlation. In short, the empirical world is noisy and complicated and it must be cleaned up to see the underlying theoretical world.

• *Artificial range truncation lowers correlations.* A second set of factors, superficial truncation of the large range of scores on one or both measures, also can dramatically reduce the observed correlation. Range truncation can occur artificially for a variety of reasons: individuals can "top out" on an objective test; insecure or untrained examiners can converge their ratings toward a safe average rating or be reluctant to use lower ratings (to fail). The range of true differences in clinical competence in a specialty also can be narrowed, and hence correlations lowered, simply because the sample population in the study was restricted, such as using only volunteers from a group of fourth-year medical students or those who *passed* a screening multiple-choice factual knowledge examination before taking the second performance assessment. These attenuating effects of observed correlations are much more difficult to estimate and correct when interpreting raw empirical correlations. They usually require independent empirical knowledge of the true population differences.

- *An example from research data.* Attenuation caused by test unreliability and range truncation of scores significantly lower empirical correlations and cause them to grossly underestimate the true structural (theoretical) relations between the two factors or constructs in our theory. In our field test involving students, residents, and practicing physicians — a very extended range of clinical competence — the observed correlation between highly reliable and valid tests of clinical knowledge (K) and ratings of clinical performance (PS) was .77. When corrected for attenuation due to the remaining unreliability, the true correlation between *tests* was estimated to be over .90. LISREL analyses of the same data set estimated the structural relationship between the K and PS *constructs* was .92! However, when we artificially restricted the range of competence in the same data set to the subpopulation that scored 75 percent correct or better on the multiple-choice knowledge test (they passed) before taking the performance assessment, then the empirical correlation drops to .40. LISREL estimated the structural relationship between K and PS in this type of restricted MCQ score data to be .52. Range truncation of one or both scores significantly affects observed correlations and hence the estimates of theoretical structural relations between constructs the tests seek to measure. One can be easily led to misinterpretations of raw empirical correlations.

What Is the True Strength of Structural Relationship Between Medical Knowledge and Clinical Problem Solving? The answer to this question is that it changes with the above measurement conditions and, within a professional peer group, throughout training and practice. At admission to medical school, a weak but positive relationship should exist; there is a common general competence factor (G) but ability to apply very limited medical knowledge to clinical treatment of patients is nearly nonexistent. As knowledge increases throughout undergraduate education but before opportunity to engage in clinical practice training, the relationship should remain relatively weak. With clinical training, the relationship between knowledge and clinical problem solving should strengthen significantly. At the end of graduate education, the relationship has been observed to be strong. During the professional career, the relationship should continue to strengthen and approach unity. In other words, it should become increasingly difficult to detect two different professional factors and an underlying general competence factor. This is because, it is hypothesized, independent bodies of medical knowledge (K) become more functional and better integrated into clinical problem-solving (PS) cognitive structures. Dysfunctional medical knowledge is forgotten. In fact, practicing physicians tend to abhor multiple-choice tests of medical knowledge and prefer to be evaluated by performance assessment methods.

Dr. Raywin Huang and I have been able to quantify the structural relationship between K and PS (with G latent) in the recertification field test involving diplomates of emergency medicine (a restricted and select group) who have been in practice five years after their specialty certification examinations. The structural relationship between K and PS at that point in career development is .85, with a standard error of the estimate of plus or minus .13. It is a very strong relationship, quite accurately measured. This changing structural relationship between K and PS throughout professional careers has very significant implications for how test methods should be used and how the resulting test scores should be combined and interpreted. Some of these implications will be suggested later in the chapter.

Scope and Limitations of the Theory

It is hypothesized that the proposed theory or measurement model will apply to any medical specialty and perhaps, with adaptation, to any comparable profession. At the very least, the theory represents a core set of constructs that can be further partitioned or built upon if the data warrant. There are, of course, many caveats and limitations to this working hypothesis; some of the more important ones are briefly discussed.

Observable Clinical Performance and Clinical Competence. When observing complex human behavior, a conventional distinction is made between a cognitive component, a psychomotor skill component, and an affective behavior component. Each tends to be conceptually structured in different ways, tends to be affected by different independent variables, requires that different dependent variables be measured, and tends to produce different types of empirical relationships. Each has its own body of knowledge to be understood.

Most but not all tests and performance assessments in medicine measure the cognitive functioning of medical students and physicians. Generally speaking, the clinical interactions of a physician with a patient are essentially cognitive, occasionally interrupted by one of many specific psychomotor skills that has been cognitively determined as appropriate. All such patient interactions seek to be "professional" with respect to their affective nature. Affective variables are, however, in specific situations and with specific patients or clients, important determinants of professional behaviors. The proposed theory does *not* address psychomotor skills or affective behaviors of the physician that may or may not be rated in performance assessments or measured in tests and questionnaires. It follows that clinical competence as we use the term means cognitive

competence to provide patient care during direct interactions
with the patient.

Applications to Other Medical Specialties and Professions. The
theory assumes that all tests and performance assessments are
content-valid for the specialty or subspecialty of the profession
in question. These specializations within professions, as in medicine, are usually defined by specialized bodies of knowledge
and procedures. It is hypothesized that the theory should apply
within these bodies of knowledge and procedures using the
appropriate test formats and assessment methods.

Errors of Measurement and Theoretical Predictions. As discussed
earlier, all practical measures of knowledge and performance
contain errors in estimating true scores or universe means. Test
reliabilities, examiner rating errors of many types, and variability of professional performance from case to case or situation to situation all combine to produce different sources of
variability in the data and attenuate correlations among the
data sets. As individual measures become more reliable and
valid, the observed correlations should converge on theoretical
predictions rather than diverge from those expectations. Corrections for attenuation and range truncation and the control
or elimination of the many sources of errors of measurements in
rating performance should strengthen observed relationships
in the direction expected by the theory. If the corrected relationships diverge from expectations, then we have added to our
knowledge of the nature of clinical competence, and the theory
should be changed.

Use of the Theory in Predicting Subsequent Patient Care. Needless
to say, an estimate of cognitive clinical competence is only one
of many variables involved in a specific patient interaction.
Since actual clinical performance, the criterion to be predicted,
does vary from patient to patient (medical problem solving is
not always easy), a reliable and valid performance assessment
must be conducted on many patients — we estimate five to seven
as a minimum in emergency medicine — and then averaged to

minimize extraneous errors of measurement and specific case selection. Only then do systematic relationships confirming predictions begin to appear.

Predictions of *average* quality of care to be provided to a *large* sample of patients, based on measures of general clinical competence alone, are moderate at best. Interpretation of individual test scores to predict subsequent quality of care to be delivered to specific patients is unwarranted and should be avoided. However, at the present time it would appear that gross differences in average quality of care to be provided to a universe of patients appropriate to the specialty can be predicted with marginally acceptable accuracy by combining medical knowledge test scores and clinical problem-solving performance assessments. The predictive validity of licensing and specialty certification examinations is supported by our research and they do serve a useful social and professional function. Reliable and valid tests can detect those who probably will not be able to practice medicine at a minimum acceptable level of quality of care for a high percentage of patients they will see.

Implications of the Theory for the Measurement of Clinical Competence. The theory presented in Figure 4.2 has many implications that differ from current conceptions and practices in the measurement of clinical competence. A few of the more important are summarized below to serve as a conceptual guide for the use of test methods and the interpretation of test scores.

- All content-valid tests and performance assessments measure a general competence factor (G). However:
    - All clinically relevant objective written tests measure amount of knowledge remembered and the G factor.
    - All clinical performance assessments involving real or simulated patients measure a performance factor identified as a problem-solving ability and the G factor.
- Empirically, the amount of clinical knowledge (K) and the ability to apply that knowledge in clinical encounters (PS) should vary as a function of education, training, and experience. Very early in the educational process the structural correlation

between K and PS should be relatively low and primarily determined by the presence of the G factor. Tests should be interpreted separately. As education proceeds through clerkships, residency training, and practice experience, K and PS become more highly correlated and add to the G factor effect. Later in a practice career the three factors should virtually merge into a single G factor with K and PS so highly correlated as to be inseparable. Test scores should be combined to estimate general clinical competence (GCC). In the later stages of training very low correlations between test scores measuring K and performance ratings measuring PS may be due to the unreliability of scores, range truncation of scores, or lack of construct validity of one or both measures. Researchers should account for the influence of G, K, and PS and potential errors of measurement before asserting that a test measures some new or unique cognitive ability or factor.

• It is better to add or average test scores across different objective test formats to better measure K and to average all performance ratings on a sample of cases to obtain a more accurate estimate of PS. Attempts to interpret a less reliable but more detailed competency profile of individual test format scores and performance ratings should be discouraged as predictors of subsequent care.

• An accurate measure of general clinical competency (GCC) is obtained by combining all objective test scores and performance assessments. It is the best predictor of the average quality of care to be provided to future patients. From the predictive validity study (Maatsch, Huang, Downing, and Barker, 1982), a reasonably accurate estimate of problem-solving ability using a simulated patient encounter format is the second best predictor. Reliable objective knowledge tests will improve prediction of the average quality of care provided to patients but are the weakest of the three alternatives if used alone.

• Educators, test designers, and organizations assessing professional competency should choose the test formats or performance assessment methods that most conveniently, cost effectively, and accurately measure the cognitive content and evaluation objectives of their specialty or subspecialty. Written objective test formats measure the same construct (K) and hence are interchangeable; scores can be combined. The same generalization applies to comprehensive performance assessment formats that accurately simulate the time-sequential availability of critical information sought by the physician during patient encounters. Specific ability ratings by examiners on these formats are relatively insensitive to the specific cognitive attributes defined and rated. A sum or average of all attributes rated best measures the performance factor identified as problem-solving ability (PS) on a specific case, but at least five cases should be rated and averaged to obtain a marginally reliable estimate of PS.

Summary

In summary, this chapter has traced the background research and literature that led to the development and evaluation of a theory of clinical competence. The theory identifies three highly interrelated cognitive constructs that underlie all test scores and performance assessment ratings conventionally employed to measure the clinical competence of physicians: a clinically relevant knowledge factor (K), a clinical performance problem-solving factor (PS), and a general competence factor (G) representing individual differences in background. When scores measuring these constructs are averaged to produce an estimate of general clinical competence (GCC), it is possible to predict with marginal accuracy the average quality of care to be provided by a physician. Some implications of the theory are identified to guide evaluation of the theory as well as the use and interpretation of test methods and test scores. This chapter is also intended to provide a conceptual background for the one that follows.

References

American Educational Research Association, American Psychological Association, and National Council on Measurement in

Education. *Standards for Educational and Psychological Testing.* Washington: American Psychological Association, 1985.

Burg, F. D., Lloyd, J. S., and Templeton, B. "Competence in Medicine." *Medical Teacher,* 1982, *4* (2), 60–64.

Hubbard, J. P., Levit, E. J., Schumacher, C. F., and Schnable, T. G. "An Objective Evaluation of Clinical Competence." *New England Journal of Medicine,* 1965, *272,* 1321.

Joreskog, K. G., and Sorbom, D. *LISREL.* Chicago: University of Chicago Press, 1978.

Levine, H. G., and McGuire, C. H. "The Validity and Reliability of Oral Skills in Assessing Cognitive Skills in Medicine." *Journal of Educational Measurement,* 1970, 7 (2), 63–74.

Levine, H. G., and McGuire, C. H. "Use of Profile System for Scoring and Reporting Certifying Examinations in Orthopedic Surgery." *Journal of Medical Education,* 1971, *46,* 78–85.

Maatsch, J. L. "Toward a Testable Theory of Physician Competence: An Experimental Analysis of a Criterion-Referenced Specialty Certification Examination." Symposium presented at the 17th Annual American Association of Medical Colleges — Research in Medical Education Conference, New Orleans, La. Oct. 1978.

Maatsch, J. L. *Model for a Criterion-Referenced Medical Specialty Test,* A Final Report on Grant No. HS-02038-02. Washington: National Center for Health Services Research, 1980.

Maatsch, J. L., Huang, R., Downing, S. M., and Barker, D. *Predictive Validity of Medical Specialty Examinations,* A Final Report on Grant HS 02038-04. Washington: National Center for Health Services Research, 1982.

Maatsch, J. L., Munger, B. S., and Podgorny, G. "On the Reliability and Validity of the Board Examination in Emergency Medicine." In B. W. Wolcott and D. A. Rund (eds.), *Emergency Medicine Annual: 1982.* Norwalk, Conn.: Appleton-Century-Crofts, 1982.

Neufeld, V. R. "Historical Perspectives on Clinical Competence." In V. R. Neufeld and G. R. Norman (eds.), *Assessing Clinical Competence.* New York: Springer, 1985.

Senior, J. R. *Toward the Measurement of Competence in Medicine.* Philadelphia: National Board of Medical Examiners, 1976.

5

Mary Ann Reinhart
Carole Wingate Keefe

Measuring Individual Differences in Clinical Competence: The Case of Emergency Medicine

In the previous chapter, Maatsch described the research from which his theory of physician competence evolved. The theory posits that general clinical competence is composed of three factors: medical knowledge (K), clinical problem solving (PS), and general competence (G); it is based on research showing that measures of both professional knowledge and clinical problem solving must be used to develop a valid measure of general clinical competence. Maatsch's conclusions, based on extensive research investigating the development and predictive validity of a medical specialty examination, leave at least one important question on assessment of professional clinical competence.

Note: The research reported here was supported by a grant from the American Board of Emergency Medicine (ABEM) to the Office of Medical Education Research and Development, Michigan State University. Jack L. Maatsch, Ph.D., was the principal investigator; Robert G. Bridgham, Ed.D., had primary responsibility for the development and investigation of the clinical problem-solving measures; and Raywin R. Huang, Ph.D., was responsible for the construction and analyses of the knowledge examinations. Benson S. Munger, Ph.D., executive director of ABEM, was an active participant in every phase of the research project. The opinions and interpretations expressed here are ours, and they do not necessarily reflect those of our colleagues or the position or policies of ABEM.

Will a physician, once certified in the specialty, maintain the level of clinical competence measured in the certification examinations? In response to concerns about assessment of continuing clinical competence, the American Board of Medical Specialties has urged that physicians who are certified by specialty boards be subject to assessment of continuing competence for the purpose of recertification. In this chapter, we briefly describe how one specialty board measured clinical competence for recertification. We also examine the degree of stability and change in physician competence since specialty certification, and attempt to determine which professional experience variables are related to these changes. That is, our primary goal in this chapter is twofold: (1) to describe the degree and nature of change in emergency physicians' professional competence that occurred between specialty certification and the field tests of the recertification assessment methods, and (2) to describe the ability of the experience variables to predict degree of professional competence five years after certification.

Introduction

The American Board of Emergency Medicine (ABEM) has from its inception endorsed a policy of a time-limited specialty certificate. The first certificates were issued in 1980 and will expire in 1990. In order for those certified in 1980 to be recertified in 1990, the board initiated a three-year research project designed to produce reliable and valid recertification assessment methods by 1987. The project built on and extended the research performed by Maatsch and his colleagues (see Chapter Four).

The recertification research project was funded by ABEM and was conducted by the Office of Medical Education Research and Development (OMERAD) at Michigan State University. Based on the results of previous research (Maatsch, Munger, and Podgorny, 1982), the recertification project was designed in part to investigate two issues: changes in the professional competence of emergency physicians over the course of five years, and the effects of certain professional experience components on these changes.

Maatsch's theory of general clinical competence provided the structure for this short-term longitudinal study. A schematic of the components of the theory and the model of the recertification study are presented in Figure 5.1. At Time 1, the diplomates in the recertification sample were certified as specialists in emergency medicine by passing a written comprehensive examination and a structured oral examination using simulated role plays. Shortly before the recertification field test, several measures of the diplomates' professional experiences were measured. At Time 2, the diplomates sat for their recertification examinations.

Most recertification assessments currently used by specialty boards or believed to be predictive of continuing medical competence were included in the study, along with several new measures. We expected that the experience variables could be organized into four internally reliable clusters; these four experience clusters and the recertification assessment methods are also listed in Figure 5.1. As indicated in the model, we expected to find changes in performances on the measures of the knowledge (K) and the problem-solving (PS) components, and we expected that both performances on the original certification examinations and professional experiences would influence performances on measures of clinical competence at the time of the recertification field tests.

While the measures and predictions described above are necessarily specific to the American Board of Emergency Medicine recertification field test, the types of assessment methods and the general nature of the predictions are expected to be generalizable to most clinical professions. For example, we would expect that engineers', educators', or nurses' general professional competence, as measured by knowledge and professional problem solving, would change, and that the nature of the change would be predicted both by their initial level of competence and their professional experiences over time. We would expect that a more challenging professional environment, practice of needed skills, and continuing education in key areas would contribute to continued professional competency. However, we would also predict that an engineer's, educator's, or

Figure 5.1. Hypothesized Relationships Between Physicians' Professional Experiences and the Clinical Components of Maatsch's Theory of General Clinical Competence.

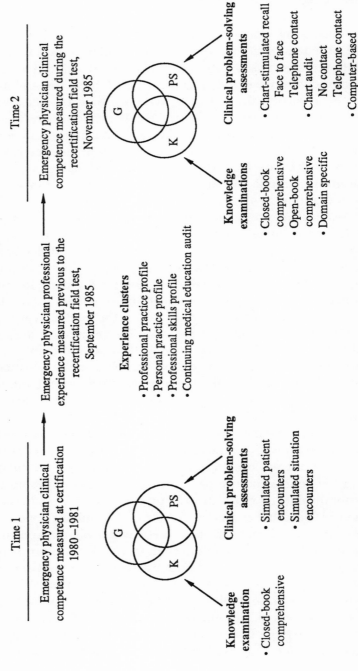

Time 1

Emergency physician clinical competence measured at certification 1980–1981 ⟶

Time 2

Emergency physician professional experience measured previous to the recertification field test, September 1985 ⟶

Emergency physician clinical competence measured during the recertification field test, November 1985

Experience clusters

• Professional practice profile
• Personal practice profile
• Professional skills profile
• Continuing medical education audit

Clinical problem-solving assessments

• Simulated patient encounters
• Simulated situation encounters

Knowledge examination

• Closed-book comprehensive

Clinical problem-solving assessments

• Chart-stimulated recall
   Face to face
   Telephone contact
• Chart audit
   No contact
   Telephone contact
• Computer-based examination

Knowledge examinations

• Closed-book comprehensive
• Open-book comprehensive
• Domain specific

G — General competence   •   K — Clinical knowledge   •   PS — Clinical problem solving nurse's initial level of competence would be the strongest predictor of continued competence. These predictions are similar to those that drove our investigations of the emergency medicine recertification field test. We expected that clinical competence at Time 1 would be the strongest predictor of clinical competence at Time 2, but that measures of certain professional experiences would also contribute significantly to the measures of competence at Time 2.

Measurement of Clinical Knowledge and Problem Solving

Knowledge Examinations. As can be seen in Figure 5.1, both clinical knowledge and clinical problem solving were measured with multiple assessment methods. All the knowledge examinations used in the recertification field test consisted of single, best-answer multiple-choice questions taken from the American Board of Emergency Medicine's certification test item bank. The test items were randomly drawn such that the mean item difficulty level could be balanced across all tests, including the diplomates' certification knowledge examination. The test items were also drawn according to a sampling plan based on the medical content of the test items. That is, some items were drawn from the entire pool and were used to form comprehensive examinations; others were drawn from within specific content domains and were used to form domain-specific examinations.

Because changes in the item bank over the five-year period were not documented to indicate knowledge new to emergency medicine, we were not able to sample items that would specifically assess either the diplomates' degree of retention or their degree of updating. Because the item pool is continuously updated, we know that some items used in the recertification study assessed information new to emergency medicine since the time of certification. Unfortunately, items that tap retention of previously learned information and items that tap updating of new knowledge are averaged in the results reported here. We had expected that the professional experiences related to retention would be different than those related to updating. For example, we had hoped to examine predictions that a diplomate's relative percent of time in clinical practice and use of professional skills would be related to retention, and amount of continuing education and teaching would be related to updating. Research still needs to be performed either in medicine or other professional fields to determine whether different professional experiences influence retention of previously learned knowledge and updating of new knowledge differentially.

We were able to select test items that would allow us to measure the degree to which the diplomates possessed a comprehensive base of current emergency medicine clinical knowledge. Test items selected according to the sampling plan described above were used to design four proctored examinations: a closed-book comprehensive, an open-book comprehensive, and two domain-specific examinations, each containing two separate emergency medicine content domains.

Problem-Solving Examinations. Multiple measures of clinical problem solving with varying degrees of examiner contact were used in the recertification study: (1) chart-stimulated recall with face-to-face examination, (2) chart-stimulated recall conducted by telephone, (3) chart audit with telephone follow-up of selected questions, (4) chart audit with no examiner-participant contact, and (5) the National Board of Medical Examiners' computer-based examination, which is discussed at length in Chapter Six. Chart-stimulated recall was developed by Maatsch and colleagues (Maatsch, Munger, and Podgorny, 1982) to be an in-depth examiner evaluation of the health care provided. It is based on participant-supplied medical charts of actual patient cases managed by the physician. Because chart-estimated recall with face-to-face examination (CSR face-to-face) provides the greatest amount of examiner-physician interaction around the examination of the physician's management of specific patient cases, it is the clinical problem-solving variable on which this chapter will focus. A more extensive discussion of the problem-solving measures used in emergency medicine research is given in Chapter Four.

Assessment of Professional Experience

Medical specialty boards use or propose a variety of methods and procedures for assessing the continuing clinical competence of board-certified diplomates who are applying for recertification of their specialty credentials. In addition to a range of oral and written comprehensive examination formats and direct audits of patients' charts, some specialty boards have also collected information on variables related to physicians' professional experiences—documentation of hospital privileges, information about professional procedures performed, numbers and types of patients cared for, credit hours of continuing medical education, and allocations of professional time to various aspects of medicine, including clinical practice, teaching, research and administration (American Board of Medical Specialties, 1981).

In the emergency medicine recertification study, four general areas of professional experience were measured and used to predict both the degree and nature of change in professional knowledge since certification, as well as the participant's current level of clinical knowledge and problem solving. Individual questionnaire items were selected to assess professional setting (emergency department profile), type of professional practice (personal practice profile), type and number of professional skills regularly used (professional skills profile), and amount and nature of continuing professional education (continuing medical education audit). The information was collected in a mailed questionnaire approximately two months before the field test of the knowledge and performance examinations.

Emergency Department Profile. The emergency department profile was developed to measure the size and complexity of the emergency physician's practice environment. It was hypothesized that continuing competency in emergency medicine would be positively related to the size and complexity of the primary emergency department practice base. The profile was developed using guidelines for categorizing hospital emergency capabilities (Commission on Emergency Medical Services, 1982) and in consideration of the levels of emergency department services defined for hospital accreditation (Joint Commission on Accreditation of Hospitals, 1985). Information was collected about patients treated during the previous twelve months: total number of patients treated in the emergency department, number of patients presented through an emergency medical system, number of patients who were treated in the department and subsequently admitted to the associated hospital, and number of patients who were transferred to another hospital for clinical reasons after initial stabilization in the emergency department. Information was also collected about the types of physician specialist coverage available to the emergency physician and whether the specialty coverage was available in hospital twenty-four-hours-a-day or on call and available within thirty minutes. The emergency department was further characterized by the availability of specialized technological resources and capabilities, such as round-the-clock operating room facilities.

Personal Practice Profile. The personal practice profile was developed to assess how emergency medicine diplomates divide their time among various aspects of emergency medicine. The study respondents were asked to indicate what percentages of their total professional time were allocated to emergency medicine clinical practice, emergency medicine teaching, emergency medicine research, and emergency department administration. It was hypothesized that continuing competency in emergency medicine would be positively correlated with the amount of clinical practice time.

Professional Skills Inventory. The professional skills inventory was designed to explore whether the actual numbers of procedures performed by emergency physicians related to continuing competency in emergency medicine. It was hypothesized that frequency would be positively related to continuing competency. ABEM had already developed a list of skills relevant to emergency medicine, and that list was evaluated and revised for the recertification study. Practicing, board-certified emergency physicians served as expert reviewers to indicate skills that should be added to or deleted from the list. Some additional items were eliminated on the basis of a pretest in which we randomly selected a sample of completed forms from emergency physicians applying to ABEM for original certification. Those items that the physicians indicated they never or very rarely performed were eliminated because they would contribute no useful discrimination among diplomates.

Continuing Medical Education Audit. The continuing medical education (CME) audit was included to determine the number and types of continuing professional education hours the recertification study physicians had accumulated over the two years prior to the study. The five categories of CME defined for the recertification study were based on the five categories established by the American College of Emergency Physicians (ACEP), the national membership organization of emergency physicians, which sponsors professional and scientific meetings and provides continuing education in emergency medicine.

Category 1 is the most formalized, and certain numbers of Category 1 credit hours are required of diplomates by several medical specialty boards, as well as some licensing boards. ACEP Category 1 accredited hours include programs, educational materials, and portions of scientific meetings reviewed and formally approved for ACEP Category 1 credit. Category 2 includes programs "planned" but not preapproved by ACEP. This category also includes hour-for-hour participation in hospital-based conferences and lectures as well as seminars and workshops in emergency medicine. Category 3 credits are obtained for teaching in emergency medicine. Category 4 credits are for published book chapters and papers or major presentations and exhibits related to emergency medicine. Category 5 is individual, nonsupervised study, self-directed continuing education activities in emergency medicine reported on an hour-for-hour basis — reading journals, for example. It was hypothesized that total CME credit hours would be positively correlated with continuing clinical competency.

Relevance to Other Professions. While the areas of professional experience that were examined in the recertification study were drawn primarily from reviews of what medical specialty boards use in assessing clinical competence, the general categories that we examined may be useful across a number of professions, such as engineering, nursing, education, and law. Several interesting questions can be asked of all these professions. Do different job settings or practice environments contribute to or detract from job performance? Do individuals perform similarly over time in different types of professional settings? Do certain demanding settings tend to build and enhance competencies? Does allocation of professional time to various aspects of one's profession improve general competence? Does teaching or performing administrative tasks make one a better practitioner? If a profession requires certain psychomotor skills, what frequency of demonstration or practice is necessary for maintaining optimal performance levels? Does the type or amount of continuing education contribute differentially to maintenance of professional competence? All these questions were examined in the recertification study and may be relevant to other professions. The answers, and their possible meaning to other professions, will be discussed shortly.

Sample Selection for the Recertification Field Test

The sample of emergency physicians for the recertification field trials was chosen to meet two primary criteria: generalizability and sufficient passage of time from certification to evaluate decay in knowledge and degree of updating. To be able to generalize the results of the field test to all diplomates, it was necessary to draw a random sample. Because it was also necessary to assure as wide a range of variability in clinical competence as possible, we decided to stratify participants on their original certification examination scores. Finally, to assess change in the level of clinical competence that occurs over time, the sample had to be reasonably far from the diplomates' certification examinations. Research on decay of knowledge in the preretirement years of adulthood indicates that most memory decay in a specific content area occurs in the first three to five years after acquisition (Bahrick, 1984). We selected diplomates who were four to five years beyond their certification examination, based on the assumption that passage of four to five years would allow us to assess decay of previously known knowledge and updating on new knowledge, and to determine which experience variables would be related to these changes. To meet all these criteria, we selected a stratified random sample of diplomates drawn from the 1980 and 1981 certification pools to participate in the 1985 recertification field test.

Findings of the Recertification Field Trials

Based on previous work and power analyses, we enlisted ninety-three emergency physicians from the population of 1980 and 1981 diplomates to participate in the recertification project. Each one participated in all aspects of the project. The participants were divided into two groups. Group 1 (N = 45) clearly passed their certification examinations, and Group 2 (N = 48) barely passed.

Generalizability of the Sample to the Population. Comparisons of certification test scores indicate that our sample (N = 93) results can be generalized to the population of 1980–1981 diplomates (N = 507). The means and standard deviations of the sample and population test scores were nearly identical, as were the distribution patterns of the scores of the two groups, giving us confidence that our sample was a valid representation of its population. Consequently, we are comfortable generalizing our findings from the recertification field test to the general population of emergency medicine diplomates.

Stability and Change in Professional Knowledge. Our analyses of the field test data show that all the proctored written examinations are highly intercorrelated and yield similar levels of performance. That is, the results confirmed Maatsch's model, which predicts that all written tests of clinical knowledge measure a single factor (see Chapter Four). All the knowledge tests were therefore combined into a single comprehensive measure. This 392-question, single-best-answer, multiple-choice examination was highly internally reliable and had a relatively small standard error of measurement. The diplomates' certification knowledge examination also was internally reliable and had a small standard error of measurement, assuring us that measurement error was a small factor in our findings.

To assess the degree of change in knowledge since certification, we subtracted the diplomates' recertification scores from their certification knowledge scores. There are at least two interesting questions to ask concerning these data. On the average, do emergency physicians gain or lose professional knowledge over the five-year period after initial certification? Which individuals gain or lose relatively large amounts of professional knowledge—that is, which experience variables appear to be closely associated with individual gains and losses?

Our finding shows no difference between the average scores of diplomates on the certification knowledge examination (mean = 82; standard deviation = 4.1) and the recertification knowledge examination (mean = 82; standard deviation = 5.3). That is, for our sample of ninety-three emergency medicine physicians, we saw no average gain or loss in professional knowledge. This finding was not what we had expected. Based on some research in adult cognitive development (Bahrick, 1984), we were expecting to see a modest decrement in comprehensive emergency medicine knowledge in our sample.

In our study, the two knowledge tests were drawn from the same item pool, were carefully matched for specific medical content sampling and for item difficulty, and had high internal reliabilities; also, our sample is representative of the population of diplomates from which they were drawn. As a consequence, we expect our finding to be replicated with future samples of diplomates. Assuming Bahrick's findings (1984) that if loss of knowledge occurs, it will happen within three to five years after acquisition, we also do not expect that the general population of diplomates will show an average loss in knowledge over time periods longer than the five years that had elapsed in this study.

The degree of generalizability of our finding to other

professions is difficult to assess. We are confident that the diplomates did not prepare for the recertification examinations,
although they had prepared for the certification examinations.
They were explicitly directed not to study for the recertification
field tests, and their feedback to us indicated they were pleased
to comply with our request. Thus it appears we were assessing
the core of everyday working knowledge. It seems that emergency physicians, on the average, maintain a comprehensive
core of emergency medicine knowledge, perhaps because of
professional demands to retain old knowledge and regularly
update new knowledge in their field. It is possible that on the
average other professionals also maintain a current store of
everyday working knowledge, at least for four to five years.

There are some important circumstances in emergency
medicine that might differentiate it from other professions.
First, from the time our diplomates sat for their certification
examinations, they knew they would have to pass recertification
within ten years. This position is highly likely to motivate professionals to keep current in their given field. Second, emergency
physicians, as well as some other specialty physicians and those
licensed by some states, must take a certain annual number of
medical education credits specifically designed for practicing
clinicians. The findings of similar research for professionals
who do not have to meet these expectations could be quite different. Data from other professions would be welcome to confirm or refute the validity and generalizability of our findings.

Although we found no average change in knowledge, this
does not preclude the fact that some individuals experienced a
gain or loss of knowledge. Indeed most diplomates did gain or
lose some percentage points. The distribution of these changes
is given in Figure 5.2. The distribution is interesting from two
perspectives — the symmetry around zero change and the general tightness of the distribution, again around zero change.
Eighty-six percent of the diplomates fall within the range of
having lost four percentage points to having gained three. Few
diplomates fall outside this range, and those who do are balanced between those who gained and those who lost: seven

Figure 5.2. Diplomates' Five-Year Gains and Losses
on Written Examinations.

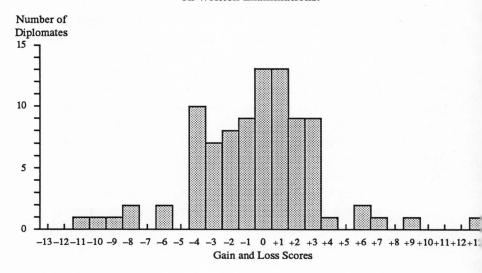

Number of
Diplomates

Gain and Loss Scores

diplomates lost six to eleven points, and six diplomates gained
four to thirteen points.

*Experience Variables Related to Extreme Gains and Losses in
Knowledge.* To understand the practice-setting differences that
might exist between these two groups of diplomates, we examined certain individual experience variables related to emergency departments and types of practice. Because our interest
was in drawing a picture of these two relatively extreme groups
of diplomates which are small in number, we did not use in-
ferential statistics to test differences between the groups. Instead
we examined the variables of interest to see if we could draw a
consistent portrait of the practice settings in which these two
groups functioned.

Of the eight experience variables in which we were particularly interested, seven tended to differentiate these two sets of
diplomates. The eighth — the number of patients transferred to
another facility for clinical care after stabilization — did not. We
had expected that diplomates in relatively nonenriched settings

would transfer more patients than those in large hospitals. Generally, this variable was not associated with the others that described the emergency department setting, and, more specifically, it did not discriminate these two groups of diplomates. The reasons for these findings are not clear to us.

Compared to those who lost the most points, those who gained an exceptional number of points saw more total patients (27,352 versus 16,957), saw more patients who were subsequently admitted to the hospital for care (4,795 versus 2,167), and had more specialist coverage and special facilities available to their emergency departments. The exceptionally good diplomates also tended to spend some time (10 percent) in clinical teaching, were somewhat less involved in clinical practice (62 percent versus 85 percent of their professional time), and were slightly more involved in administration (18 percent versus 11 percent) than those who lost a significant number of points. The diplomates who lost or gained fewer points tended to have average values on these experience components between the values of the two extreme groups. That is, it appears that enriched practice settings and practices that include some teaching and some administration are associated with improved performance over time on tests of professional medical knowledge, and it appears that these associations tend to be linear in nature. However, these results are based on very small numbers of diplomates who gained or lost a significant number of points on the knowledge examinations. Because the numbers of diplomates in these groups are very small and our study has yet to be replicated, these data must be interpreted somewhat cautiously.

What we find most interesting and comforting about these linear trends is the consistent picture they paint of an emergency physician who maintains a high level of competence over time. This specialist is in an enriched environment (number of patients, number of admitted patients, available specialist coverage, and available special facilities), and takes a relatively small but significant portion of time from clinical practice to teach medical students or residents in a clinical setting and to do some administrative work. As always, the causal direction of this picture (if it continues to be replicated with future samples of diplomates) cannot be determined without additional longitudinal data. That is, we do not know if exceptionally good emergency physicians are called to stimulating environments and perform multifaceted work, if they are exceptionally good because they have these opportunities, or if the causality is interactive and works both ways. Future research is needed to answer these questions.

Stability and Change in Clinical Problem Solving. To this point, our investigations of gains and losses have focused on measures of medical knowledge. Unfortunately, we are not able to make a direct study of the diplomates' gains and losses on measures of clinical problem solving. The certification and recertification performance examinations are not identical measurement methods. Although both problem-solving examinations evaluate a physician's care delivered to a patient, the certification examination uses structured patient cases; the chart-stimulated recall used in the recertification study is based on actual patient cases. Therefore, the examination procedures for the two methods are necessarily slightly different. Without further evaluation, we are not comfortable considering these two formats as exactly parallel tests, and therefore cannot assess gains and losses on clinical problem solving. For a more elaborated discussion of the nature of the examinations, see Maatsch, Munger, and Podgorny (1982) and Chapter Four in this book.

Predictors of Physician Competence. Our final question concerned the ability of the experience variables to predict degree of medical knowledge and clinical problem solving at the time of recertification. Recall that we predicted that diplomates' performance at certification would be the strongest predictor of performance at recertification, and that measures of professional experience would also contribute predictive information. To use our most reliable measures of professional experience, we used the data from the total sample and combined individual experience items into three large clusters of items. To answer our question, the knowledge and problem-solving recertification data were separately regressed against the three experience clusters, the total amount of continuing medical education, and the diplomates' knowledge and problem-solving certification scores. The first step in this process was to construct internally consistent clusters from the three groupings of individual experience variables.

Predictors of Emergency Medicine Competence. The items within the emergency department profile, the personal practice profile, and the professional skills profile were standardized and then submitted to separate confirmatory cluster analyses, using typical least squares analysis with communalities in the diagonals. Based on interitem and item total correlations, item communalities, and internal reliabilities (Cronbach's alpha), items that formed internally consistent clusters were retained.

The emergency department profile, a measure of the richness of the physician's setting, has an internal reliability of .86. The final cluster of items contains most measures of the number and types of patients who were seen, degree of coverage of the emergency department by fourteen different medical specialists, and the availability of eight clinical capabilities, such as computerized tomography (CAT scan) and twenty-four-hour operating room facilities. The personal practice profile, a measure of the diversity of the physician's practice, has an internal reliability of .77 and contains six items measuring the diplomate's involvement in clinical practice, teaching, and research. The professional skills profile measures amount of use of the typical psychomotor skills employed by an emergency physician; for example, catheter placement and oral or nasal intubation. This cluster has thirty-seven items and an internal reliability of .91.

After the clusters were formed and the total hours of continuing medical education were standardized, we performed separate stepwise multiple regressions in which we regressed the recertification knowledge and performance scores against all of our newly formed independent variables; that is, the emergency department, personal practice, and professional skills profiles, and total hours of continuing medical education. We also added knowledge and problem-solving certification scores to our list of experience variables. We hypothesized that the diplomates' original certification scores would strongly predict their recertification scores and the experience variables would contribute a small but significant amount of variability.

Predictors of Medical Knowledge. Our results tend to confirm our predictions, especially in the case of the diplomates' performance on the recertification knowledge examination. Our analysis yielded three predictors that account for 63 percent of the variance in the knowledge recertification data. Confirming the expected predictive ability of the certification examinations, the two certification tests account for 60 percent of the variance in the recertification examination. The certification knowledge examination accounts for 51 percent and the certification problem-solving examination contributes an additional 9 percent. The emergency department profile contributes a significant but small amount of variance (3 percent) to the recertification knowledge examination. No other experience variables contributed meaningfully or significantly to the regression equation.

Our primary hypothesis concerning these data was upheld: past demonstrations of competence are the best predictors of future demonstrations of competence. We expected and found that the certification knowledge examination predicts most of the variance in the recertification knowledge examination and the certification problem-solving examination predicts a smaller but significant amount of variance. Interestingly, the only experience variable that influences the diplomates' scores is the profile of the emergency department setting. The nature of the physician's personal practice, the amount of use of professional skills, and the hours of continuing medical education add no further information.

Predictors of Clinical Problem Solving. The results of the regressions of the problem-solving data on the independent variables support the predictive ability of the certification examinations, but not so conclusively. For the chart-stimulated recall (CSR) data, we are able to predict less than half of the amount of variance predicted in the knowledge examination data. One likely explanation *for these results* is the relatively lower reliability and higher standard error of measurement in the CSR face-to-face data compared to the knowledge data. We are quite confident that systematic changes in the examiner preparation methods used in the recertification field test will both raise CSR reliability and lower its standard error of measurement. At the present we can only await future research to confirm this expectation.

Using the certification examinations and the experience variables, we were able to predict 29 percent of the variance in CSR face-to-face data. The certification problem-solving examination predicted 14 percent of the variance, the total amount of continuing medical education predicted an additional 11 percent, and the skills profile accounted for 4 percent. Given the low predictive ability of the independent variables, it appears that all of the existing relationships have been attenuated due to the relatively low reliability of the criterion measure. Nevertheless, it is still instructive to look at the relationships found. Not surprisingly, the certification problem-solving scores contribute the most information to the recertification problem-solving scores. Contrary to our hypothesis, the certification knowledge examination does not add significant predictive ability to the regression equation. We expect that this result is due to attenuation of a relatively small correlation between the measures, but the answer awaits further analyses of these data and future research with CSR face-to-face after new examiner training methods have been implemented.

Two experience variables predict scores on CSR face-to-face: amount of total continuing medical education (CME) taken within the past twenty-four months and use of emergency medicine skills during this time period. Both CME and skills maintenance are means of remaining current in the practice of emergency medicine. Through CME, physicians learn the clinical implications of new research results and new and improved treatment practices. The regular use of emergency medicine skills keeps physicians current in treatment procedures and also implies involvement in a multifaceted clinical practice. As expected, both variables are associated with clinical problem solving as measured by the CSR face-to-face measure.

Conclusions

The research from the American Board of Emergency Medicine's three-year recertification project reported here was primarily focused on two issues. The first concerned the measurement of stability and change in clinical competence over five years. We were particularly interested in measuring change in competence and drawing a profile of the professional experiences of the physicians who gained or lost the most knowledge between specialty certification and the field test of recertification. Our second primary focus concerned predicting the degree of the diplomates' current clinical competence using certain experience and competency variables. All this research was based on Maatsch's model of general clinical competence, discussed in Chapter Four.

Contrary to one of our most fundamental hypotheses, our sample of emergency physicians on the average showed no change in clinical competence as measured by clinical knowledge examinations. Given the high measurement quality of the examinations, we expect this finding to replicate with future samples of board diplomates. Although this result is reassuring from a general medical viewpoint, we do not believe that licensing and certifying boards should drop plans for mandating relicensure of recertification. Two factors prompt us to this conclusion. First, emergency physicians have always known that they would have to stand for rigorous tests of recertification. We have no means to determine the validity of our findings under conditions of no recertification requirement. Second, our data show clear individual differences in stability and change. Average gains and losses are interesting from a theoretical perspective, but individual differences are critical from the perspective of professional practice.

We were able to draw a profile that contrasted the physicians who made extreme gains and losses. Consistent with our hypotheses, those who made exceptional gains in clinical knowledge over the course of five years were in enriched professional settings and had enriched personal practices. While all physicians were highly involved in clinical practice, those who made exceptional gains in knowledge tended to be somewhat more involved in clinical teaching and emergency department administration, not totally involved in clinical practice. We had not expected this finding, and it warrants further research.

Our second major focus was to describe the research in which we attempted to predict the diplomates' current level of competence using their certification test scores and their scores on several measures of professional experience since certification. Confirming our hypothesis, past demonstration of competence is the best predictor of current demonstration of competence. Also as expected, professional experience variables augment entry competence, but the major contributor to current competence is previous degree of demonstrated competence.

Three of our four experience variables contribute small but significant amounts of information to emergency physicians' degree of continuing clinical competence. The emergency department setting in which board diplomates practice medicine, their total hours of continuing medical education over the previous twenty-four months, and their use of emergency medicine clinical skills contribute to their clinical competence five years after certification. The only experience variable that did not contribute to competence measured at the field test of the recertification examinations is the profile of the diplomate's personal practice. This cluster of variables includes the relative amount of time physicians spend in clinical practice, teaching, and research. It is likely that the contributions that these factors make to physicians' competence are measured by the three variables that do contribute to the regression equations. A measure of practice is given by the emergency department profile and the professional skills profile. Total amount of continuing medical education includes amount of teaching and presentation of research results, as well as private reading of the professional literature, a necessary component of both teaching and research. More research is needed to determine how these variables interact with physicians' competence at certification and ultimately contribute to their continuing clinical competence.

The results of our analyses demonstrate the continuing importance of the level of knowledge and problem-solving competence that a physician brings to emergency medicine. The relative stability of this level of competence and the relatively small influence of the experience variables measured in this study also highlight the importance of professional training and rigorous certification examination.

At this time, the generalizability of these findings to other medical specialties and to other professions is difficult to assess. Given the results of our studies, we are comfortable that we have validly assessed the broad constructs of competence and experience that we set out to measure. We see no reason that these constructs—professional knowledge, professional problem solving, the professional practice environment, the allocation of professional activities, use of professional skills, and continuing education—should not be equally relevant to other practicing professionals.

References

Accreditation Manual for Hospitals. Chicago: Joint Commission on Accreditation of Hospitals, 1985.

American Board of Medical Specialties. *Annual Report and Reference Handbook—1981.* Evanston, Ill.: American Board of Medical Specialties, 1981.

Bahrick, H. P. "Semantic Memory Content in Permastore: Fifty Years of Memory for Spanish Learned in School." *Journal of Experimental Psychology: General*, 1984, *113*, 1–9.

Commission on Emergency Medical Services. *Provisional Guidelines for the Optimal Categorization of Hospital Emergency Capabilities.* Chicago: American Medical Association, 1982.

Maatsch, J. L., Munger, B. S., and Podgorny, G. "On the Reliability and Validity of the Board Examination in Emergency Medicine." In B. W. Wolcott and D. A. Rund (eds.), *Emergency Medicine Annual: 1982.* Norwalk, Conn.: Appleton-Century-Crofts, 1982.

6

Using a Computer-Based
Simulation Model of Assessment:
The Case of CBX

In the practice of medicine, the tools for diagnosis and prevention are as important as the tools for treatment. The same relationship applies in dealing with the maintenance of competence in the health professions. Professional development requires not only "treatments" — a variety of approaches to providing continuing education — but also "tests" for preventive screening and diagnosis. These tools must be sensitive enough and specific enough to detect incipient obsolescence or the risk factors leading to obsolescence, and to diagnose areas of incompetence that develop during the professional's career.

In the same way that we must detect a risk factor before preventive intervention or disease before treatment, we must determine needs for maintaining professional competence before we begin educational interventions. Furthermore, once an educational intervention has been applied, we should be able to measure its effectiveness at remedying or preventing the professional "disease" or risk factor it was meant to modify.

Acceptance Through Customization

An important issue in the development of tools to maintain competence of professionals who have already surmounted the entry barriers of their profession is the acceptability of those tools to their target audience. Particularly in professions where the effort to maintain currency is voluntary, the instruments used for continuing education and assessment must be perceived as relevant. This perceived relevance is different from a concern for educational efficacy or measurement reliability and validity. It relates to perceptions of pertinence to the practitioner's day-to-day activities, ease of use, and intuitive value in helping the professional meet self-defined goals for learning and self-assessment.

Two factors determine the perception of relevance to practice. First, the content of the educational materials or test must be based on the professional's current practice profile or its desired expansion. Second, the form of the education or measurement intervention will be best accepted if it resembles the familiar turf of day-to-day activities. In continuing education and assessment for physicians, this means that the content should be keyed to the clinician's practice profile (for example, specialty and demographics) and that the teaching or testing environment optimally will resemble the actual day-to-day practice of the physician.

Few systems for maintaining competence in medicine are tailored to the specific profile of the clinician's practice. While programs offered by specialty societies at least focus on a constrained content domain, they rarely are customized for the specific practice characteristics of the individual physician. The constraints of traditional media—classroom and print—have made such customization of content prohibitively expensive. Customization based on a profile of the physician's strengths and weaknesses within the specific practice setting is even more uncommon, even though it represents the most common-sense approach to the maintenance of professional competence.

Few systems for the continuing education of physicians or the assessment of continuing competency resemble the actual environment of patient care. Most educational programs use classroom or text. The techniques that emulate the environment of day-to-day practice—for example, role playing, simulation, and bedside rounds—are also prohibitively expensive.

An ideal system should be tailored to both the content and the demonstrated needs of the individual professional, and it should teach and test in an environment reminiscent of actual practice. It should also provide feedback designed to continue the customization of the professional development process by continually assessing strengths and weaknesses. Strengths should be reinforced, and weaknesses should lead to tailored remediation. The professional should be able to assess his or her mastery against peer and criterion standards.

The major impediments to reaching this ideal are the costliness of adequately individualized educational programs and the unavailability of effective measurement instruments for many components of professional competence. While current research has not fully defined a taxonomy for clinical competence in medicine, it is widely accepted that several distinct, albeit overlapping, domains exist: knowledge base, problem solving, interpersonal communication skills, and manipulative skills. Effective and widely accepted measurement instruments exist only for the knowledge base. Methods of assessment of other components of clinical competence have been proposed, developed, and used, but none has been demonstrated to have adequate reliability and validity to gain widespread acceptance as a measurement tool.

So we are left with measurement tools that allow us to measure only a limited component of clinical competence; therefore, our ability to tailor education and remediation is limited even if resources are available. Developments in electronic technology show considerable promise in making an individualized assessment and teaching program feasible. Our ability to store large amounts of information, whether test questions or updates on the latest clinical advances, allows the selection of only that information best suited to a professional's needs. Advances in audio and video technology, linked with small, inexpensive but powerful computers, can provide realistic portrayals of real-life situations that are highly interactive.

The same technology also makes possible new measurement tools that broaden the ability to effectively assess components of clinical competence beyond knowledge base.

Computer-based simulations allow the standardized, objective assessment of problem-solving skills, thus complementing test formats that assess knowledge base. With both techniques, a physician's knowledge base and clinical management skills can be profiled. Based on this assessment, a professional development program can be customized to meet the documented needs of the professional.

Development of a New Assessment Tool

The National Board of Medical Examiners (NBME) was chartered in 1915 in order to develop examinations of such high quality that they would be accepted in all jurisdictions as evidence of competence for medical licensure. Throughout its history, the NBME has sought to improve the breadth and depth of the formal assessment process by using a variety of measurement instruments. As its experience and expertise grew, the NBME increasingly provided evaluation services for entry-level certification of health professionals other than physicians. In addition, evaluation components of continuing education programs for health professionals have been developed, as well as evaluation tools for reassessment and recertification of health professionals' competence.

The major evaluation tools used during the last several decades have effectively measured the knowledge base for health professionals. When the knowledge base of a discipline can be clearly defined, short-answer or multiple-choice questions can be devised to effectively measure it. Both the types of effective questions and the statistical techniques to analyze performance on these items have been perfected. However, in the health professions as in other professions, mastery of a knowledge base represents only one of many dimensions of competence.

Unfortunately, the assessment tools honed to a fine state of perfection during the last four decades are singularly limited in their ability to effectively measure aspects of competence beyond knowledge base. In its early days, the NBME used tools perceived to measure additional components: essay questions, oral examinations, and practical bedside observations. For many years, these methods satisfied the desire to assess the complete range of competence; however, increasing concern with reliability and the cost and logistical difficulty of scoring them resulted in their exclusion from most evaluation programs. For several decades, the NBME has sought new techniques for assessment of clinical management skills. Most of this research has centered on various formats of clinical simulation. The end result of this effort is CBX, the NBME's computer-based simulation examination system.

How does it work? The physician interacts with the simulated CBX patient while sitting at a personal computer linked to a videodisc player and two television monitors, one for textual information and the other for medical images retrieved from the videodisc. The simulation begins with a brief description of the patient and the reason for this clinical encounter. For example: "A young woman carrying a small boy in her arms walks into the emergency department and says, 'My son fell down and hit his head about twenty minutes ago. I can't bring him out of it.' The patient is unconscious and has a bruise on the left temple." The time and day and the patient's current location are constantly displayed on the computer screen. In our example, it is Tuesday, day 1 of the simulation, at 10:00 A.M., and the patient is in the emergency department.

Before caring for simulated patients at CBX General Hospital or the CBX office, physicians are provided with information on the facilities and services available, and their clinical privileges, the procedures they may perform without assistance. These clinical privileges may be tailored to the setting in which the simulations are used. For example, when used for assessment of general competence for medical licensure, a limited list of procedural privileges is provided that is consistent with the privileges that might be granted to a general practitioner. If the simulations were used for cardiologists, the privileges could include many cardiac diagnostic procedures (such as cardiac catheterization, pacemaker insertion) not afforded the general practitioner.

With this background information in mind, the physician

sets out to assess and manage the CBX patient. The system never directs the physician to take any specific action. At every point, the physician may perform a procedure such as history, physical examination, lumbar puncture, and insertion of a central venous catheter, or write orders for tests, treatments, nursing procedures, or consultants. As the case progresses, the computer collates all information in a medical record format, which can be reviewed by the physician at any time.

In our example, the physician might "look" at the patient. "General appearance: An unconscious boy with a bruise and slight swelling of the left temple; appears small for age with no apparent deformities." He might then ask the nurse to obtain vital signs while he obtains a brief history from the mother. Each time a procedure is initiated, time moves forward an appropriate amount. "Looking" at the patient requires one minute; obtaining the brief history take five minutes. The nurse reports the vital signs, which were obtained while the physician acquired the history.

With the information from these actions in hand, the physician might proceed to further examine the child. A complete examination can be performed or one or more components specified. Time moves forward as appropriate for the physical examination performed. Alternately or subsequently, the physician may choose to write orders.

Orders are written by typing the name of the request. The computer recognizes abbreviations, common misspellings, and generic and trade names of drugs. In addition, an internal search algorithm allows the system to provide lists of best matches for the item requested by the physician when the request cannot be perfectly identified by the program. As a result, the physician will be able to identify and verify his request if the first three characters of the requested item or any of its synonyms are correctly typed.

In writing orders, the practitioner can select from the entire range of tests and treatments available in a modern health care setting. More than two thousand individual tests, procedures, and treatments are available at all times. Each item is available as in real life. Certain tests are unavailable in certain locations or at certain times. For example, routine X-rays are not available on weekends in the outpatient setting but are available in the hospital or emergency department; intravenous therapies can generally not be administered while the patient is at home.

After writing a series of orders and confirming their identity with the system, the physician is asked to verify various parameters. For tests and some procedures, the physician may write a STAT (perform immediately) order. Tests can also be ordered to be done recurrently or at some later date. The method of administration of therapies must be specified; for example, intravenous, oral, subcutaneous. Drugs can be given once or repetitively. Dose and frequency of drug administration may also be required.

When orders are completed, the physician is notified that tests have been sent or scheduled and that therapies are being initiated. Results of tests will not be reported until the appropriate amount of time passes. When procedures have been performed and orders written, the practitioner specifies when he next wishes to evaluate the patient. The clock then advances to the specified time. When the clock stops, all information accumulated during the movement of time is displayed, including results of laboratory tests, X-ray reports, and consultant responses.

With this new data available, the physician decides to reexamine the patient or write additional orders. As time passes, the condition of the patient changes in response to the underlying pathology present and the orders written by the physician. The physician must evaluate his course of action with each change in the patient's condition. In many cases, the changes are not apparent to the physician unless he specifically monitors the patient for a change in condition.

In some instances, realism dictates that the physician be notified of radical changes in the patient's condition. For example, if there is a sudden change in the level of consciousness of a hospitalized patient, the nurse will notify the physician. On such occasions, the advance of time may be interrupted. An appropriate message will be displayed to the physician, who can then reassess the patient, write new orders, or resume the advance of time.

When results of physical examination procedures or certain tests that are presented visually in real life are displayed, the system can access a linked interactive videodisc to display the medical image. This image can stand alone, as in the case of physical examination findings, or may be accompanied by text, as in the case of an X-ray with its report. In some cases, the image is available earlier than the textual description. The videodisc can store 54,000 single images, thirty minutes of full-motion sequences, or combinations of both image types. We have successfully used X-rays, microscopic materials (allowing scanning of the microscope slide by the physician), physical examination parameters, electrocardiograms, and other graphic materials.

In addition to performing procedures, writing orders, and controlling the frequency of follow-up encounters with the patient, the physician can move the patient among the available locations at will. As the patient's location is changed, the availability of tests and treatments may also change.

Returning to our example, normal values are reported for the boy's vital signs. The mother gives some additional history, describing a temper tantrum during which the child fell and hit his head. Brief past and developmental history are also provided. A neurologic examination reveals a comatose child without any physical examination evidence suggesting a specific intracranial lesion.

At this point, the physician will develop a hypothesis, the differential diagnosis of the problem as it is currently understood, and will set out to assess this hypothesis. For example, he may wish to rule out the presence of intracranial hemorrhage. He must specify, without cue, how this will be done. Will a lumbar puncture be performed? A skull X-ray? An echoencephalogram? Computerized tomography of the head? None of these options is suggested; the physician must decide what to do and specify it for the system.

In this patient, studies prove that no intracranial mass lesion is present. Additional hypotheses may be tested serially or in parallel, as determined by the student. A physician might wish to test for metabolic abnormalities, hyperglycemia, or ingestion of some toxic substance. Initial treatment and monitoring orders might also be written. Nurses can be asked to monitor vital signs and neurologic status at a specified frequency. An intravenous line may be inserted to allow the rapid administration of drugs should the clinical situation deteriorate.

At some point, after procedures are done and orders written, the physician will decide that there is nothing more to do for the patient until more information is available. The physician may specify when he will reevaluate the patient, in minutes, hours, or days. In our example, the physician returns to see the patient in one hour. At that time, the results of the blood studies excluding major metabolic abnormalities will be reported if they were ordered initially. On reexamination, the physician finds no change for the better or worse.

Our physician decides to admit the patient to the intensive care unit for observation. On admission, the physician must consider routine orders. He may choose to ask a consultant for advice. If he has already performed appropriate diagnostic studies for intracranial mass lesion, the consultant will agree with his admission and advise a period of neurologic observation. If appropriate studies have not yet been performed, the neurologist says, "I suggest that you order a CT scan of the head and contact me again after the results are available."

After the admission, and depending on the sequence of actions already taken, it may be 2:00 P.M. The examinee may decide to return to check on the patient in the evening. As the clock moves forward, it stops at 4:00, and the following message is displayed: "NURSE'S NOTE: The patient is awake intermittently and indicates that his head aches."

The physician may now continue to move time forward to see the patient as originally planned or may abort the planned clock advance and reevaluate the child. These actions continue, fully controlled by the physician, until the following message appears, usually in the evening of day 2: "The case has ended; thank you for taking care of this patient."

Throughout this case, the computer has maintained an

accurate record of all actions taken by the physician, the time they were done, and their sequence relative to other actions. This transaction record can be used to analyze the physician's performance. After the case ends, the computer can optionally display a description of the key events and expected performance.

The key features of the CBX simulation model are: time realism, including the timing of test results; dynamic response of the patient consistent with the natural history of the under-lying disease and the physician's interventions for good or for bad; ability to present visual materials without interpretive text; open-ended availability of all tests, procedures, and treatments without cuing; and the ability to record sequence and timing of actions.

Simulated patients have been developed for a broad range of clinical disciplines. Surgery, internal medicine, pediatrics, obstetrics, gynecology, emergency medicine, and family practice are all represented. Because of the limitations of representing interpersonal communication with a computer, cases focusing on behavioral problems have been difficult to create. Cases may be acute, lasting only a few minutes of simulated time. Other cases are chronic, taking place primarily in the ambulatory setting and lasting for months or even years.

Simulations are developed by a team of content experts and technicians. The content experts craft the outline of the case and the major internal events. The technicians use an extensive medical data base to research the efforts of the disease being modeled on the more than two thousand individual elements in the simulation data base. This information is then encoded for the computer by the technical specialists. Each case must be extensively tested to assure clinical realism, even in the face of actions not anticipated by the development group.

This developmental process is expensive. Each case must be used by a large number of physicians to effectively amortize its cost. Our experience suggests, however, that modest changes in the identifying features of simulated patients will allow the same basic simulation to be reused without easy recognition by the physician.

Assessment with CBX

At this point, the physician has had a realistic experience mir-roring the care of an actual patient. A complete record of actions taken has been made. Qualitative feedback may have been provided. While the experience of managing the simu-lated patient may be of educational value, practitioners prefer a more quantitative assessment of their performance. Such a quantitative measure also allows easy comparison of perfor-mance within specified groups and development of profiles of clinical competence. Therefore, to be of optimal value, the simulation must be systematically scored. Scores must be based on an assessment of how the actions taken in the case com-pare with actions defined as optimal, less than optimal, or contraindicated.

This assessment requires the development of perfor-mance criteria for each case. An independent group of content experts reviews the case as an unknown. Using a structured group process, they then define the actions and combinations of actions representing optimal care of the patient. Optimal is defined as the actions that must be taken, given the information available to the student, to safely manage the patient to the best possible outcome. This definition does not reward thorough-ness except as thoroughness affects safety for the patient.

Several optimal courses of action are defined, along with additional sets of actions defined as less desirable but still beneficial for the patient. Other actions are identified that place the patient at risk. The expert panels also identify actions that are considered inappropriate because of cost, redundancy, or lack of pertinence but do not place the patient at risk. Another group of actions are identified that are thought to be of some importance, although the expert committee cannot reach consensus.

Actions are judged according to their timing and their relationship to other actions. In our sample case, the child is found to have sustained a fractured arm in addition to a concus-sion. If the arm is placed in a cast before the neurologic status stabilizes, that action is considered a risk. If the arm is placed in a cast after the child awakens but before any overt complaints by the child, assuming that the physician was thorough enough to detect the fracture without an external cue, optimal credit is given. If immobilization of the arm is delayed for too long after the child awakens, less credit is earned.

In most cases, different actions are ranked in importance with one another but specific weights are not applied. The committees specify when certain key actions should not be overwhelmed by the combination of several less important actions. Any action of the physician can be used as a scoring element, including procedures performed, orders written, changes in patient location, and intervals selected for reassessing the patient.

When the performance criteria have been defined, they are encoded using Boolean algebraic statements so that the computer can compare the criterion list with the physician's transaction list. The result is an "answer sheet" showing the match of the physician's actions with the criteria established by experts.

The criteria are validated using several methods. The expert panel includes representatives from multiple clinical disciplines who must reach consensus on criterion actions. They must reconcile their own blind performance on the case with the performance standard established by the group process. The scoring keys are also validated in the field. A group of subjects manage the simulated patient. The elements of the scoring key are then subjected to a "fit" analysis using an item response theory (Rasch) analytic model. Those elements that do not perform as expected are returned to the expert panel for further review. The complete transaction lists of all field trial subjects are also reviewed to identify actions taken that were not anticipated by the expert panel but that should be included in the criterion set.

After a criterion set has been developed for the simulation, the computer compares the practitioner's actions with the criteria. The result is a list of the elements of the criterion set met by the individual student. Related actions can be rank ordered and assigned partial credit. The ranking can be for related actions, for actions across time, or for a combination of both parameters. In our example, the physician might receive full credit for an element relating to management of the fractured arm if he obtains an orthopedic consult in an appropriate time frame. If he chooses to reduce the fracture and set it in a cast himself, he will receive only partial credit for these actions. For full credit, equivalent to asking the consultant to manage the problem, he must reduce and cast the fracture as well as obtain a postreduction X-ray.

When the individual elements are combined in different ways, either within individual patients or across several patients, different scores can be developed. We have assessed the groupings of those elements judged beneficial to the patient and those judged risky. Other groupings on a patient-by-patient basis under study include the elements judged to be inappropriate but not risky, those that related only to timing or sequencing, items weighted by perceived relative importance, and elements grouped by clinical problem. Scores based on actions across several cases that are perceived to be related to specific clinical competencies (for example, data collection or setting of treatment priorities) are also being studied. It is hoped that these scores may establish a competence profile, allowing definition of both content and skill deficiencies.

To date, we have found that scores based on benefits or risks on a patient-by-patient basis, standardized and combined for a group of simulated patients, appear to be a valid measure of some components of general clinical competence. Furthermore, it appears that tests using these scores can have adequate reliability to serve as one parameter in making decisions about the practitioner's competence.

In a field trial conducted in 1987, several indications of the validity of CBX simulations were observed. Performance on the simulations differentiated physicians at different levels of clinical experience (third-year medical students versus first-year postgraduate trainees). While the performance distribution of these subjects overlapped considerably, the means of the two groups were substantially different.

In comparing the simulation test with other measures of

clinical competence (multiple-choice question test and written patient simulations using latent image printing), CBX was positively correlated, although the correlations were low. After correction for the attenuation caused by method unreliability, the correlation coefficient of CBX with multiple-choice questions was 0.49; the correlation coefficient for CBX with written patient management problems was 0.56. In an analysis of CBX with several multiple-choice measures of competence administered at various points in the medical education continuum, all other methods accounted for only 22 percent of the variance detected by CBX.

Studies of various techniques of measuring clinical problem solving have demonstrated that many clinical problems must be presented to obtain a reliable measure. Using a set of eight CBX cases, we found the alpha reliability coefficient to be 0.75. The length of test using CBX cases will vary depending on the required reliability of the measure obtained from the test. However, it is safe to assume that the use of clinical simulations for assessment of management skills will require substantial testing time. Additional studies of the precision of measurement of CBX show that the measure is more precise at the bottom of the performance range than at the top. This characteristic is desirable when the instrument is to be used to diagnose marginal competence.

Field trials demonstrated that neither prior use of computers nor computer anxiety alters performance on the clinical simulations. Furthermore, those with no prior computer experience were effectively oriented to the system quickly. It was apparent, however, that the uniqueness of the simulation environment required acclimatization. Performance measures did not stabilize until the physician had completed two or three simulations. This learning effect did not appear to be related to computer experience or anxiety.

Application of CBX

CBX promises to provide reliable and valid measures of clinical competence. It is hoped that ongoing research efforts will allow us to more fully understand the measures derived from the simulations and to assess their utility in developing profiles of physician management skills. With the rapidly increasing availability of microcomputers in physicians' homes and offices and in institutional health care settings, the logistics of self-assessment using computer-based simulations do not appear to be a significant impediment to use of this technology. The NBME has succeeded in developing a large library of several hundred simulations. While the development is expensive, widespread use of this technology would result in a very reasonable unit cost.

CBX simulations are seen by physicians as providing a realistic representation of clinical practice. The system is engaging, drawing on the full range of the physician's problem-solving skills. It can provide tailored feedback in addition to quantitative assessment. The measures derived from CBX can be compared with criterion or group performance data to allow comparison of individual performance. Students and residents using CBX in our field trials rated it very positively as a tool for self-assessment and continuing education. CBX was rated favorably when compared with currently used measurement instruments.

In the near future, we will be able to combine traditional testing formats with computer-based simulations to profile the physician's knowledge and patient management skills. This profile can serve as a basis for a prescription for the prevention of professional obsolescence. When marginal competence is identified, appropriate remediation can be identified. The power of modern information technology will allow this assessment process to be precisely focused on the practice characteristics of the professional. The same technology can be used to quickly provide direction for continuing education activities keyed to the specified deficiencies.

Computer-based simulations increase the breadth of our assessment of clinical competence. They do not fill all the gaps. Future efforts should be directed toward perfection of techniques for the measurement of other components of competence, particularly interpersonal skills and procedural skills. When such tools are available, an ideal system for the assessment of professional competence in medicine will have been achieved.

7

Donna S. Queeney
Wayne D. Smutz

Enhancing the Performance
of Professionals:
The Practice Audit Model

The purposes of continuing professional education are quite clear — to ensure competence and enhance performance of professionals. The means by which those are to be achieved, however, have been evolving over the last twenty-five years. The most prevalent approach since continuing professional education began to receive concerted attention in the early 1960s has been labeled the update model (Houle, 1983). It suggests that professionals must continuously engage in ongoing learning activities that keep them current in order to avoid professional obsolescence caused by the phenomenal growth of knowledge and the massive infusion of technology into professional practice. Importantly, this approach rests on the assumption that professionals must possess the most recent knowledge in their fields if they are to be effective practitioners. The mandatory continuing professional education movement that began in the early 1970s, then slowed, and more recently regained momentum (Phillips, 1987) was spawned by charges from citizens and government officials that professionals were not keeping up to date and thus were delivering inadequate service (Frandson, 1980; Olesen, 1979).

Although the update model continues to dominate continuing professional education (Nowlen, 1986), a rising tide of criticism over the last decade suggests that this approach in and of itself is not sufficient to ensure professional competence. Certainly there is acceptance that acquisition of knowledge provides a foundation for enhanced practice. At question, however, is whether possession of new knowledge will guarantee adequate performance (Caplan, 1983). More specifically, critics have charged that equating knowledge acquisition with competence is erroneous at best and foolish at worst (Klemp, 1979; Pottinger, 1980). From this perspective, professional competence is action oriented and is demonstrated in terms of what professionals do (their practice and performance), rather than simply by what they know. Consequently, continuing professional education must focus its efforts accordingly by attending to the context in which professionals work — the practice setting.

By identifying learning needs based on performance deficiencies and developing programs that are directly related to practice, continuing professional educators are more likely to help professionals engage in learning experiences that lead to competency and enhanced performance than would be the case if they participate solely in knowledge-acquisition experiences. This notion is based on the premise that practice deficiencies can be identified, along with the learning needs that might address them. These are not simple tasks. An array of assessment tools and methods is required to identify the variety of deficiencies that could exist within even one profession.

A different approach to continuing professional education, developed in response to this challenge, is described in this chapter. The uniqueness of the approach rests with its practice orientation to needs assessment and program development, and thus it represents an alternative to the update model. Called the Practice Audit Model, it was initially developed at The Pennsylvania State University during the late 1970s in work with the pharmacy profession. It subsequently was implemented extensively in the course of the 1980–1985 Continuing Professional Education Development Project, conducted at Penn State and funded by that institution and the W. K. Kellogg Foundation.

The Relationship of Continuing Professional Education to Practice

Continuing professional education programs often have been criticized for not being closely related to daily practice. University-based offerings in particular have been subject to pronouncements that they are too theoretical in orientation. What exactly does it mean to assume a *practice orientation* to continuing professional education? Several perspectives can be offered.

First, it means that continuing professional education must be tied to the context in which practitioners perform. This requires a thorough understanding of the entire scope of practice for the profession being addressed. For example, it is not enough to know that accountants need interpersonal skills. One must consider the specific tasks for which an accountant uses these skills, then tailor educational programs to those applications.

Second, a practice orientation requires that professionals' learning needs, the foundation for programs, be derived from a determination of their strengths and weaknesses. Specifically, it focuses on performance deficiencies. Yet decisions about professionals' continuing education needs often are based on surveys asking respondents what topics interest them, or on faculty members' perceptions of what practitioners should be taught. While such procedures can be useful, total reliance on them may result in programs that focus more on perceived wants than on actual needs.

Third, the practice orientation recognizes the importance of integrating new knowledge and skills into practice. Because continuing professional education is designed for professionals with established patterns of practice, whatever is taught must be integrated into existing practice patterns. This is quite different from entry-level education, where students have not yet developed their individual modes of professional practice and are just beginning to consider weaving job proficiencies into a coherent style of practice.

Higher Education/Profession Collaboration

How might such a practice-oriented approach be developed? Given the complexity of the task, one possibility is by combining the efforts of higher education and professional organizations. Through such a collaborative effort, different types of expertise can be brought to bear on the problem of developing practice-oriented continuing professional education. For example, continuing education professionals are experienced in the delivery of programs, university faculty members work to uncover new knowledge, professional associations are in the closest touch with practicing professionals' concerns, and regulatory bodies are knowledgeable about assessment methods. Because each has something valuable to contribute, working together collaboratively they are likely to produce a better product than they can individually (Smutz and others, 1981).

Such collaboration is not casually or easily achieved, however. If two or more groups are to work together in a truly collaborative fashion, each must have some resources (expertise, facilities, funding, contacts, materials) to contribute to the relationship. Each must be unable to satisfactorily accomplish alone the goal being addressed; each must need the other or others. And while collaborating groups must share compatible goals and interests, they should not have identical goals that would put them in the position of competing with one another to accomplish the same thing (Lindsay, Queeney, and Smutz, 1981).

Even when appropriate groups for collaboration have been identified, careful orchestration is required to enable collaboration to occur and be sustained. Steps must be taken to ensure that all parties have and maintain equivalent roles, and that a sense of ownership of the effort is developed by all participants. Collaboration must be built around a commonly held purpose, and the work of the collaborating body must be structured so that it moves forward smoothly.

Origin of the Practice Audit Model

With these concerns about the need for a practice orientation to continuing professional education and the importance of a higher education/profession collaboration to the optimum development and delivery of continuing professional education, Penn State in 1975 began work with the four Pennsylvania schools of pharmacy and the American Pharmaceutical Association to define a process for determining pharmacists' practice-related needs and "to develop an organized, accessible, and ongoing program of continuing professional education for all pharmacist practitioners which would enable them to maintain the necessary competencies to fulfill their role optimally" (Smutz and others, 1981, p. 21).

The work of this group continued for several years. As the group reached the point of delivering programs designed to meet identified needs, they reviewed the steps they had taken. The result was the Practice Audit Model (Figure 7.1), a seven-phase process intended to guide the systematic development of continuing professional education programs that would assist practitioners in maintaining competence. Its key features are (1) identification of professional practitioners' learning needs through performance assessment, (2) design of practice-oriented programs based on the identified needs, and (3) collaboration between educational institutions and professional organizations with regard to program development and delivery.

The first systematic application of the Practice Audit Model occurred from 1980 to 1985, during the Continuing Professional Education Development Project. Two of its major goals were directly relevant to the model:

1. To develop and implement practice-oriented continuing professional education through the application of the Practice Audit Model to selected professions.
2. To establish collaborative relationships between the university and the professions in order to strengthen the development and implementation of continuing professional education programs.

Figure 7.1. Practice Audit Model.

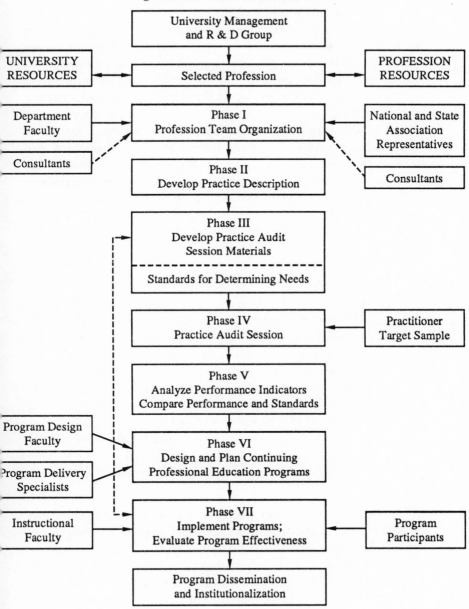

Although the purpose of the Continuing Professional Education Development Project was to implement the seven-phase Practice-Audit Model, consideration first had to be given to selecting the professions to which the model would be applied. To do this, specific selection criteria were established to identify professions most developmentally ready to undertake a systematic, practice-oriented approach to continuing professional education. Criteria varied somewhat according to specific situations and applications. In the case of the Continuing Professional Education Development Project, criteria of two types were used: *essential* (criteria that the profession and the academic base must meet in order to be considered) and *supporting* (criteria considered beneficial in that they represented an important asset, but not required for the profession to be suitable for application of the model) (Queeney and Melander, 1984, pp. 11–12).

Three criteria were deemed essential:

1. The profession had to have addressed the issue of practice standards or developed a role delineation because of the effort's focus on performance. (A role delineation is a hierarchical description of a profession's activities organized into major domains of activity, responsibilities, and tasks.)
2. An academic department that prepared individuals for the given profession had to be present at Penn State to facilitate access to appropriate faculty members.
3. A willingness to cooperate had to exist within the profession so that representatives from higher education and the associations could work together effectively.

Using these criteria, project staff members identified five professions or profession specialties for potential participation: accounting, architecture, clinical dietetics, clinical psychology, and nursing. Academic departments at Penn State, state and national professional associations, and regulatory agencies, where relevant, were contacted, and all parties representing the five professions agreed to participate. Thus, the context was set for implementation of the needs assessment and program development phases of the model.

Phase I: Profession Team Organization. To carry out the work of the project, for each profession the relevant academic department, professional associations at the state and national levels, and the national regulatory agency (where appropriate) appointed one or more representatives to a "profession team." It was these teams, ranging from six to ten members, that executed project activities. Each profession team met at least two times yearly, for two and one-half days each time, to make key decisions and outline the work to be done. Profession team members assumed responsibility for various tasks identified in these meetings, and accomplished the necessary work between meetings.

Two project staff members were assigned to each profession team to (1) organize the activities of the teams to ensure that the project remained on schedule, (2) provide background information and resources so that the teams' decisions and actions would be well grounded, (3) establish decision-making frameworks for the teams during each phase of the Practice Audit Model so that team activities remained focused within the parameters of the project, (4) facilitate access to other university academic departments and service units, and (5) serve as catalytic agents to maintain interest, enthusiasm, and productivity among team members throughout the extended life of the project. However, because of the collaborative nature of the project, it was essential that project staff members not be viewed as being in charge of the project. The active participation of all team members was critical, and steps were taken to encourage this.

To illustrate, the profession teams were designed to operate by consensus throughout the project, to build team members' commitment to the effort. A group process consultant was hired to conduct the early meetings of all teams. She was viewed as neutral, and thus was able to minimize any perceptions of staff ownership of the project. In addition, she encouraged all team members to participate in the discussion, ensured that all viewpoints were expressed, and minimized any conflicts that arose. As the teams progressed through successive meetings, team members began to take charge of their meetings and to function as truly collaborative, consensual groups. As this occurred, the consultant withdrew from each team.

For many of the professions, these teams represented the first time that the academic departments and professional associations had worked together in an organized, ongoing fashion. While there may be several reasons for this historic dearth of collaboration between higher education and the professions, three primary reasons may be cited:

1. Collaboration requires a conscious bringing together of groups (or individuals) around a common problem or task, so that they might share complementary resources to address a unifying concern. Without this deliberate action, all will proceed as separate entities.
2. Historically, professional practitioners often have viewed academics as operating in an ivory tower, removed from realities and practical applications of what they teach. Conversely, academicians have considered practitioners to be overly pragmatic, functioning in a task-oriented fashion with little attention to the theoretical foundations of their work. While there may be kernels of truth in these observations, they are obstacles that can be overcome through concerted effort by everyone.
3. Academicians are concerned with education; professional associations often focus on training. The two need not be mutually exclusive, but a belief that they are may have kept them from looking at the commonalities, rather than the differences, in what they do.

In our project, these types of problems were effectively addressed. One profession team even brought together representatives of a professional association and a regulatory agency with a joint history of opposition. In virtually all cases, the collaborative relationships worked exceedingly well and have continued beyond the life of the project.

Phase II: Develop Practice Description. The first task faced by each profession team was to develop a practice description through utilization of role delineation procedures. A practice description outlines the scope of practice of a given profession. Although each practitioner within the profession might not do all tasks included in the document, the profession as a whole is committed to addressing all the tasks indicated. The development of a practice description is critical in the competency-based approach to continuing professional education because the types of activity in which a given set of professionals engage must be defined before performance deficiencies can be determined (Menges, 1975).

The practice descriptions for the professions participating in the project were created by utilizing the expertise of profession team members and the relevant existing literature, which provided much of the base from which to begin. Four of the five project professions had developed or were developing role delineations for entry-level practice prior to their commitment to the project.

The profession teams' task involved using consensual decision making to modify these documents to reflect practice beyond the entry level. While much of the practice description for a midcareer professional remains similar to that for the entry-level practitioner, some important differences exist. For example, management and administrative skills, not needed for beginning professionals, become necessary as professionals advance in their careers and assume a management role. Likewise, more experienced practitioners may need preparation for supervision of students and interns. Mature professionals also become involved in issues internal to their profession and in representing the profession in the practice context and beyond. Thus preparation in group dynamics, professional relations, and influencing legislation is useful.

Each practice description was structured to include three levels: (1) proficiency domains, broad areas of practice within a profession; (2) responsibilities, more specific portions of practice; and (3) tasks, specific behaviors or actions of daily practice. For example, within nursing one domain would be "provide direct patient care." Under that domain, one responsibility would be "assess the patient," and a task within this responsibility would be "interview the patient." Generally, the practice descriptions consisted of 3 or 4 major domains, 10 to 15 responsibilities, and 70 to 120 tasks.

After each team drafted a practice description, a survey of Pennsylvania practitioners was conducted to determine how accurately it portrayed professional practice. A written questionnaire was designed for each group, asking respondents to answer two questions for every task included in the practice description: (1) How important is this task to your practice? (2) How often do you perform this task? Respondents also were asked to identify additional tasks of practice not included in the practice description. High agreement among respondents on both questions increased team members' confidence in their descriptions. For all five professions, the data collected indicated that the practice descriptions did indeed serve to delineate the responsibilities and tasks of daily practice.

Phase III: Develop Performance Assessment Materials. A one-day assessment session, called a Practice Audit Session, was to be conducted for each of the five professions, to assess the performance of sample groups of practitioners. Identification of practitioners' strengths and weaknesses in the areas selected for assessment was necessary so that those areas of weak performance could be addressed by educational programming. Because practitioner proficiency in all responsibilities and tasks could not be assessed in one iteration of the Practice Audit Model, the initial assessment had to be restricted in scope. The teams chose a limited number of tasks and responsibilities for the assessment, primarily by examining the survey data to identify the tasks and responsibilities that practitioners believed most important, and that they performed most frequently.

Once the content areas were identified, the task facing the profession teams was twofold: (1) to create exercises that would measure practitioners' performance in the specific areas selected for assessment, and (2) to establish performance standards that defined the point at which practitioners' performance as a group was deemed acceptable, and the point at which it was considered weak. This second step was critical because the assessment process was intended to measure the performance of the group of practitioners studied rather than individual performance, thereby leading to identification of the group's educational needs.

Because of the project's performance orientation, Practice Audit Sessions were designed following assessment center concepts, with specific exercises developed to simulate the practice situation as closely as possible. Each Practice Audit Session included a range of exercises, focused not on what participants knew but on how they applied what they knew. Most of them had at least one live simulation, with an actor portraying a patient or client with whom each participant was required to interact. In these live simulations, the participant was given written material describing the case and a specific assignment for working with the client or patient, then asked to meet with the individual (portrayed by an actor or actress) for a specified length of time. For example, clinical dietitians were asked to teach a "diabetic patient" about proper diet for this condition. Accountants met with the "president" of a business to discuss his tax returns. These live simulations were videotaped and later evaluated by trained raters, using evaluation criteria developed by profession team members.

Another form of exercise was the trigger film, where participants were shown a film portraying a particular practice situation. The film was stopped at specific intervals, and participants were asked questions regarding their perceptions of the situation and the steps they would take in that situation. Case studies, in which participants were asked to prepare a patient care plan or an accounting report, for example, also were used. The entire Architecture Practice Audit Session was based on one case study, which involved designing a town hall for a fictitious community.

Phase IV: The Practice Audit Session. Identification of individuals to participate in the Practice Audit Sessions was accomplished by inviting Pennsylvania practitioners to apply for the opportunity. For each profession, from forty to fifty participants were chosen from the pool of those who responded or were nominated. An effort was made to obtain a sample of practitioners representative of the profession in terms of practice setting, education, age, and years of experience.

Each Practice Audit Session was a full day in length, and the schedule for each session was carefully coordinated and structured to make optimum use of the time. In all cases, participants were divided into small groups at the start of the Practice Audit Session. Each group was led by a member of the profession team to facilitate administration of the assessment instruments. Although the exercises were completed by each individual working alone, the groups gave participants an opportunity for peer interaction between activities and reduced the likelihood of participants feeling threatened by the assessment experience.

Participants in the Practice Audit Sessions viewed them as a learning experience. The small groups were considered particularly helpful because they provided an opportunity for exchange of ideas among the practitioners. From these participant observations, profession team members gained some insights into methods that might be applied to the delivery of the educational programs they were about to develop.

Phase V: Analyze Performance Indicators, Compare Performance and Standards. Once the Practice Audit Sessions had been completed, it was necessary to evaluate participants' performance on each exercise. Rating scales, scoring sheets, and other appropriate devices had been developed and were applied. Profession team members subsequently reviewed the results of each exercise, considering how the group of participants performed. From these data, and using the performance standards established by the profession team, it was possible to identify areas where participants did well and those where they exhibited weakness.

Across the professions deficiencies were identified, particularly with regard to the skills practitioners perform on a daily basis. Some examples of specific findings include the following:

1. Among architects, weaknesses were found in problem defi-
    nition and methodology in the area of project scheduling,
    and low performance ratings were associated with data
    collection (building an information base for cost estimat-
    ing). Architects' responses also indicated that they did not
    regularly fulfill their obligations to keep clients informed of
    cost changes that occurred in the course of a project.

2. With respect to clinical dietitians, the findings indicated
    that practitioners had difficulty particularizing their re-
    sponses to individual situations. For example, in the case
    studies they were able to identify the nutritional problems
    of their clients but then offered standardized care plans that
    often ignored the unique features of the client's case. Simi-
    larly, in the client simulations dietitians demonstrated an
    ability to structure an interview, ask open-ended questions,
    and establish a dialogue, but exhibited a tendency to com-
    pletely control the situation without adequately exploring
    clients' concerns, involving them in goal setting, demon-
    strating empathy, or obtaining feedback.

3. The assessment of nurses caring for older adult patients
    indicated that general knowledge regarding gerontological
    patients was not at the level anticipated. Deficiencies also
    were uncovered related to nurses' development of care
    plans. Problems here related to several issues including
    establishing goals and evaluating outcomes of nursing ac-
    tions. In terms of interacting with patients, nurses demon-
    strated good verbal and nonverbal skills and were respectful
    and nonjudgmental, but performed less well in terms of
    active listening and information gathering. Other areas
    of demonstrated need included understanding the scope of
    nurses' professional authority and client advocacy.

4. Data suggested that although accountants plan their audits,
    they frequently fail to plan systematically and to document
    their planning. Specific needs were identified in the areas of
    familiarity with client/industry, identification of client
    changes from year to year, and establishing audit priorities.
    In the area of data gathering, respondents failed to demon-
    strate ability to move beyond identification of major issues.

For example, they did not use their technical expertise to fully explore the issues, identify salient points and technical details, and perceive the broader context in which the issues were embedded. Accountants appeared to be somewhat better at identifying client goals in the goal assessment process than at developing financial plans to meet those goals, and they exhibited difficulty applying technical information in the area of tax return review.

5. Results of the clinical psychologists' assessment indicated that they performed satisfactorily in certain areas, such as collecting information necessary for clinical inferences, but that problems surfaced in other areas. For example, some deficiencies were identified with respect to integrating sources of clinical information, recognizing one's own limitations in providing clinical services, and understanding legal and ethical issues (Lindsay, Crowe, and Jacobs, 1987). In addition, the performance assessment experience led profession team members to conclude that increasing psychologists' sensitivity in making clinical observations and helping them gain new insights into available therapist actions, regardless of current level of proficiency, were important issues to be addressed by future continuing education programs.

On the basis of the information gleaned from the Practice Audit Sessions, specific areas were selected for educational programming.

Phase VI: Design and Plan Continuing Professional Education Programs. The profession teams gave considerable thought to the selection of appropriate methods for teaching and delivering their programs because of the project's practice orientation. The nature of the weaknesses uncovered in the Practice Audit Sessions and participants' responses to the sessions themselves indicated that teaching needed proficiencies through the standard lecture format would not be sufficient to ensure that practitioners would learn the necessary skills and integrate them satisfactorily into practice. Profession team members subsequently developed programs that used a variety of instructional techniques to enhance development of proficiencies. They can be thought of as characteristics of practice-oriented programs, and include:

- Demonstration models to illustrate the application of specific skills.
- Frequent interaction among program participants to provide a forum for integrating skills with practice and for exchanging alternative approaches and perspectives.
- High ratio of instructors to participants in order to provide individualized attention.
- Guided practice both during and after formal instruction through case studies and client simulations.
- Frequent feedback from instructional personnel to shape participants' use of the desired skills.
- Small-group activities to facilitate the interactive nature of the instruction.

For several of the professions, expertise to address some of the areas of identified weaknesses was based not in the academic discipline of the profession but in another academic department. However, because a faculty member with the necessary knowledge was not likely to understand the profession being addressed, it was deemed advisable to have the instruction designed and provided by a combination of faculty members and practitioners representing both disciplines. In all cases, profession team members were not hesitant to identify individuals with greatest expertise in the areas to be addressed, whether within the university, the professional association, or the profession at large.

Phase VII: Implement Programs; Evaluate Program Effectiveness. In the course of the project itself, seven different programs were delivered at several Penn State locations across the Commonwealth. Upon completion of each program, participants were asked to provide an evaluation. Although traditional measures of program quality were used, primary attention was focused on determining the practice orientation of the programs. On this issue, the programs were rated exceptionally well; participants indicated that the programs clearly had a greater emphasis on specific proficiencies than other continuing education programs in which they had participated, were more relevant to practice, and overall were of higher quality.

Because of the strong emphasis on practice orientation, a follow-up evaluation was conducted for a number of the programs. Participants were sent a questionnaire approximately six months after the program asking how they had used the information presented in the program. These evaluations also were quite favorable, with participants reporting that the programs indeed had an effect on their patterns of practice.

Teachings of the Model

With the delivery and evaluation of continuing education programs to all five professions, the Continuing Professional Education Development Project came to a conclusion. Over a five-year period, each of the professions had proceeded through all seven phases of the Practice Audit Model. As a result, the project provided an opportunity to learn about the efficacy of the model in general, and about its three key features: performance-based needs assessment, practice-oriented continuing education programs, and collaboration. Many lessons were learned.

Evaluation of the Model

As a means of identifying professionals' performance deficiencies and developing practice-oriented programs to meet those needs, the model is highly effective. It offers an iterative process to address the entire scope of a profession over time in an exceedingly thorough and comprehensive fashion. It recognizes the limitations of individual institutions and organizations, and hence provides for meaningful collaboration among several groups to ensure that the full range of considerations is included.

Implementation of the Practice Audit Model is, however,

costly. The assessment-center approach to identifying needs, while optimum for this purpose, is labor intensive and requires expensive equipment and facilities and sophisticated evaluation instruments. Practice-oriented continuing professional education programs share many of these characteristics, and thus must either carry high registration fees or be subsidized. Alternative ways of assessing needs and presenting practice-oriented programs must be explored if the model is to be within the reach of professions.

Use of the model also is time consuming. This need not be seen as a deterrent, but rather as a factor defining appropriate uses of the model. It is not intended to provide immediate responses to professionals seeking state-of-the-art knowledge and technology. It is designed to view the total scope of the profession on an ongoing basis and focus on fundamental proficiencies. Those interested in responding quickly to practitioners' needs for continuing education on the most current topics would be ill advised to use the model for this purpose.

While the model stresses a comprehensive approach to the entire scope of practice of a profession, it does not ensure a curricular orientation to continuing professional education. For too long continuing professional education has been approached as a series of isolated experiences, rather than as a coherent course of learning that occurs throughout the practitioner's professional life (Queeney, 1984). If continuing professional education programs are to be related to practice, they also must be related to an ongoing, integrated program of learning to enhance that practice. Future revisions of the model must take this issue into consideration.

Each profession is unique, and the model is flexible enough to accommodate that individuality while still providing strong guidance to those following it. Given the diversity of the professions that implemented the model during the project, their completion of the entire effort is testimony to its adaptability. This characteristic suggests that it can be successfully used in the future by many professions.

Perhaps the Practice Audit Model's two greatest strengths, however, are its attention to a practice orientation for continuing professional education, and its use of a collaborative approach. The two are intertwined; without the collaboration of those who practice the profession and those who teach and do research in it, the practice orientation could not be realized. The centrality of competence and enhanced performance to continuing professional education has escalated the practice orientation concept to an issue of substantial importance among the education and professional communities and the public at large. The Practice Audit Model represents one useful response to the concerns of those groups.

Performance Assessment

The model uses an approach to needs assessment that focuses on what professionals can and cannot do, rather than what they think they may or may not need in continuing education. Several different types of findings emerged from implementation of this approach in the project.

Assessed Needs versus Perceived Needs. Frequently professional practitioners are certain about what they do not know; if asked which areas they are weak in, they will provide answers with confidence. However, when Practice Audit Session participants were asked to identify their learning needs and then were assessed, using the variety of instruments included in each session, the results were quite different. Generally professionals identify as weak areas those procedures and knowledge they use infrequently but might perceive as necessary for a higher-level position (such as management skills), or those that are new to the profession (such as new tax laws for accountants). Few professionals perceive themselves as lacking proficiency in the tasks they perform regularly.

Both approaches to needs assessment—perceived and performance based—have value. One does not replace the other; rather, each identifies a different type of learning need, thereby underscoring the importance of using a variety of assessment methodologies. Perceived needs are real and must be attended to, and may in fact serve as a positive means of encouraging practitioners to recognize the importance of continuing professional education. However, professionals tend not to think in terms of needing improvement with the skills of their daily practice, perhaps because they self-defensively want to believe that what they do, they do well. Thus when assessment identifies weaknesses in these areas, it may be difficult to motivate practitioners to enroll in programs to strengthen the relevant proficiencies.

This is a significant problem and one that will not be easily overcome. In the short term it might be addressed by developing programs that combine the content of currently fashionable topics with that of fundamental proficiencies in need of attention. In the long run, though, the problem must be addressed directly by helping individual professionals better understand continuing professional education's multiple dimensions. This means preparing professionals before they enter practice with the mindset to be knowledgeable and responsible consumers of continuing professional education and reinforcing that orientation once they are in practice. Anything less is unlikely to instill the responsibility for maintaining competence and ongoing professional development that must accompany professional status.

Commonality of Professionals' Needs. The disciplines participating in the Continuing Professional Education Development Project were a varied group. Yet across these five professions a commonality of learning needs was identified: interpersonal skills, problem-solving skills, and ability to integrate information into a coherent plan (be it for patient care or design of a building). This finding has two implications that could be perceived either as conflicting or as providing additional opportunities.

First, while the needs may be generic (such as communication skills), they must be addressed educationally in terms of specific professions. Accountants use communication skills differently than clinical dietitians, for example. Accountants must be able to communicate with their clients sufficiently to determine their true accounting needs; frequently clients report the symptoms of their problems, rather than the problems themselves. While clinical dietitians generally have good interviewing skills, they tend to lack the communication skills necessary to help clients become committed to a new action plan that would change their eating behavior. Thus educational programming might be developed and delivered cooperatively by persons representing the discipline of the need, in this case communications, and the specific profession, accounting or clinical dietetics.

Second, shared needs can provide an opportunity for interprofessional educational programming. Particularly in cases of professions that are related or whose practitioners may work together, opportunities for exchange of ideas and increased understanding of another's perspective can be quite valuable. For example, nurses and clinical dietitians, both of whom may work with hospital patients, could benefit from joint educational programming.

Individualized Needs of Experienced Professionals. As noted earlier, the Practice Audit Model as implemented in the Continuing Professional Education Development Project assessed group needs. Increasingly, however, individual practitioners need assistance in assessing their own specific needs, and they need to be able to do so without participating in group assessment sessions at centralized locations.

The Practice Audit Model could incorporate such an approach, but substantial initial development costs would be required. Thus an area in need of further study is that of self-assessment of learning needs or self-administration of assessment instruments. Ideally, an assessment instrument could be sent to practitioners for completion at home or office. It would be returned for scoring, and they would receive not only feedback on their performance, but also information on learning opportunities to strengthen areas of weakness identified. Such a process would be quite useful in improving individual practitioners' performance, but it is an expensive proposition, at least initially. Some work in this area is being pioneered by the

American Institute of Architects and Penn State's Office of Continuing Professional Education.

A related issue has to do with expectations about acceptable levels of performance by practicing professionals. Results of the assessments performed during the project revealed that the practice context had a powerful impact on the performance of practitioners. Once professionals enter practice, they often begin to concentrate their efforts on particular types of content or particular types of clients. As a result, knowledge and skills related to other areas in which they do not work diminish. Thus the question for those concerned with competency is whether practicing professionals need to maintain acceptable levels of performance across common areas of the profession or whether attention should be focused on areas of specialization. In essence, the issue here also is one of individualization. Performing group assessments and hence delivering group programs run the risk of focusing on common problems and offering uniform solutions to what are idiosyncratic needs (Smutz, Crowe, and Lindsay, 1986).

Practice-Oriented Programs

The Practice Audit Model provides for, and the project delivered, practice-oriented programs that addressed fundamental proficiencies of professionals. The programs were rated quite favorably by participants, but attendance was less than expected. One reason may be that the nature of the continuing professional educational experience offered — fundamental proficiencies — was not congruous with professionals' expectations of the continuing education they think they need — state-of-the-art developments.

What is responsible for this discrepancy? While higher education, the professions, regulatory agencies, and employers are highly concerned with providing practitioners with optimum continuing professional education experiences, most individual professionals do not appear to adequately understand the challenge posed by continuing professional education

and thus do not make effective use of the many different opportunities available. There is little evidence, for example, that
professionals are knowledgeable consumers of continuing professional education. They often are unaware of the range of their
learning needs, and thus may have trouble determining which
programs will be most useful to them in their daily practice. In
addition, there seems to be limited understanding that skill-
based programs must be structured differently from knowledge-
update programs and that they require different types of commitment in terms of time and cost. Most skills simply cannot be
effectively learned from a one-day seminar or a four-hour au-
diotape. Three things need to happen to ameliorate this situation: (1) support services should be provided to help practitioners select the programs best suited to meet their needs; (2)
continuing professional education curricula should be developed for individual professions to lend continuity to each professional's ongoing learning; and (3) individual assessment tools
and feedback mechanisms must be developed and made available to professionals.

Efforts to help professionals understand the complexity
of the challenge posed to them by continuing professional
education need not wait until they have begun to practice. For
too long higher education has been guilty of educating students
for entry into the professions without preparing them for the
task of ongoing learning. The notion of continuing professional
education should be introduced as part of entry-level education;
this will happen only if those responsible for continuing professional education take an active role in implementing its
introduction.

Collaboration

The Practice Audit Model demonstrated the feasibility of collaboration between the professions and higher education. The
groups that initially entered into collaborative relationships at
the start of the project are still collaborating, some time after the
project ended. If such collaboration is to be successful, a
number of conditions must be met. Collaborating parties must

be selected with care, and collaboration, like any other human relationship, requires nurturing and work to maintain. A genuine sharing of purpose is central to any collaborative effort.

Experience during the Continuing Professional Education Development Project revealed two areas of adjustment that must be addressed in future efforts using the collaborative approach. First, only professional associations, regulatory agencies, and academic departments are specified as the collaborative parties in the Practice Audit Model. However, the experiences of the five professions using the model indicate that employers of professionals, or representatives of the practice setting, should be included in future endeavors. The reason is quite simple: regardless of the value of the proficiencies taught, the likelihood of their implementation is limited if they are not accepted by the employer or supervisor. Thus the employer viewpoint is critical to the development of practice-oriented continuing professional education. Second, while the project was successful in terms of collaboration among individual representatives from different organizations, it is less clear to what extent there was effective *organizational* collaboration. How individual representatives can more closely involve their organizations throughout the process must be addressed in future efforts.

Summary

The Practice Audit Model, a seven-phase, needs assessment/program development process, has proved to be a useful tool for delivering practice-oriented continuing professional education to practitioners. As applied in the Continuing Professional Education Development Project at The Pennsylvania State University, it was effective in meeting this goal and others. While the model as initially developed could be applied across the professions and across the country, it is considered by those most familiar with it as representative of a growing, changing process intended to optimize the quality and usefulness of continuing professional education. Its successful application to five professions is evidence of its efficacy. Perhaps most important, the

Practice Audit Model also raises new questions and suggests new directions to be pursued in the quest for lifelong professional competence.

References

Caplan, R. M. "Continuing Education and Professional Accountability." In C. H. McGuire, R. P. Foley, A. Gorr, R. W. Richards, and Associates (eds.). *Handbook of Health Professions Education: Responding to New Realities in Medicine, Dentistry, Pharmacy, Nursing, Allied Health, and Public Health.* San Francisco: Jossey-Bass, 1983.

Frandson, P. E. "Continuing Education for the Professions." In E. J. Boone, R. W. Shearon, E. E. White, and Associates. *Serving Personal and Community Needs Through Adult Education.* San Francisco: Jossey-Bass, 1980.

Houle, C. O. "Possible Futures." In M. R. Stern (ed.), *Power and Conflict in Continuing Professional Education.* Belmont, Calif.: Wadsworth, 1983.

Klemp, G. "Identifying, Measuring, and Integrating Competence." *New Directions for Experiential Learning: Defining and Measuring Competence.* P. S. Pottinger and J. Goldsmith, ed. San Francisco: Jossey-Bass, 1979.

Lindsay, C. A., Crowe, M. B., and Jacobs, D. F. "Continuing Professional Education for Clinical Psychology." In B. A. Edelstein and E. S. Berler (eds.), *Evaluation and Accountability in Clinical Training.* New York: Plenum Press, 1987.

Lindsay, C. A., Queeney, D. S., and Smutz, W. D. *A Model and Process for University/Professional Association Collaboration.* University Park: Continuing Professional Education Development Project, The Pennsylvania State University, 1981.

Menges, R. J. "Assessing Readiness for Professional Practice." *Review of Educational Research,* 1975, *45* (Spring), 173–207.

Nowlen, P. M. "A Continuing Professional Education Agenda for the Future." Paper presented at the National Conference on Continuing Professional Education, University Park, Penn., Oct. 1986.

Olesen, V. "Employing Competence-Based Education for the

Reform of Professional Practice." In G. Grant and others (eds.), *On Competence: A Critical Analysis of Competence-Based Reforms in Higher Education.* San Francisco: Jossey-Bass, 1979.

Phillips, L. E. "Is Mandatory Continuing Education Working?" *Mobius,* 1987, 7 (Jan.), 57–64.

Pottinger, P. S., and others. *The Assessment of Occupational Competence.* Washington: National Center for the Study of Professions, 1980.

Queeney, D. S. "The Role of the University in Continuing Professional Education." *Educational Record,* 1984, 65 (3), 13–17.

Queeney, D. S., and Melander, J. J. *The Profession Selection Process.* University Park: The Pennsylvania State University, 1984.

Smutz, W. D., Crowe, M. B., and Lindsay, C. A. "Emerging Perspectives on Continuing Professional Education." In J. C. Smart (ed.), *Higher Education: Handbook of Theory and Research.* Vol. 2. New York: Agathon Press, 1986.

Smutz, W. D., and others. *The Practice Audit Model: A Process for Continuing Professional Education Needs Assessment and Program Development.* University Park: The Pennsylvania State University, 1981.

Part Three

FACILITATING
THE MAINTENANCE OF
PROFESSIONAL COMPETENCE:
KEY APPROACHES

Three Approaches to Maintaining Competence

In Part Three, three approaches to the maintenance of professional competence are presented. The first focuses on manipulating features of the work environment that foster enhancement of competence. This approach is discussed in Chapters Eight, Ten, and Eleven. The second approach involves training specific skills that are considered to be deficient in some mid-career professionals. Examples of this, the structured learning approach, are described in Chapters Seven and Twelve. Structured learning involves well-defined procedures for acquiring specific skills considered essential in certain fields. For example, empathy skills have been successfully taught to nurses; counselors have been trained in confrontation strategies and techniques; and the management skills of industrial supervisors have been enhanced. The components of the structured learning approach include modeling, role playing, performance feedback, and transfer of training.

The third approach to maintenance of competence involves self-directed updating. This approach involves the accessing of the most current and salient literature on a given professional topic, via electronic information systems, and is discussed in Chapter 13. Self-directed learning, where the professional acquires new knowledge via the printed (or on-line) word, is the most common approach to updating, yet has received little attention or research. As the volume of information expands exponentially, an important feature of updating will be choosing and accessing the most relevant information from the mass of available data. Electronic data bases and retrieval systems are becoming increasingly important in this process. Chapter Thirteen discusses variations in the types and sources of information needed by professionals at different levels of competence — expert, specialist, generalist, and uninformed. The potential of electronic data bases and retrieval systems to assist the professional in the updating process is described. The authors remind us that developing competencies in using these electronic information systems will become increasingly important as the volume of information in all professions continues to expand.

Work Environment Factors That Enhance
Professional Competence

The first approach has received the most consideration in the current literature. In this volume, the role of the work environment in facilitating the maintenance of professional competence has been considered for four professions: engineering (Chapters One and Eight), business (Chapter Ten), medicine (Chapter Five), and education (Chapter Nine). Certain common features of the work environment that foster competence have been identified.

Challenging Work Assignments. There is consensus among various authors (see Chapters One, Eight, Ten, and Eleven) that the most powerful incentives for maintaining professional competence are intrinsic — tied directly to the work itself — rather than involving external rewards, such as money. Challenging work assignments have been found to be the strongest motivators that the work environment can offer for maintaining professional

competence. Intrinsic satisfaction comes from competent performance in a challenging work assignment and the achievement of new learning goals associated with the assignment.

What, then, characterizes a "challenging" work assignment? The work demands are broad and complex, but not
overwhelming. They involve novelty, such that the professional
must acquire some new information and skills. Professionals are
given sufficient autonomy in carrying out the assignment that
they can determine their own scheduling and sequencing of
tasks. Enough time is given for the assignment that new information and skills can be acquired. Some risk taking is encouraged
so that professionals can explore alternative strategies and
solutions.

The assignment often involves working with ideas and
people, rather than in isolation or solely with equipment. Work
assignments involving interaction with other people have been
found to be the most challenging. A challenging work assignment requires professionals to summarize and to document the
completed assignment, thereby fostering the integration of findings and clarifying what was learned and achieved in the assignment. Finally, specific rewards or incentives are linked to successful accomplishment of the assignment.

The findings from Reinhart and Keefe's research on work
environment factors associated with professional competence
in emergency medicine personnel (see Chapter Five) provide
support for the importance of these characteristics of the work
environment. Emergency care physicians found to be more up
to date seven years after initial certification saw, on average,
more patients, worked in an environment that involved collaboration with more specialists and special facilities, and also were
more likely to be involved in teaching activities. Likewise, the
types of academic work assignments described by Votruba
(Chapter Nine) as fostering faculty members' vitality, such as
developing a new course or a new interdisciplinary specialty,
involved many of the characteristics of a challenging work assignment described above.

**Communication and Collaboration Among Peers and with Manage-
ment.** An organizational environment that facilitates open com-

munication and exchange among professionals and between management and professionals fosters the maintenance of competence in a number of ways. First, this type of environment encourages the exchange of ideas, information, and skills among professionals in various parts of the organization. The interchange of ideas and skills facilitates the successful accomplishment of challenging work assignments. The interaction among professionals from diverse backgrounds as they approach a common problem from different perspectives or methods fosters intellectual stimulation and enhances motivation to maintain competence.

Open communication and exchange with management not only helps professionals clarify the goals and requirements of particular work assignments, but also involves them in institutional planning and governance. As noted by Votruba (Chapter Nine), control and autonomy in one's work becomes increasingly important to midcareer professionals. Open exchange with management and the involvement of professionals in institutional decision making fosters a sense of control and autonomy.

An open flow of information and communication among professionals and with management is also useful in maintaining accurate and realistic expectations and beliefs about management's perspective on work responsibilities and the outcomes (rewards) for competent performance. According to expectancy theory, motivation to maintain competence is a function of the professional's expectations and beliefs about the process. As Farr and Middlebrooks note (Chapter Eight), factors in the work environment are important in fostering both positive and realistic expectations and beliefs.

Organizational Flexibility. The organizational structure and management policies must be flexible enough to permit reassignment of people and work responsibilities. Flexibility maximizes the utilization of current professional competence and promotes the development of further professional skills through new and challenging work assignments. Votruba (Chapter Nine) emphasizes the need for open career paths within academia.

Institutional Commitment to Professional Development. Both Chapters Nine and Ten point out the importance of organizations and their management being involved with professional development at the individual level. Since intrinsic, rather than extrinsic, motivation and reward are more potent forces for maintaining professional competence, the institution's awareness and involvement at the individual level are particularly effective. Concern for the career development of the individual must reflect an awareness of individual differences. Professionals differ widely in the goals and rewards they seek from their careers, and organizations must be responsive to these individual differences.

Miller (Chapter Ten) argues that "flat organizations" with fewer administrative levels and thus broader responsibility domains are more effective in fostering professional vitality. Open or flexible administrative structures that permit lateral career moves and interdepartmental (interdisciplinary) collaboration on work assignments are helpful in enabling midcareer professionals to acquire new competencies or to explore alternative career opportunities.

Although all the authors emphasize that enhancing professional competence involves an interaction of individual characteristics and environmental factors, most chapters focus more directly on organizational or environmental issues. Votruba, however, does consider two individual characteristics that are particularly relevant to the midcareer college faculty member: the increasing desire for control and autonomy in one's work, to define one's own professional goals, and to be self-directed, and a renewed need to find meaning and purpose in one's professional activities (see Chapter Nine). Finding meaning and purpose in work are important factors in sustaining professional vitality and the motivation to remain professionally competent and up to date. Once certain career achievements are attained, many midcareer professionals reevaluate prior goals and give greater attention to the meaning and purpose of professional activities and responsibilities.

8

James L. Farr
Carolyn L. Middlebrooks

Enhancing
Motivation to Participate
in Professional Development

People in professional positions must make decisions: should they invest time in activities that enhance professional competence, or run the risk of obsolescence? Factors affecting motivation are central to this decision process. Motivation, in this context, is the process of allocating personal resources (time and energy) to maximize anticipated outcomes (Naylor, Pritchard, and Ilgen, 1980). People allocate their available time and energy to the various tasks, interests, and interactions that they believe will result in outcomes they value. Thus, we can think about updating (enhancing and maintaining professional competence) as one activity, among many, competing for a share of a professional's time and energies.

What factors influence the outcome of this competition? In this chapter we apply a motivation theory — expectancy theory, probably the most generally accepted theory of work motivation over the past two decades. Expectancy theory has been applied to professional updating by several researchers, including Porter (1971), Arvey and Neel (1976), Fossum, Arvey, Paradise, and Robbins (1986), Farr and others (1980), and Farr, Enscore, Steiner, and Kozlowski (1984).

Although professional updating can be viewed as a choice made by the individual, it is clear that this choice is not made in a vacuum. Professionals are influenced by a variety of organizational and work group factors as well as their own past experiences and expectations about the future (Dubin, 1973). A particular strength of expectancy theory for understanding professional updating is that its framework can incorporate characteristics of the work situation and the individual. This theory can also be used to guide organizational management in the design and implementation of programs that encourage professional updating.

Basic Assumptions of Expectancy Theory

Expectancy theory states that an individual's behavior is strongly affected by his or her anticipation that one particular action will result in more desirable consequences than others. Thus, it is a motivation theory based on the concept of behavioral choice. The individual chooses from among various options the behavioral alternative that is expected to have the most favorable outcomes. In the more specific case of professional updating, expectancy theory predicts that the amount and type of updating engaged in by professionals are influenced by their beliefs about the consequences of maintaining professional competence. If they believe that updating activities will result in more favorable consequences than obsolescence, then they are more likely to engage in activities that enhance competence.

Expectancy theory suggests that three kinds of information are necessary to understand motivation and behavior: expectancy beliefs, instrumentality beliefs, and outcome valences. Expectancy beliefs refer to the belief that expending personal effort will result in attaining some level of performance or knowledge state. With reference to professional updating, an expectancy belief refers to the degree to which professionals believe that participating in some specific activity (for example, taking a course at a local university) will result in becoming or remaining professionally up to date.

Instrumentality belief refers to the belief that attaining a particular performance level or knowledge state will affect rewards or outcomes. Applying this to professional updating, instrumentality belief refers to the extent that professionals believe that their level of professional competence influences the kinds and amounts of rewards and outcomes (work related or otherwise) they will receive.

Outcome valence refers to the desire for or aversion to some consequence of behavior. These consequences may be work related (for example, pay raise, promotion, peer rejection, supervisory praise, assignment to routine tasks) or not (for example, opportunity for leisure, respect of spouse, reduced time with family, and the like).

Expectancy theory predicts that the three factors — valence, instrumentality, and expectancy — combine in a multiplicative fashion to influence a person's motivation toward some course of action. This means that, for professionals to be motivated toward a certain level of performance, they must believe that they can attain that level of performance and that the level of performance will result in desired outcomes. If they believe that the performance level is impossible to achieve, no matter how hard they try, then their motivation toward that performance level will be nonexistent (expectancy will equal zero).

Also, if they believe that attaining the performance level will *not* produce the desired outcomes, then they will not be motivated toward that performance level (instrumentality will equal zero). Finally, if reaching a certain performance level produces only nonvalued outcomes, then people will not be motivated to perform at that level (valence will equal zero). In summary, for people to be motivated toward some particular course of action (for example, engaging in an activity to enhance job proficiency), they must believe it is possible to accomplish and that accomplishing it will lead to an outcome that has value to them.

Consider this example: an executive suggests that a sales manager enroll in a two-day seminar on telemarketing. If the sales manager views the seminar as a challenging opportunity to learn about a new technique that is likely to lead to increased sales, then he will be motivated to enroll. If he has doubts about whether telemarketing will actually improve sales, or if he views attending the seminar as an admission that he cannot competently perform his job, he will be motivated only to avoid the seminar.

Expectancy theory does not attempt to specify the individual characteristics that affect motivation or the outcomes people seek as a result of their behavior. It only describes the process by which an individual is motivated. This focus on processes of motivation gives expectancy theory an advantage over motivational theories that prescribe that everyone should be motivated to achieve similar outcomes. Thus, expectancy theory can easily account for individual differences, while not ruling out the possibility that certain outcomes or rewards may be important for many.

Individual differences in motivation toward updating activities may be caused by differing beliefs about the instrumentalities and expectancies existing in the work setting or by differing valences about various outcomes. Instrumentality and expectancy beliefs are, at least in part, influenced by the individual's past work experiences. Thus, although expectancy theory predicts motivation on the basis of beliefs about what will happen in the future, what the individual has experienced in the past is important in determining those beliefs. Differences in these work experiences, as well as differences in personality and motive structures, explain why two professionals in the same work situation may have different views about the value of updating. Therefore, expectancy theory assumes that choice behavior is a subjective process, but one that is systematic at the level of the individual—meaning that the individual always chooses the alternative that he or she expects to yield the maximum payoff.

Expectancy Theory and Dubin's Model

Expectancy theory is concerned with the process of motivation; it does not specify the factors in the work setting that may influence motivation toward professional updating. To examine these factors, we must complement expectancy theory with a more content-oriented view of updating: the professional updating framework suggested by Dubin.

Dubin (1973) proposed that professional updating is affected by five aspects of the work environment: supervisory behavior, peer interactions, work assignments, management policy, and organizational climate. These five elements can enhance or inhibit the individual's motivation for updating.

For example, the supervisor who constantly labels university courses as "ivory-tower nonsense unrelated to the real world" is not likely to have many subordinates who take these courses. However, when supervisors make work assignments that require professionals to be aware of recent developments in fields outside their usual specialization, subordinates are likely to be actively involved in various kinds of updating activities.

In Dubin's model the work environment directly affects motivation. Farr, Enscore, Steiner, and Kozlowski (1984) suggested a modification of Dubin's model based on expectancy theory; Figure 8.1 presents their model. In this model the work environment factors do not act directly on the motivation toward updating; instead they influence the individual's beliefs about the efficacy and utility of updating for obtaining valued outcomes. These beliefs then influence motivation as expectancy theory would predict.

Thus, in our example, the supervisor's labeling university courses as "ivory tower" is likely to affect subordinates' expectancy belief ("I don't believe that taking a university course will result in my being more up to date in job-relevant proficiencies"). This changed belief then reduces the likelihood that they will participate in this type of updating activity. However, a challenging work assignment that calls for knowledge outside the normal range of expertise is likely to increase beliefs about the instrumentality of being up to date ("I had better learn this new material if I want to succeed at this task and be promoted"). Such beliefs would increase general motivation for professional updating and thus participation in updating activities.

This model has several implications for better understanding motivations toward professional competence. First, we must recognize that it is the individual's *perceptions* of the various

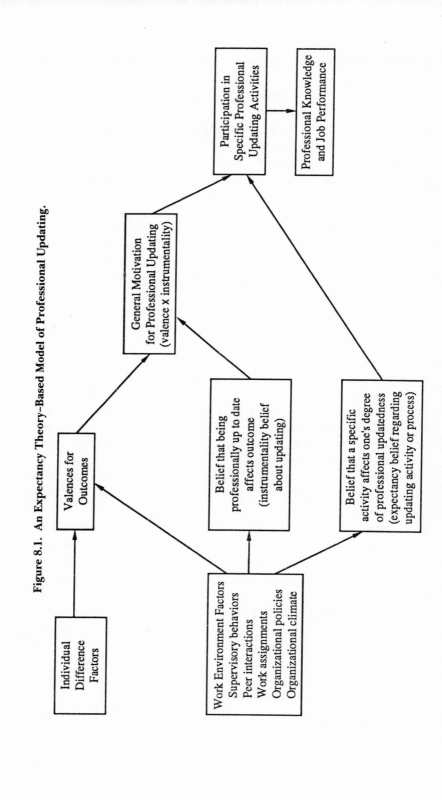

Figure 8.1. An Expectancy Theory–Based Model of Professional Updating.

work environment factors that are important in affecting updating motivation, not necessarily the "true" nature of the work environment. For example, good-faith efforts by management to promote people who are most up to date may be for naught in terms of enhancing updating motivation if staff members believe that promotion is primarily a function of who you know, not what you know. Related to this is the important role of individual differences. We cannot expect that all will respond similarly to a common work environment.

The question is often asked, "Why don't professionals update their job-related proficiencies?" Expectancy theory reminds us to ask, "Why should they update?" To understand the level of professional updating that occurs in a given setting, we must consider the expected payoffs from remaining up to date and from not being up to date. Various techniques can be used to assess these beliefs and expectations. Organizational management can use these methods to determine whether its professionals believe there is value in being up to date.

For example, engineers have been surveyed about the relationships between participation in various updating activities and remaining professionally up to date (expectancy beliefs) and between being up to date and attaining desired outcomes (instrumentality beliefs) (Farr, Enscore, Steiner, and Kozlowski, 1984). Similar questionnaires could be developed for other professions to determine whether professionals in an organization believe the time and effort they spend in updating activities will result in outcomes they value. Once these beliefs are determined, the motivational level of the organization's professionals toward updating activities can be assessed. Periodic surveys of such beliefs are also useful ways to monitor whether programs implemented to enhance the motivation toward updating are having their intended effects.

Enhancing Professional Updating Activities

Traditionally, organizations have used retraining and continuing education to prevent or remediate the obsolescence problem (Fossum, Arvey, Paradise, and Robbins, 1986). Mentorships, sabbaticals, and training and development advisory councils are other frequent remedies (Dalton and Thompson, 1971; Rosen and Jerdee, 1985). Although these approaches are common and are often used, they frequently fall short of accomplishing the intended results. An expectancy theory perspective offers some insight into possible causes of these failures.

To be effective, methods must alter a person's intrinsic motivation to enhance and maintain professional competence. Intrinsic motivation is defined as the motivation to perform a task when no apparent reward is received except that which is directly derived from the task itself (Daniel and Esser, 1980). By affecting professionals' perceptions of valences, instrumentalities, and expectancies, organizations may be able to alter their intrinsic desire to partake in updating activities. Unfortunately, many organizational efforts only remove possible constraints and inhibitors of updating rather than enhance intrinsic motivation in this way.

For example, consider tuition reimbursement. Although reimbursement eliminates the monetary cost to the individual, if a person chose not to take classes, no cost would be incurred either. In either case, the person is not paying for the class. Thus, tuition reimbursement, in and of itself, provides no motivation.

Only methods that offer positive outcomes for becoming more professionally competent, rather than merely reducing the constraints for doing so, will increase the motivation to update. The limited success of traditional approaches may be accounted for by the fact that they only reduce the negative outcomes of professional development rather than increase the positive outcomes.

Methods of increasing these positive outcomes do not need to be complex. An organization can note the professional development efforts of its employees in the company newsletter or on the bulletin board or in other simple ways recognize those who have participated. These practices, although certainly not elaborate, help emphasize the organization's belief in the importance of professional development. These approaches are not intended to be extrinsically rewarding for the employee;

they recognize individual effort, which can be intrinsically motivating.

Another problem stemming from the more traditional approaches is the lack of a system-oriented perspective. For instance, the performance evaluation system is often at the root of the obsolescence problem and is usually not addressed by the more common methods. The evaluation system has a pivotal role in forming employee expectancy and instrumentality beliefs. Often performance evaluations peak when technical professionals are at a relatively young age, remain constant for a while, and then decline. This can lead to what Dalton and Thompson (1971) call the negative spiral effect. When an individual first receives a low evaluation, or is left on a dull assignment for a long period of time, an initial burst of individual effort may result. However, this effort often goes unrecognized, and so the belief that that effort leads to a good evaluation is reduced. The lowering of this expectancy often results in an indifferent attitude, which in turn results in still lower ratings, which lead to lower self-confidence, and so on. If the efforts of older professionals are not recognized, their resulting indifference may be interpreted as a lack of ability to contribute ("Money," 1985). Thus, the evaluation system exacerbates a continuous downward spiral of expectations, performance, and judgments about the older professional's capabilities (Dalton and Thompson, 1971). Managers should be explicitly alerted to the negative spiral effect so that they can be sensitive to the experienced professional's efforts and needs for recognition and stimulating assignments.

Problems such as the negative spiral effect make it evident that we must consider the bigger picture when attempting to alter expectancy and instrumentality beliefs. The organization should be viewed from a systems perspective. An innovative culture that maintains the intellectual curiosity of professionals and provides adequate reward and recognition for technical excellence is an essential part of this system (Zelikoff, 1969). It is the interaction between the work environment factors and individual difference factors that determines motivation for en-hancing professional competence (see Figure 8.1).

Group Effectiveness Factors. Hackman and Walton (1986) have discussed some general group effectiveness factors that are drawn from a systems-oriented perspective. In particular, they found that three factors improve the effectiveness of task-performing groups.

First, groups should be given *clear, engaging direction.* In-structions should be unambiguous and group members should be informed of their goals and the overall purpose of the proj-ect. Direction must also be engaging, or motivating. Objectives are motivating when they allow enough leeway for individual or group interpretation and when the task outcome will signifi-cantly affect members of the group and others in the organiza-tion. Hackman and Walton found that clear objectives do not decrease motivation, as might be expected, but instead "an engaging, authoritative statement of purpose orients and em-powers teams" (p. 82).

An *enabling performance situation* is also essential. This is fostered by a group structure that facilitates competent task work, an organizational context that supports and reinforces excellence, and available, expert coaching and process as-sistance. The second element, organizational context, is es-pecially relevant to overcoming professional obsolescence. The reward system, the educational system, and the information system of the organization should provide employees with the appropriate recognition, knowledge, and data to competently complete their tasks. In addition, interaction with fellow profes-sionals may also enhance their interest and motivation to under-take updating activities.

Finally, *adequate material resources* are needed for effective performance. Adequate resources may also increase the expec-tancy and instrumentality beliefs of professionals. For instance, if the organization obtains the most contemporary equipment for its labs, professionals are more likely to be motivated to explore the capabilities of the equipment and, thus, to remain closer to the cutting edge of knowledge in their field.

The main point is that differences in effectiveness and motivation cannot be understood in terms of single variables; multiple, often redundant conditions operate in concert to determine how well professionals will be able to perform and the extent to which they will be motivated to enhance professional competence. Thus, one or even a few methods aimed at reducing incompetence and obsolescence are not going to be effective. Redundant systems that reinforce the organization's commitment to professional development are essential.

Emphasis on Learning Goals. Related to a systems perspective is the need to emphasize learning goals as well as performance goals. Many organizations are concerned only with how their employees perform, not what they know or how they might use that knowledge. Through learning goals, individuals seek to increase their competence or to master something new. Performance goals are tied to favorable judgment of their competence or to avoidance of negative judgment (Dweck, 1986). Highlighting performance rather than learning goals works against the pursuit of challenge and knowledge. To benefit from performance objectives, people must believe their ability level is high or else they will try to protect themselves from possible negative evaluation by avoiding challenges. Performance goals, in other words, tend to promote defensive behavior.

Learning goals, however, encourage people to put forth the effort to acquire skills and knowledge without fear of negative evaluation. Satisfaction is directed toward the effort expended rather than toward present capabilities. Dweck notes that intrinsic motivation is more difficult to obtain with performance goals. This could be caused by the effect of extrinsic rewards on intrinsic motivation. A sole focus on external rewards or performance goals may limit a person's intrinsic motivation for highly interesting and unstructured tasks (Daniel and Esser, 1980). Therefore, learning goals, by directing satisfaction toward mastery of new tasks, tend to increase intrinsic motivation. An increase in intrinsic motivation leads to a more innovative work environment (Amabile, 1986).

Climate for Professional Development. Environmental qualities that promote creativity and innovation include freedom, good project management, sufficient resources, encouragement, recognition, sufficient time, challenge, and pressure (Amabile, 1986). "Innovation is best served . . . by fostering the conditions which enable and inspire technical professionals to contribute their creative efforts" ("Money," 1985, p. 66). To increase professional motivation about competence, the organizational climate must foster the conditions that are conducive to professional development activities and that are consistent with individual expectancies, valences, and instrumentalities. An important component of such a climate is the luxury of being wrong—risk taking is encouraged and errors are allowed. If professionals are punished for every failure, even small ones, they are unlikely to apply new knowledge or skills—or even to want to acquire them.

The organizational climate encourages updating and innovation primarily by enhancing the valence of professional development activities to the professional. As Vroom noted in his original formulation of expectancy theory (1964), the valence of a first-order outcome of effort, such as updating, is a function of the valences of the second-order outcomes, such as recognition and feelings of achievement, that result from the first-order outcome. These second-order outcomes can be either intrinsic or extrinsic. Of course, expectancy theory also suggests that increasing the belief that a valued outcome will result from a particular activity enhances the likelihood that the person will engage in the activity. Since intrinsic motivation to update may be more strongly linked to subsequent professional development activity than is extrinsic motivation, we will concentrate on intrinsic motivation, with the understanding that extrinsic motivation is also important.

Challenging Work Assignments. One way to affect positively later performance and the motivation for lifelong learning is to increase the degree of technical challenge (Berlew and Hall, 1966). Designing challenging jobs uses the intrinsically motivating factors of the work itself to enhance the professional's interest in updating. Kozlowski and Farr (1988) found that task challenge was positively influenced by the technological demands on engineers' knowledge and skills, the level of uncertainty on how to accomplish task goals, and the degree of discretion or autonomy allowed them for determining procedures for task accomplishment. So task challenge relates directly to technical performance, as evaluated by supervisory personnel, and to the amount of professional development engaged in by the engineers.

Research has shown that extrinsic rewards do not always increase the motivation to continue professional development. In a study of technical professionals in ten organizations, the most important sources of motivation were the nature of the work itself, organizational processes such as how work was allocated and evaluated, and career development and planning. In general, motivators such as recognition for individual expertise and sense of personal accomplishment were more highly valued than monetary rewards ("Money," 1985).

In addition, time constraints must be recognized, particularly the likelihood of professionals engaging in activities that involve nonwork time, as do most university-based graduate or continuing education programs. Clearly, the feasibility of engaging in professional development activities is a major concern for the employed professional. Recall that professional development is but one activity competing for the time and energy of professionals. The expectation, tacitly held by many organizations, that they will enhance technical skills on their own time is not likely to be met.

It can also be argued that unfocused learning, not directed toward specific projects or assignments, is less likely to be approached enthusiastically than learning for which an application can be perceived. Challenging work assignments provide a focus for the professional's learning, allow updating and task accomplishment to occur simultaneously, and may be less costly for the organization than many other approaches to professional development. This is not to say that actively attempting to provide challenging work for each professional is easy. In the short run, it is easier and faster to assign a project to someone who already knows how to do its every aspect. This may, however, sacrifice the long run for the short.

Management must be sensitive to the nature of work assignments and attempt to provide the proper level of stimulation through work challenge to each professional. Some professionals may resist challenging assignments. It is safer to work on tasks that one knows how to do in their entirety, but in the long run the professional can become narrow and overspecialized. Management must communicate to professionals that technical assistance can be made available, that it is safe to acknowledge uncertainty about how to proceed on a project, that learning and personal growth are valued, and that static technologies, markets, and products are things of the past (Farr, Enscore, Steiner, and Kozlowski, 1984).

Professionals are becoming more aware of the usefulness of task assignments as a means of enhancing professional development. Engineers rated challenging work as the best way to maintain up-to-date technical skills (Farr, Enscore, Steiner, and Kozlowski, 1984). It is the task of organizational management to provide professionals with these kinds of assignments.

It must also be recognized that in any one organization not every professional can be assigned to challenging and interesting tasks at any one time. A possible approach to dealing with the relative scarcity of challenging tasks is suggested by the Premack Principle, which states that individuals may be motivated to perform a less interesting or desirable activity (as professional development may be for many) if they are later rewarded with desirable tasks (Premack, 1962). Thus, challenging or interesting work could be used as a reward for involvement in the less desirable development activities. In this way, professional development could be viewed as a path to the more innovative assignments.

Perhaps an even more engaging task could be developed by instituting a program in which those individuals who meet established criteria for participation in professional development activities would be eligible to submit proposals for work projects. These projects could be innovative approaches to organizationally relevant problems or products to which the professional would be assigned full or part time. Not all such proposals need be supported by the organization, although a reasonable proportion should be so as to maintain strong instrumentality beliefs about professional development.

Challenging work as a means of encouraging professional development may be especially important for more senior professionals. Professionals near the beginning of their careers may be more amenable to formal types of development, such as workshops, university courses, and advanced degree programs. Experienced professionals may be threatened by a return to the classroom and may view professional development in general as an indication that they cannot perform their jobs satisfactorily. They may be more attracted to informal activities that are directly linked to job duties, such as work that encourages them to learn new skills.

Organizational Reward Systems. Although we have argued for the primacy of task assignments as a means of encouraging professional development, the organizational reward structure must not be overlooked. It remains an important factor that influences a person's expectancies, instrumentalities, and valences. The functional (updating) reward system of the organization is the individual's perception of the outcomes that will accrue as a result of their efforts (in this case, continued professional development [Dubin, 1972]) and must be strongly related to that effort if professional development is to be encouraged. The reward structure should have enough flexibility to permit individually valent rewards (Fossum, Arvey, Paradise, and Robbins, 1986). A prime duty of the organization is to ensure that professionals have accurate expectations about rewards and performance goals and then to fulfill those expectations by rewarding individuals appropriately and consistently.

Although the reward structure is an extrinsic motivator of professional development, it has another important function: providing feedback about personal performance, including recognition for accomplishment. Reward systems can be more than monetary in content; the creative provision of recognition for professional achievement and growth goes a long way toward fostering a climate for continued professional development.

A method that incorporates both reward and evaluation systems has been used to recognize technical excellence in several large corporations: the dual career ladder promotion plan. It establishes technical career paths that attempt to parallel those of management. Companies such as Xerox, Texas Instruments, and Honeywell have recently instituted such plans (Deutsch, 1986). These plans reward excellence in technical performance by providing professionals in these jobs with the same salaries, titles, and perquisites normally reserved for managerial personnel. The dual career ladder tries to solve the problem of how to reward outstanding professionals without moving them out of the types of jobs they prefer. Professionals can be rewarded in a fashion similar to managers while continuing to perform the tasks for which they are best prepared and which they generally enjoy doing.

Steiner and Farr (1986) found that many engineers employed in industry regarded the managerial reward structure more favorably and, not surprisingly, desired to move out of their technical positions into managerial careers. Moreover, the engineers planning such career changes were evaluated by their superiors as *more* technically proficient than those planning to remain in a technical career. If other professions experience similar findings, organizations face a potential loss of those incumbents who are the better performers—not an encouraging prospect. The key to fighting professional obsolescence lies in developing an environment that supports innovation, that ensures that professionals have challenging tasks, and that rewards professional achievement.

Conclusion

The continuous proliferation of new technologies and the unlikely event of a decrease in this acceleration are reasons to believe that obsolescence among professionals is going to be a continuing problem for organizations.

This chapter has shown how the basic assumptions of

expectancy theory can serve as a useful guide for developing solutions to this problem. The framework illustrates the need to consider individual expectancy beliefs, instrumentality beliefs, and valences toward professional development activities. The multiplicative relationship conveys the importance of considering all three components of the model, since exclusion of one element will dramatically reduce professional motivation to remain up to date, if not eliminate it altogether.

The expectancy theory model also makes evident the importance of redundant systems of enhancers that reinforce motivation to participate in professional development activities. Research has suggested that the most effective means of enhancement are those that affect intrinsic motivation. A system that emphasizes learning goals is one such mechanism. Other methods that positively affect individual perceptions of the valence of remaining up to date will also facilitate the intrinsic motivation to update.

Traditional approaches to the problem seem to have primarily reduced the negative outcomes of professional development activities without increasing the positive outcomes. Challenging task assignments, an effective reward structure, and adequate feedback are ways that the organization can strive to correct this imbalance. By rewarding and enhancing individual efforts and beliefs regarding professional development activities, the organization can increase professionals' intrinsic motivation to enhance professional competence. Most important, organizations must first recognize those work environment factors that influence professionals' beliefs about the utility of professional development activities for obtaining valued outcomes, and then restructure the professionals' work environment appropriately.

References

Amabile, T. "A Model of Organizational Innovation." In J. L. Farr, "Innovation and Creativity in Work Organizations." Symposium presented at the Annual Meeting of the American Psychological Association, Washington, D.C., Aug. 1986.

Arvey, R. D., and Neel, C. W. "Motivation and Obsolescence in Engineers." *Industrial Gerontology*, Spring 1976, pp. 113–120.

Berlew, D. E., and Hall, D. T. "The Socialization of Managers: Effects of Expectations on Performance." *Administrative Science Quarterly*, 1966, *11*, 207–223.

Dalton, G. W., and Thompson, H. (1971). "Accelerating Obsolescence of Older Engineers." *Harvard Business Review*, 1971, *49* (5), 57–67.

Daniel, T. L., and Esser, J. K. "Intrinsic Motivation as Influenced by Rewards, Task Interest, and Task Structure." *Journal of Applied Psychology*, 1980, *65*, 566–573.

Deutsch, C. H. "Holding on to Technical Talent." *The New York Times*, Nov. 16, 1986, p. 4.

Dubin, S. S. "Obsolescence or Lifelong Education: A Choice for the Professional." *American Psychologist*, 1972, *27*, 486–498.

Dubin, S. S. "Defining Obsolescence and Updating." In S. Dubin, H. Shelton, and J. McConnell (eds.), *Maintaining Professional and Technical Competence of the Older Engineer: Engineering and Psychological Aspects*. Washington: American Society for Engineering Education, 1973.

Dweck, C. S. "Motivational Processes Affecting Learning." *American Psychologist*, 1986, *41*, 1040–1048.

Farr, J. L., Enscore, E. E., Jr., Steiner, D. D., and Kozlowski, S.W.J. "Factors That Influence the Technical Updating of Engineers." Final report to National Science Foundation, Grant no. SED-80-19680. University Park: The Pennsylvania State University, 1984.

Farr, J. L., and others. "Relationships Among Individual Motivation, Work Environment, and Updating in Engineers." Final report to National Science Foundation, Grant no. SED-78-21941. University Park: The Pennsylvania State University, 1980.

Fossum, J. A., Arvey, R. D., Paradise, C. A., and Robbins, N. E. "Modeling the Skills Obsolescence Process: A Psychological/Economic Integration." *Academy of Management Review*, 1986, *11*, 362–374.

Hackman, J. R., and Walton, R. E. "Leading Groups in Organizations." In P. S. Goodman and Associates, *Designing Effective Work Groups* (pp. 72–119). San Francisco: Jossey-Bass, 1986.

Kozlowski, S.W.J., and Farr, J. L. "An Integrative Model of Updating and Performance." *Human Performance*, 1988, *1*, 5–29.

"Money Isn't the Best Tool for Motivating Technical Professionals. *Personnel Administrator*, 1985, *30*, 63–66.

Naylor, J. C., Pritchard, R. D., and Ilgen, D. R. *A Theory of Behavior in Organizations*. New York: Academic Press, 1980.

Porter, L. W. "A Motivational Theory for Updating." Paper presented at Seventeenth International Congress of Applied Psychology, Liège, Belgium, 1971.

Premack, D. "Reversibility of the Reinforcement Relation." *Science*, 1962, *136*, 235–237.

Rosen, B., and Jerdee, T. H. "A Model Program for Combating Employee Obsolescence." *Personnel Administrator*, 1985, *30*, 86–92.

Steiner, D. D., and Farr, J. L. "Career Goals, Organizational Reward Systems and Technical Updating in Engineers." *Journal of Occupational Psychology*, 1986, *59*, 13–24.

Vroom, V. H. *Work and Motivation*. New York: Wiley, 1964.

Zelikoff, S. B. "On the Obsolescence and Retraining of Engineering Personnel." *Training and Development Journal*, 1969, *23*, 3–14.

9

James C. Votruba

Strengthening Competence and Vitality in Midcareer Faculty

The faculty are the lifeblood of any college or university. It is they who define the curriculum, teach and advise students, generate new knowledge through research and scholarship, and reach out in a variety of ways to serve the larger society on whom higher education depends for legitimacy and support. In many essential respects, a college or university *is* its faculty. Faculty members who are highly productive, adaptive, enthusiastic, creative, curious, and regenerative produce a climate that fosters academic excellence. Encouraging ongoing faculty competence and vitality, particularly at midcareer, is a complex challenge that campus leaders must confront if they hope to produce and maintain energetic and productive institutions.

The issue of ongoing competence and vitality is not new to higher education, but it has never been more important. Recent literature on the status of American higher education reports that faculty morale is low, productivity is diminished, and future prospects are constricted. The projected decline in student enrollments has led institutions to hire fewer new faculty right out of graduate school, and fewer experienced faculty are able to advance in their careers by moving to new positions

at other institutions. Gaff (1985) reports that the 1984 employment outlook issued by the U.S. Department of Labor listed
college faculty among the occupational groups facing greatest
percentage of decline in numbers by 1995. In addition, the
growing pressure on collegiate institutions to reduce expenses
has led to reports that faculty are being asked to assume heavier
teaching and committee loads and to conduct their research
efforts with obsolete equipment, fewer support services, and
diminished financial resources (Austin and Gamson, 1983).
Centra (1985) and others also reported that institutional programs and funds for faculty development have been greatly
reduced in recent years. Development program staff numbers
have been reduced, fewer sabbaticals are being granted, and less
money is being made available for conferences and other professional activities.

In today's colleges and universities, the challenge of encouraging faculty development and renewal is made more complex because larger numbers of faculty are in the middle and
later stages of their careers. In the 1960s, thousands of new
faculty members were hired to teach the baby-boom generation
that was enrolling in record numbers. Today, those same faculty
are in at least the midcareer stage. Keller (1983) notes that by
1990 35 percent of the faculty will be over 55. By the year 2000,
this figure will be approximately 52 percent, perhaps even
higher if the current mandatory retirement age for faculty (70) is
lifted. The fact that larger numbers of faculty are in midcareer
has implications for how we encourage continued faculty development and renewal. While there is a pronounced lack of literature on this subject, it is safe to assume that as faculty members
progress through various personal and professional life stages,
their needs, interests, and priorities are likely to change. Programs designed to encourage midcareer faculty development
must keep these changes in mind.

In Chapter Eight, Farr and Middlebrooks draw on expectancy theory to describe the process by which individuals
choose to either remain current in their field or risk atrophy and
obsolescence. For those who hope to design successful professional development strategies, the strength of expectancy theory

as a conceptual model is its emphasis on both the intrinsic motivation of the individual and the conditions of the work environment that influence that motivation. This emphasis on both the individual and the work environment provides the framework for our discussion of faculty development.

Enhancing Personal Motivation

The appropriate place to begin considering how to enhance faculty competence and vitality is with the faculty members themselves. Commenting on the general phenomenon of self-renewal, John W. Gardner wrote, "What is it that keeps alive in some people the natural spark of curiosity, eagerness, hunger for life and experience and how may we rekindle that spark when it flickers out?" (1963, p. 11). This is the fundamental question that we must confront if we hope to enhance faculty competence and vitality on our campuses. What is it that causes some faculty members to remain energetic and productive throughout their professional lives while others sink into semi-retirement soon after tenure is granted? While there is yet no definitive answer to this question, it is clear from the faculty development literature that the answer lies in a combination of the intrinsic developmental needs of faculty members and environmental factors that either enhance or inhibit the achievement of those needs (Claxton and Murrell, 1984).

Need for Control and Autonomy. Lawrence (1985) suggests that the themes of control and search for meaning provide a useful framework for understanding the intrinsic developmental needs of faculty. Throughout our lives, there is a persistent need to control the environment in order to achieve transient goals and develop consistency between our social environment and our values. Guttman (1973), Levinson (1978), and Erikson (1963) all emphasize the need to establish relative degrees of autonomy and control over our environment in order to bring balance and a sense of order to our lives. Loevinger (1976) offers a developmental model that has human growth progressing through a stage of conformity and subordination to authority to more advanced stages in which behavior is the result of negotiation and accommodation.

Dalton's model of career stages (in Hayes, 1981) characterizes development in terms of movement from positions in which we are under the control of others to those in which we have responsibility for ourselves and, ultimately, for others. Baldwin and Blackburn's model of faculty development (1981) assumes that people move through initial stages in which they are under the control of others (pretenure) to ones in which they take more active and self-directed roles in the institution. The importance of control is further emphasized by research that shows that productive faculty members take an active stance with regard to their environments (Pelz and Andrews, 1976) and are most satisfied when they have the freedom to pursue self-defined goals (Clark, Corcoran, and Lewis, 1984).

Search for Meaning. If control represents one important developmental need of faculty, the search for meaning represents another. Faculty, like all human beings, need to believe that what they do is important and that their lifestyle is self-fulfilling. They need to feel a sense of purpose in both their personal and professional lives. Individuals are continually questioning the meaning of their lives but this questioning becomes even more intense during periods of transition. According to Loevinger (1976), in the early stages of development meaning is provided by others. Then, as people move through successive developmental stages they move to greater levels of individualization and self-defined meaning.

During the early stages of an academic career, activities are essentially prescribed. Junior faculty members are guided by senior faculty as well as institutional values expressed in such policies as promotion and tenure criteria. However, Braskamp, Fowler and Dry (1982) suggest that after a faculty member has achieved tenure, the need to find meaning, which may have been lying dormant during the probationary period, becomes a dominant force. It is not uncommon in the posttenure transition for faculty members to express both a newfound feeling of control over their careers and a heightened sense of anxiety and doubt about the meaning of their professional lives.

Gaff (1985) suggests that midlife crisis can strike faculty members with a special force. Even successful midcareer faculty looking ahead to twenty or thirty years of essentially the same work occasionally ask themselves, "Is this all there is?" Faculty in midcareer often feel trapped in positions that no longer seem challenging and with no opportunity for career change. In addition, they may feel an increasing sense of isolation and a concern that their field is passing them by. Younger faculty members may begin to receive increasing amounts of recognition while the midcareer faculty member is pushed to the sidelines. This problem can be exacerbated by the personal transitions that occur as faculty members move into middle age.

There is general agreement among developmental theorists that the intrinsic motivators for maintaining high work performance include such variables as achievement need, challenge, recognition, autonomy, responsibility, and a belief that one's work has meaning (Dubin, 1977). Commenting on the forces that energize people to work productively and creatively, Kanter (1979) asserts that faculty who conceive of themselves as among the "moving" rather than the "stuck" will be likely to keep their aspirations high, have positive self-esteem, work hard, take appropriate risks, remain engaged in their interests, remain involved with their students and colleagues, and advocate constructive organizational change.

Howard (1984) came to essentially the same conclusions in her longitudinal study of successful executives. She found that in the early stages of their careers, those who eventually became highly successful were not dramatically distinguished from those who would eventually be less successful. However, over the course of a career, successful executives were able to develop and sustain an intense drive to meet the challenge of their jobs and a motivation to succeed that resulted in sustained work involvement at a time when many of their colleagues were beginning to look for satisfaction and reward from other dimensions of their lives.

To keep midcareer faculty among the "moving," the institution must develop and maintain an opportunity structure that opens career paths, provides developmental activities, facilitates lateral movement across fields if vertical movement is impossible, involves faculty in planning and governance, fosters collegiality and cohesiveness, and acknowledges good performance in a variety of ways. How they can provide this kind of support is the topic of the next section.

Enhancing Institutional Support

Colleges and universities that want to enhance faculty competence and vitality must begin by making continuous faculty development and renewal an integral part of the institutional culture. Far too often, the responsibility for faculty development has been housed in a middle-management office that is understaffed and underfunded. In times of budget crunch, these offices are often the first to go. If faculty development is a campus priority, it must be woven into the fabric of the institution at every level, from individual faculty members to the president and board. All must feel a sense of ownership and responsibility for its achievement. Faculty vitality and institutional vitality must be seen as both interrelated and interdependent. High-performing organizations, including colleges and universities, manifest a culture of excellence that is people centered and includes continuous attention to personal as well as professional development. In short, the campus must represent a generative environment (Claxton and Murrell, 1984).

Clark, Corcoran, and Lewis (1986) argue that the concept of academic competence must go beyond concerns with efficiency to those of productivity, effectiveness, and quality. Measures of faculty competence and vitality should include value-added, quality-associated concerns with careers over the long term, skill development at different career stages, internal opportunities for both vertical and lateral mobility, relationships that promote a psychological sense of community, and participation in shaping the direction of one's own unit and the institution at large. Incentives that promote narrow, special-purpose scholarship and faculty competition must be balanced by incentives that favor cooperation, collegiality, and a collective identity for the faculty (Toombs, 1985).

Colleges and universities that are committed to enhancing faculty development must offer a broad range of incentives that respond to the intrinsic needs of faculty who are at various career stages. Tuckman (1979) argues that incentives for productivity are strongest early in the academic career because professional accomplishments at that stage contribute to promotion and may open up new career opportunities for young professors. Economic incentives are also strongest in the early stages of an academic career. As professors move into midcareer, they are more apt to be attracted by opportunities to work across disciplinary boundaries, negotiate their work schedule in order to develop new professional directions, work in collegial teams, and contribute to the direction of their academic unit or the broader institution. The point is that institutional incentives must be diverse and responsive to the distinctive developmental needs of faculty at various career stages.

What types of incentives are most likely to motivate midcareer faculty to maintain their productivity and enthusiasm? While the faculty development literature is not definitive in this regard, there appears to be a variety of both tangible and intangible incentives that support the needs of midcareer faculty.

Providing Release Time for New Initiatives. Midcareer faculty often need to infuse a new sense of meaning and direction into their professional lives. This renewal process can be stimulated by providing faculty with release time to develop new perspectives on their professional field or new directions in their teaching or scholarship. While the sabbatical system has been the traditional approach for granting release time, there are a variety of other approaches that should be considered as well. For example, a popular program on many campuses is faculty study in a second discipline. For the past decade, faculty members at the University of Illinois at Urbana-Champaign have been able to propose a program of study in a related field, generally for a semester or a year. Release time is provided for this activity with the expectation that the effort will lead to new directions in teaching or research. A similar approach is to provide release time for faculty to experience their field from a different perspective. For example, faculty members might be encouraged to spend time working in a state or federal agency, a foundation, or a professional association that relates to their field. Again, the expectation would be that these experiences would lead to new directions in teaching or scholarship.

Another approach is to provide release time for faculty involvement on another campus as a visiting scholar. Release time is of course provided on many campuses to allow faculty members to develop new courses or teaching approaches as well as for curriculum development. Campuses that want to increase the spirit of community and cohesiveness among faculty should consider granting release time to small groups of faculty to pursue a particular project or professional activity.

The point is that release time can be a powerful incentive for midcareer faculty updating and renewal. Even modest amounts of release time can lead to new directions in teaching and research as well as provide recognition and reinforcement that the faculty member is a valued resource. Release time also gives faculty a greater sense of control over their lives and an opportunity to break patterns that by midcareer may have become stifling.

Several years ago the Rochester Institute of Technology eliminated its sabbatical system and replaced it with a program of professional development leaves that take many forms and may last varying amounts of time. Where sabbatical leaves often become perceived as a right of all faculty, the professional development leave is much more discretionary and dependent on the quality of the faculty member's development proposal. This professional leave program is supported by a faculty development fund that functions much like an internal foundation.

Providing Grant Support. In addition to release time, institutions can stimulate continued faculty development and renewal through a variety of grants that are targeted at specific developmental objectives. For example, the State University of New York at Binghamton has a very successful research incentive grants program that provides seed money for new research initiatives or travel for faculty to meet with potential funding sources. Faculty at the midcareer stage often develop an increased interest in teaching. Small grants to support the development of new courses or instructional approaches have been powerful incentives at many institutions.

In recent years, many campuses have developed very successful grant programs that support the purchase of equipment, software,data bases, books, and other resources that will support a faculty member's work. These grants can be made to individuals or teams who may be working on the same project or in the same area. Grants for travel to professional meetings are also very successful on most campuses. Grants that include summer stipends seem to be particularly attractive to faculty as a way of promoting professional development as well as augmenting their academic-year salaries. It is important for administrators to keep in mind that grant programs need not involve large amounts of money to function as attractive incentives. Indeed, the College of Charleston found that making relatively small grants available to relatively large numbers of people is a powerful stimulus to professional renewal and updating.

Cross-discipline Interactions. Another strategy for stimulating midcareer faculty renewal is providing opportunities for faculty to work with colleagues from other disciplines to teach interdisciplinary courses or address problems from an interdisciplinary perspective. For example, the SUNY Binghamton Center of Education and Social Research, an organized research center, has no faculty of its own but rather draws its faculty from a variety of disciplines to address complex social and educational problems. Faculty form interdisciplinary teams to write grant proposals and conduct research. The effect is to stimulate new friendships and associations, new perspectives on one's discipline, and a new sense of community and collaboration among scholars from across the campus.

Monetary Incentives. On most college and university campuses, direct monetary incentives are another major element in faculty incentive programs. These awards are usually in the form of merit pay, added to a faculty member's base pay in recognition of achievement. There is no doubt in my mind that merit pay can be a powerful incentive for some faculty, particularly on campuses where substantial merit increases are available. However, the merit pay process can also be counterproductive and can erode the self-respect, morale, and vitality of the average faculty member. Research on faculty motivation suggests that monetary reward is not as strong an incentive as some of the other more intrinsic motivators. Research also suggests that monetary incentives are less important for midcareer faculty than for those in the initial stages of their careers. Indeed, for many, monetary incentives may be more important for their symbolic value than for their cash value. The message that faculty members get from a merit raise is that their work is important and valued.

Other Incentives. In addition to release time, grants, interdisciplinary projects, and monetary incentives, there is a host of other tangible incentives that institutions can use to enhance faculty competence and renewal, particularly at the midcareer level. Visiting professor programs can bring outside scholars to campus to provide new breadth and insight. Regular faculty forums can help break down disciplinary boundaries, develop a greater sense of collegiality, and promote increased faculty awareness of their colleague's work. Faculty development funds can be established, with banking credits for each faculty member. Awards of student assistants can be used to both stimulate and reward productivity. The quality of campus facilities, such as the library, faculty club, recreational building, computer center, performing arts center, museum, and faculty office space, can affect the quality of life on a campus and the pride that a faculty member feels in being part of the institution.

Colleges and universities that want to encourage continued faculty vitality and productivity must provide a full range of tangible incentives to support this end. However, tangible incentives are not enough. Faculty members at all levels need to feel that their work has meaning and that they are valued by the institution and by their colleagues. The nature of academic life often inhibits this type of recognition. Faculty members generally work alone in both their teaching and scholarship. The significance of their work is often not fully appreciated on their own campus. The product of their work is often hard to quantify and measure. In these circumstances, recognition and reinforcement of the value of a faculty member's work can be easily overlooked. This can be particularly true for midcareer faculty who often turn their attention from cutting-edge research to such activities as mentoring younger faculty and serving the institution through a variety of activities including committee work and special projects. If these activities are important to the institution, they must be acknowledged and rewarded.

Building Successful Programs

There is no ideal institutional program for enhancing faculty competence and vitality. Each institution must fashion its own creative approach based on its mission, resource base, and faculty developmental needs. The type of incentives that are established by a small liberal arts college may be quite different from those established in a large graduate research-oriented institution. However, there are several factors that seem to be associated with successful faculty development programs no matter what the institutional setting.

Successful faculty development efforts begin with strong and visible support from campus administrators at every level of the institution. The president, vice-presidents, deans, and department heads must continually reinforce the notion that faculty vitality and renewal are a high institutional priority. In study after study of faculty development efforts, effective administrative leadership was identified as a crucial precondition for success (Schuster, 1985).

As both the campus chief administrative officer and the primary spokesperson for institutional priorities and values, the president is in a unique position to both spark public awareness about the importance of faculty development and to ensure that faculty development initiatives receive a high priority in the resource allocation process. Presidents, working in consort with their academic vice-presidents and with input from appropriate faculty governance bodies, can establish campuswide faculty development programs that serve the needs of individual faculty members and the institution. Faculty development priorities should flow from a sense of where the institution is heading and what kind of human resource capacity it will take to get there. This kind of campuswide planning must take place at the highest levels.

On most campuses, the academic vice-president has primary responsibility for overseeing the faculty reward process, particularly salary, promotion, and tenure considerations. If faculty development efforts are not clearly tied to the faculty reward system, these efforts stand little chance of success. Faculty members generally choose where they will spend their time and energy based on the perception of benefit that is likely to accrue. Academic vice-presidents must ensure that the faculty reward system and faculty development efforts are mutually supportive.

Deans and department heads play a pivotal role in providing administrative support and stimulus for faculty development efforts. They are in the best position to know the developmental needs of their individual faculty and to take steps to try to meet them. They are also in the best position to acknowledge and reward the full range of contributions that faculty members make to the campus and to their discipline. If they are in touch with the activities of their faculty and if they are willing to invest the time and energy, deans and department heads can have a profound impact on the culture of both the campus and their own particular academic unit by continually reinforcing in a variety of ways that what individual faculty members are doing is both important and valued. While highly prestigious awards for teaching and scholarly excellence are useful faculty incentives and call attention to the fact that the institution values these activities, it is equally important that valued activities be reinforced throughout the institutional infrastructure and particularly in the day-to-day life of the college and department.

While strong administrative support is necessary at all levels, faculty development efforts are more likely to succeed if members of the faculty feel that the program is theirs, rather than something imposed by the campus administration. Developing a sense of ownership requires that faculty be involved early and often in the program design and implementation. In particular, every opportunity should be taken to involve faculty leaders. The responsibility for making the program a success must be felt by administrators and faculty alike. To involve faculty in designing their own incentive program is to encourage a sense of faculty empowerment which, in itself, is a good developmental strategy.

Successful faculty development programs are not accomplished through words alone. They require a commitment of institutional resources that are secure in bad times as well as good. Bevan (1985) suggests that faculty development efforts should be supported by resources equal to at least 1 percent of the sum spent annually for academic operations. The commitment of scarce resources requires making choices. If professional development of faculty is a major priority, it must be treated as such in the budget. Ideally, resources for faculty development should be allocated throughout the institution so that deans and department heads have at least modest amounts of discretionary funds to reward faculty productivity and initiative. The point is that successful faculty development programs require a strong resource base, not only to support the program but also to reinforce the faculty perception that continuing professional development is indeed important.

Successful programs include incentives that are tied to developmental differences. A substantial body of literature supports the claim that the needs, interests, and priorities of faculty differ at various career stages. Members of the academic profession do not constitute a homogeneous group. McKeachie (1984) suggests that differences in interests, abilities, and roles are likely to increase over time. It is unwise to assume that the same incentives will work for all. If the objective is to stimulate the productivity and updating of midcareer faculty, then incentives must support their individual needs. It is not enough for administrators to *think* they know what the developmental needs are. Faculty must be given the opportunity to voice those needs and administrators must listen carefully. This is yet another reason to involve faculty early and often in the program design.

To be successful, faculty development programs must be compatible with institutional priorities. For example, efforts to improve teaching effectiveness are unlikely to have any substantial impact unless it is clear that the institution values teaching. There are countless examples of institutions that have mounted teaching improvement programs only to see them fail because faculty know that teaching effectiveness counts for little at salary, promotion, and tenure time. Faculty development and institutional development should be mutually supportive.

Successful programs for ongoing faculty development tie rewards to performance. Rather than focusing only on low-performing faculty, they offer opportunity and reward to faculty who are making solid, substantial contributions. They give faculty a sense that their efforts are valued and that the institution will reward excellence. But to reward excellence, an institution must be able to identify it. This is a relatively straightforward matter in research and scholarship, where performance measures are quite well defined. However, evaluating performance in teaching and service can be more complex. If institutions want to enhance faculty vitality in teaching, research, and service, they must be able to identify outstanding performance in all three areas. At Utah State University, faculty members develop annual performance plans in consort with their department head and dean. These plans include not only mutually agreed upon objectives in teaching, research, and service but faculty developmental goals as well.

Finally, faculty development programs stand a better chance of success if implemented at various levels within the institution. While the president and academic vice-president may set overall faculty development policy and administer certain campuswide incentive programs, much of the effort has to take place at the college and departmental level. It is here that direct and active intervention, based on the needs of individual faculty members, can occur. Deans and department heads who are doing their jobs and are in touch with their faculty should be among the first to know when a faculty member is in need of encouragement or reward. They need resources that allow them to take initiative on behalf of an individual faculty member without having to go through a complex and time-consuming campus bureaucracy. If deans and department heads are to shoulder a major responsibility for faculty development, they must be selected and trained with this function in mind.

How does one know when attempts to enhance faculty competence and vitality are succeeding? Unfortunately, there is no easy answer. Developing convincing evidence that a particular strategy has led directly to improved teaching or scholarship is complex. However, several approaches to program evaluation can yield useful evidence. If the program is focused on enhancing the vitality and productivity of midcareer faculty, evidence of success can include such indices as increases in scholarly publications, external grant proposals and awards, new course preparations, and involvement in departmental, college, and campus affairs. Deans, department heads, and other designated campus personnel can collect anecdotal and case study evidence that reflects the program's impact. Faculty development teams at the campus, college, and departmental level can monitor program success and report findings on a periodic basis.

Keeping in mind that institutional vitality is dependent on ongoing faculty development and vitality, it is also important to continually evaluate the overall institutional culture with special emphasis on the attitudes of faculty toward the institution. Is there a culture of pride in the institution? Are faculty pleased with their institutional affiliation? Do faculty at every career level feel that they are able to pursue an active and productive career within the institutional setting? Do faculty feel empowered, with a sense of control over their professional direction? Do they feel that their work is meaningful and valued by the institution? This is the kind of evidence that can point to the success of faculty development efforts and the need to strengthen or reorient particular dimensions. Many campuses find it useful to enlist the help of external consultants to pursue these questions periodically.

Conclusion

Maintaining the productivity and vitality of midcareer faculty is one of the most complex yet fundamental challenges facing higher education. As the number of midcareer faculty on most campuses continues to increase, their impact on overall institutional vitality will continue to increase as well. The enhancement of competence and vitality requires a broad range of incentives that capitalize on those developmental needs that motivate faculty naturally: the need for control over one's life, the need to feel that one's work is important and valued, the need to feel appreciated, the need to break out of the routine and take advantage of new opportunities and new challenges. Attempts to enhance productivity and vitality are unlikely to succeed unless they address these developmental needs.

Much of the faculty development literature is prescriptive with the general admonition that more is better. In fact, the agenda should not be simply to argue for more faculty development programs. Rather, we need programs that more creatively address the developmental needs of faculty at various career and life stages. To accomplish this, we need to know more about adult learning and development, more about the way academic careers are structured, more about how faculty are socialized, and more about how the academic institution affects faculty vitality.

Most colleges and universities would acknowledge that the faculty are their most important human resource. Indeed, most would argue that they are committed to continued faculty growth and vitality. However, faculty development remains a relatively low priority on most campuses. It is generally understaffed, underfunded, and lacking in the creativity and informed leadership that is necessary for its success. It is ironic that those institutions which in recent years have become so heavily involved in meeting the continuing education needs of society often do so poorly in attending to the ongoing developmental needs of their own faculty and staff. Colleges and universities that are committed to enhancing the development and vitality of faculty at all career levels must create and nurture an institutional culture that supports this goal.

References

Austin, A. E., and Gamson, Z. T. *Academic Workplace: New Demands, Heightened Tensions.* ASHE-ERIC Higher Education Research Report no. 10. Washington: Association for the Study of Higher Education, 1983.

Baldwin, R. G., and Blackburn, R. T. "The Academic Career as a Developmental Process: Implications for Higher Education." *Journal of Higher Education,* 1981, *526,* 598–614.

Bevan, J. M. "Who Has the Role of Building Incentives?" In R. G. Baldwin (ed.), *Incentives for Faculty Vitality. New Directions for Higher Education,* no. 51. San Francisco: Jossey-Bass, 1985.

Braskamp, L., Fowler, D., and Dry, J. "Faculty Development and Achievement: A Faculty's View." Paper presented at annual meeting of the American Educational Research Association, New York, Apr. 1982.

Centra, J. A. "Maintaining Faculty Vitality Through Faculty Development." In S. M. Clark and D. R. Lewis (eds.), *Faculty Vitality and Institutional Productivity: Critical Perspectives in Higher Education.* New York: Teachers' College, Columbia University, 1985.

Clark, S. M., Corcoran, M., and Lewis, D. R. "Critical Perspectives on Faculty Career Development with Implications for Differentiated Institutional Policies." Paper presented at the annual meeting of the American Educational Research Association, New Orleans, Apr. 1984.

Clark, S. M., Corcoran, M., and Lewis, D. R. "The Case for an Institutional Perspective on Faculty Development." *Journal of Higher Education,* 1986, *57* (2), 176–195.

Claxton, C. S., and Murrell, P. H. "Development Theory as a Guide for Maintaining the Vitality of College Faculty." In C.M.N. Mehrotra (ed.), *Teaching and Aging. New Directions for Teaching and Learning,* no. 19. San Francisco: Jossey-Bass, 1984.

Dubin, S. S. "A Learning Model for Updating Older Technical

and Professional Persons." Paper presented at the American Psychological Association, San Francisco, Aug. 1977.

Erikson, E. H. *Childhood and Society.* (2nd ed.) New York: Norton, 1963.

Gaff, J. G. "Faculty: Ongoing Development and Renewal." In J. S. Green and A. Levine (eds.) *Opportunity in Adversity: How Colleges Can Succeed in Hard Times.* Jossey-Bass, 1985.

Gardner, J. W. *Self-Renewal.* New York: Perennial Library, 1963.

Guttman. D. *In the Country of Old Men.* Occasional Papers on Aging. Ann Arbor: Institute of Gerontology, University of Michigan and Wayne State University, 1973.

Hayes, J. "Over Forties in Professional, Managerial, and Administrative Work." In G. Cooper and D. Torrington (eds.), *After Forty: The Time for Achievement.* Chichester, England: Wiley, 1981.

Howard, A. "Cool at the Top: Personality Characteristics of Successful Executives." Presentation at annual convention of the American Psychological Association, Toronto, Canada, Aug. 1984.

Kanter, R. M. "Changing the Shape of Work: Reform in Academe." *Current Issues in Higher Education,* 1979, *1,* 3–9.

Keller, G. *Academic Strategy: The Management Revolution in American Higher Education.* Baltimore, Md.: Johns Hopkins University Press, 1983.

Lawrence, J. H. "Developmental Needs as Intrinsic Motivators." In R. G. Baldwin (ed.), *Incentives for Faculty Vitality.* New Directions for Higher Education, no. 51. San Francisco: Jossey-Bass, 1985.

Levinson, D., and others. *The Seasons of a Man's Life.* New York: Knopf, 1978.

Loevinger, J. *Ego Development: Conceptions and Theories.* San Francisco: Jossey-Bass, 1976.

McKeachie, W. J. "The Faculty as a Renewable Resource." In M. Waggoner, R. Alfred, and M. Peterson (eds.), *Academic Renewal: Advancing Higher Education Towards the Nineties.* Ann Arbor: School of Education, University of Michigan, 1984.

Pelz, D., and Andrews, F. *Scientists in Organizations.* Ann Arbor: Institute for Social Research, University of Michigan, 1976.

Schuster, J. H. "Faculty Vitality: Observations from the Field." In R. G. Baldwin (ed.), *Incentives for Faculty Vitality*. New Directions for Higher Education, no. 51. San Francisco: Jossey-Bass, 1985.

Toombs, W. "Faculty Vitality: The Professional Context." In R. G. Baldwin (ed.) *Incentives for Faculty Vitality*. New Directions for Higher Education, no. 51. San Francisco: Jossey-Bass, 1985.

Tuckman, H. P. "The Academic Reward Structure in American Higher Education." In D. R. Lewis and W. E. Becker, Jr. (eds.) *Academic Rewards in Higher Education*. Cambridge, Mass. Ballinger, 1979.

U.S. Department of Labor. *Occupational Outlook Handbook*. Washington: U.S. Government Printing Office, 1984.

10

Donald Britton Miller

Organizational, Environmental, and Work Design Strategies That Foster Competence

In part, the need for continuing professional development is created by the way organizations use — or fail to use — the knowledge and skills of their people. An unused or underused capability deteriorates with time. Work that fails to stretch, to challenge, fails to motivate people to learn and grow. Continual learning and individual development are the keys to renewal and vitality, both for the organization and for the individual. (We are talking about adaptability energy — the power to be successful tomorrow.) For example, in response to business needs some organizations leave significant numbers of professionals on technical byways while others pursue new technology. Under these circumstances new learning is impeded and decreased competence is assured. Any work environment that impedes individual growth invites deterioration. Managers intent on winning tomorrow's business and technical challenges must build renewal and vitality enhancement, an important part of which is continuing professional development. Managers must refuse to accept the notion that loss of capability over time is a required part of doing business.

Work environments can be designed that stimulate re-

233

newal, enhance vitality, and encourage continued development. Individual managers can design small-group work environments that put a high value on individual development and reward those who continue growing. Organization management can design work environments that reduce the pressures for short-term results. This should result in first-line managers feeling free — even required — to emphasize development of tomorrow's capabilities as part of today's goals. Such rebalancing of short- and long-term goals is absolutely necessary to support continued skill and knowledge development. Today's work world overemphasizes short-term goals. This is one of the reasons renewal, vitality, and continued development have become important contemporary management issues.

On the individual level, work assignments can be designed so that they stretch the professional and *cause the need* for continued learning and growth in capability. In this way, work can become something that creates rather than saps vitality. Vitality, the power to win tomorrow, results from a gain in the adaptability energy necessary for tomorrow's success.

Vitality is an integrating management concept that, when used as a strategy and as a guide for decision making, can assist in stimulating updating and renewal. A vitality strategy, as explained first by Miller (1977a, pp. 342–349), goes a long way toward establishing organizational values that make growth in capability important; it provides an incentive for weaving the process of continued learning into the fabric of the organization. By testing management decisions against the question "Does this action deplete or enhance vitality?" managers can create a positive force for continuing development. In this chapter the goal is to build an understanding of the power of a changed managerial outlook, one that emphasizes vitality.

Vitality as an Integrating Concept

Vitality is the power gained in the process of doing today's tasks that increases an individual's or organization's ability to succeed tomorrow. It represents the increase in capability that results from using one's skills and knowledge in an environment that puts a high value on continuing development of capability. Another way to think about vitality is as adaptability energy. In this sense, it is an increase not only in basic technical, professional, and personal knowledge and skills but also in the ability to encompass and manage change.

The discovery of the vitality concept initially came out of studies (unpublished) of obsolescence and burnout in a technical organization. It was discovered that obsolescence occurred as much from misuse of people as from the change in technology. The vitality concept also makes sense in terms of the findings in studies of quality work (Davis and Cherns, 1975). One of the definitions of quality work (Thorsrud, 1974, p. 6) is work that stretches, work that causes one to learn and grow new capabilities.

It became evident that each individual case of obsolescence was in some sense unique, and not responsive to the same type of "cure." This caused a shift toward prevention. Rather than wait until obsolescence and burnout occur, we began a search for work and environmental causes of lack of continuing development, looking for aspects of work and environment that could be changed. We believed that if we could design work assignments and a work environment with positive forces motivating continuing learning and increase in capability, then much obsolescence and burnout could be prevented. Prevention of obsolescence has proved one of the most powerful management strategies in creating vitality.

Organizational goals are a significant part of the environment and directly affect what happens and how. In these days of increased need for creativity and innovation, vitality and effectiveness become important strategic goals, especially for organizations with many technical professionals. These twin goals can be used to shape the environment and provide a force for improving creative output. They must be accepted and implemented by line management. And they must be paired; the pursuit of improved capability without its application to meaningful goals is of no value. Effectiveness requires applying the capability to goals of high value. For example, it is useless to encourage a professional to study laser optics if there is no conceivable way of applying laser optics to the organization's business. There is no static vitality. Vitality results from the application of capability to meaningful goals.

Organizational goals can encourage or depress a person's motivation for professional development. As adults we become increasingly pragmatic. We demand that there be a reason for what we do, one we can understand and agree to. Generally, adults will no longer follow the direction of another person just because that person is the teacher or the boss. Since professional development requires the study of new material, either on or off the job, the individual must agree to the need for learning, and must see the payoff.

The most powerful motivation for continuing professional development is a personal goal that requires new capabilities for its achievement. If the individual's work assignment requires learning and application of new information, then that person will be motivated to add the new capabilities. If this occurs in a work environment where people are rewarded for maintenance and enhancement of their skills, then the probability that professional development will take place is increased. An organizational strategy that emphasizes the importance of vitality establishes the base for development; enhancement of capability then takes on a high value. It is necessary to touch the individual's motivation on two levels: the level of the job itself, by making the job require new learning, and at the environmental level, through policies and programs that demonstrate a management commitment to continued individual development, including an intention to reward it.

In an earlier work, I set forth specifications for the design of vital, effective research and development organizations (Miller, 1986, pp. 186–189). Here, I restate these concepts so they are broadly applicable to all organizations. An alternate set may be found in Mastenbroek (1988). These specifications are intended to become a conceptual guide, not a specific prescription, for developing a strategic outlook and an environment supporting improvement in capability and application of that capability to meaningful goals.

Specifications for vital and effective organizations:

1. Develop participative processes for choosing important goals so that the members of the organization become owners of the goals and can create a congruence between personal and organizational goals.

2. Develop processes for achieving a creative amalgam of funding, leadership, people, and facilities, and applying these to the mission and goals of the organization in a way that both achieves results and enhances the capability of achieving future goals.

3. Create an image of vitality, excitement, and achievement of results that helps the organization attract, develop, and retain vital people.

4. Design and implement environments that institutionalize caring and nurturing in ways that support individuals in improving capability and career management. Implementing this requirement requires support of learning on the job as well as support of continuing formal education in business, technology, personal, and professional skills.

5. Develop environments that support the individual in being sufficiently secure to risk experimentation, to try approaches different from the past, and to push at the frontiers of application of new concepts and technologies to the needs of customers and clients.

6. Choose vitality and effectiveness as goals and give them an importance equal to product, system, service, and financial goals. In other words, find a way to balance long-term goals of increased capability with short-term results goals.

7. Create an open communications climate that supports the transmission, use, and storage of information about the business so that data become useful feedback for organizational learning and individual development.

8. Create policies and human resource systems that ensure a good match of people with work so that their skills are used, but not in such a repetitive manner that it stifles the growth of new capabilities or eliminates the variety necessary to avoid obsolescence and burnout and support renewal.

Organization and Work Design Concepts

Flat organizations, ones with fewer layers and broader responsibilities, are generally believed to support development of capabilities and increase vitality. The spread of responsibility provides the variety that stimulates vitality and learning. Deep organizations, ones with many layers and narrow responsibilities, are generally believed to impede the development of capabilities and decrease vitality. In a deep organization responsibilities are narrowly defined and individuals are not encouraged to look beyond these narrow confines. In fact, deep organizations tend to have more than enough people monitoring what one does, making sure one does not step outside a narrow role definition. Since the work is finely divided it might seem that people in deep organizations would have more time for learning. However, because of narrower scope, other aspects of the environment do not encourage development. By assuring a breadth of activity, management can, through organization design, support professional development and renewal.

Organizational units or work groups that are too small give the manager little freedom to vary assignments, to encourage learning. In fact, they tend to support assigning the work to the person who already knows how. This stifles new learning and reduces the possibility for achieving variety, a necessary component of vitality. If taken too literally this would suggest all work groups should be large. Management must understand that there are other needs and goals to be supported through organizational design. For example, in a large group it is not possible for the leader to have substantial daily contact with each individual. This makes coaching, feedback, and appraisal—which complement and support development—more difficult. Thus, appropriate size of a group can be determined only by careful review and balancing of management's goals.

Organization design affects the flow of information. If the organization is many layered, we usually find that the flow of information does not provide the individual leader with enough data to take risks and learn. Information flow in that type of organization tends to follow narrow specialty lines, thus limiting the learning about other activities. Increasing information availability is an important management tool for increasing capability.

Organization structures with too many borders or too rigid separation of responsibilities usually impede the rotation of employees for growth and development. This can support managers in hoarding human resources and blocking career development and growth. On questioning, managers in one organization told me why they did not support professional development and career growth. Each time they let someone move on to another assignment they lost head count, meaning they were expected to do the same work with less people.

Organizations can impede movement, adaptation, and change, all necessary in stimulating vitality, by making border crossings difficult. Management can also impede development with rules and controls that encourage hoarding human resources. Establishing policies that help the individual adapt and grow as the result of technical, business, and personal change supports continuing development of capability.

These general statements about organizational design are just that—general. The most direct route to affecting learning is not through organization design but through environment and job design. The lack of renewal and vitality, however, is often the result of lack of compatibility between organizational design and environmental design. In these cases, individual managers find that they are caught between inconsistent goals and measures. As a result, they support short-range goals like meeting schedule and budget and fail to support longer-range goals of capability development.

From the eight specifications for a vital and effective organization listed earlier, we can gain insights into the impact of environment on professional development. An environment is made up of elements or dimensions, for example, mission; business goals; technological base and its rate of change; management values and style; nature of work facilities and physical conditions; value systems, mores, norms, and rituals that affect how one works; human resource principles, policies, and practices; the character of the communications climate; and significant events such as business successes or takeovers.

Several of these elements can have a direct effect on professional development by stimulating or depressing certain activities. For example, organizational value systems can make continuing growth of capability important or unimportant. Mores, norms, and rituals may reinforce using up capability, or they can support enhancing it. A business goal that stresses the importance of growing people capable of technological leadership can provide the basis for creativity, exploration, and learning.

A fast-moving, changing technological base will make continuing professional development an important factor in personal success. A slow-moving technical environment will not put a premium on continued learning. This is why identification of obsolescence as a problem, an important management issue, occurred first in electronics and computer industries. Aggressive business goals can also encourage experimentation and learning if the reward and punishment climate supports the freedom to make a mistake. A merger or takeover might depress individual development because the individual feels the loss of a future. It could provide a feeling of enhanced internal opportunity. Or, by contrast, a merger could make the individual so insecure that it motivates him or her to increase time and energy spent on learning.

Management practices and style can affect the support for continual increase in capability. In one late 1950s IBM study, professionals were asked why they had dropped out of advanced study courses. Almost universally they responded that their manager required overtime or travel, making continued study almost impossible. Here short-term pressures for results were interpreted by the manager as more important than the long-term pressures for individual development. Continuing professional development suffered. These are but a few examples of how environment can affect our goal.

At the more specific level of the job, in an environment that encourages individual development, the manager can design jobs and assignments that motivate the individual to increase capabilities. If the environment really puts a high value on increased capability, the manager will be rewarded for stimulating individual development and supporting career management. One organization added to its appraisal system specific measures of the manager's activities in developing people. This forcefully demonstrated the commitment to this goal. For, in organizations, what we measure is what is important.

The manager can best affect the need for learning to do the job by understanding the aspects of the job that may stimulate the need. It is best to look at these at the task level (Miller, 1972). At that level the connection between what is expected and what the individual needs to do is most clear. Here are some of the aspects of the task that can be altered by negotiation between the manager and the individual, to increase the need for learning:

- Breadth: the task breadth should be so inclusive that it requires new learning but not so wide as to confuse objectives, exceed the individual's tolerance for ambiguity, or create a poor relationship between the task and results.
- Newness: the task should require some new behavior and new knowledge such that completing it can be accomplished only through new learning; it should not just be a repetition of past activities.
- Communication: the requirement for interaction with others can be varied in ways that increase the potential for exposure to the ideas of others. An increase in communication is usually associated with an increase in learning and stimulation for exploration.
- Time scale: requirements for results in a short time usually increase the reliance on what is already known. Appropriate increase in time for task completion can make possible exploration of alternatives and greater learning, but does not guarantee it.
- Research: the amount of study of prior work necessary to embark on the task can be varied. With an increase in research there is usually an increase in learning.
- Documentation: requiring documentation of results forces

clarification of what has been learned and thus reinforces the individual's learning.
- Reward: can be attached to short-term results, increase in capability, or a combination. By varying the timing, nature, and relationship to tasks, the manager can stimulate individual learning through rewards.

These aspects of jobs can be used to vary the relative emphasis on short-term results and long-term enhancement of capability. They have a direct effect on the motivation for personal and professional development. Some jobs, however, do not lend themselves to this type of design change. For example, it would be difficult to change a routine assembly job to increase learning, although some experiments in the quality of work life movement have moved in this direction. The job of the professional, however, the individual whom we believe *must continue individual development for survival*, is amenable to design changes using these concepts. The requirement is that both the professional and the manager understand the need. They must also be willing to put other goals in second place.

A management wishing to create vitality and renewal cannot work only at the task level but must also work at the organizational and environmental design level. The environment represents the backdrop against which all activity is seen. Environments can be designed to stimulate, encourage, and reward learning activity, or to depress it. Sometimes work environments depress individual development without management's intent, or even without understanding that this is happening. However, environments that *do* support development and renewal do not occur accidentally. The natural pressures for profit, for results, tend to run counter to what is necessary to stimulate vitality and renewal. Thus, if management wants the manager to design task assignments that stimulate development, to support career management, it must take specific steps to create an environment that supports that activity.

Management can choose not to accept the environment that exists but rather to design and implement specific types of environment through policies, practices, training, and reward and recognition systems. All these elements must be consistent. For example, a policy that pays for additional graduate education is of little value if it is blocked by managerial actions, as in our earlier example. It is of little value to put the manager in a management development program that emphasizes the need for nurturing of individual development if that manager's manager never rewards that activity. The manager's actions are affected by the immediate supervision as well as the environment. Thus, even in an environment where policies support good human resource practices, an immediate manager who emphasizes only technical matters can counteract that environmental element. Or, by contrast, a manager who wishes to encourage human development, working in an environment that supports treating individuals as disposable and nonrenewable, will be blocked and negatively reinforced.

Here are some of the elements of environment that can be used to positively affect individual development, renewal, and updating:

- Policies: a set of human resource policies that establishes a high value and provides funds and other support for continued learning, both formal and informal, and rewards individuals and managers for responding to these goals.
- Practices: implementation of training, measurement, and reward systems that reinforce those who follow the broad policies and do not block the desired capability enhancement process.
- Value reinforcement: for individuals to follow the policies and practices, they must believe in them and own them, so the organization must use communication emphasis and participation to nurture these values.

It is now possible to move from the general concepts to a more detailed discussion of job design. Matching the individual's needs and capabilities with the needs and capabilities of the organization is the most important managerial activity leading to effectiveness and vitality. This is a joint task of the manager and the individual. It involves identifying the characteristics of the job that match and those that do not. It involves, in the case of a characteristic that does not match, trying to change that characteristic so that it can more nearly meet the needs or capabilities of the individual. This change, redesign, of a job characteristic is what we call job design.

One of these characteristics, directly relating to continual professional development, is the need to learn new things to accomplish the job. Generally, good jobs, jobs that motivate professionals, stretch and challenge. Part of this challenge is the need to encompass something that has not been done before and requires learning new skills or knowledge. Through joint negotiation of the specifications for the task by manager and professional, before the work is done, it is usually possible to add activities or change the nature of activities so that the challenge is increased.

Examples of Environment and Job Design Affecting Development

Most research organizations have some system for supporting new initiatives, unplanned activity. The concept behind such systems is that people learn and grow when they are able to pursue a new idea before it has to face the rigors of budget planning and examination by those who demand to know its long-range profit potential. When such systems work, and unfortunately many do not, they do increase the probability of exploration of a new concept by an individual who is personally motivated. Exploration leads to learning and growth in capability as well as to creativity and innovation. This is an example of a deliberate environmental design action affecting what happens in an organization. The environment concretely backs up managerial statements about the importance placed on freedom to explore. The action is to provide freedom, time, and funds with limited restraints.

Another action taken by research organizations has been to establish participative mission and goal-setting processes. One of the elements of environment on which the research professional tends to place a high value is strategic autonomy.

Having strategic autonomy means having the ability to affect organizational direction. A system that truly involves the non-management professional in establishing goals responds to this need.

While this action seems to focus on other aspects of the quality of the work environment, it also can affect renewal and vitality. By responding to the individual's research interests, the need to influence what is to be done, it is possible to capture the individual's motivation for exploration and creativity. Participation builds congruence between individual and organizational goals. This is a key to individual motivation. Improving the match of needs between the individual and the organization enhances productivity and also supports the goals of vitality and renewal.

For another example of the impact of environmental design, let us look at a development organization. In IBM's San Jose facility, years ago, we wanted to communicate management's commitment to individual development, and so we created an environmental statement. This is management action that speaks louder than the words or cost involved. A corner of the technical library was redesigned and totally devoted to individual and professional development. The library added career planning and management literature, personal improvement literature, and professional improvement literature, videotapes, and cassettes. This special section of the library was painted white so it stood out in an otherwise brown room. This simple environmental design action transmitted the message that it was all right to use company space and time for continuing personal development. Did it work? People came to the library door who never had been there before! The library now had content that was valuable for them. (For other types of environmental design actions, see Miller, 1977b.)

Examples can also be drawn from other types of organizations. I was asked to work with a computer center organization where the problem was perceived to be a lack of potential for career growth. After learning about environmental design, management created a set of new policies and programs that demonstrated commitment to support career growth. In addition, both managers and professionals were trained in career management concepts and processes. This made it possible to implement a practice of annual career discussions between managers and employees. Finally, the company set up a human resource center. This center assured that the results of individual career discussions between managers and employees affected the choice of candidates for internal career opportunities. Over several years, these actions helped to modify feelings about career growth possibilities. All these actions stimulated additional emphasis on continued learning and individual development.

Ideas for new initiatives, both at the environmental design level and at the job design level, can flow from these concepts. For example, we might consider the following:

- Environmental design actions that translate the rhetoric about supporting continued learning into real support.
- Environmental design actions that support the individual in responding to changed interests, changed needs, or need for variety, with change of assignment and study.
- Policies and practices that create an open environment for people movement and reduce managerial blocking of growth and change.
- Communication of success stories where individuals have successfully evolved through change by investing in learning and career and life management.
- Programs that train individuals and managers to talk about job-to-person match and implement job design changes that improve motivation for continued learning and individual development.
- Implementing recognition and reward systems that support the manager in taking the longer-term view of enhancing capability, rather than overemphasis on short-term results.
- Long-term strategic planning, on a participative basis, that helps to demonstrate and emphasize the need for individual and organizational adaptation in order to survive.

Integrating the Concepts

It is often difficult to translate the concepts of management books into action. Sometimes the difficulty is in deciding which concepts to accept and which to reject. Perhaps the examples used to illustrate the concepts may not seem to be applicable to the specific organization. Putting concepts to work is also difficult because each organization has a different culture. How and where one starts is different for each organization; change actions must be culture specific.

Still another aspect of implementation difficulty occurs as a result of the position in the organization of the person who desires to implement change. From some positions it is possible to implement change, from others it is not. It depends on the sphere of influence, the ability to communicate and be heard. To be motivated to change and to work to make it happen, those who will be affected by the change should respect the change agent as a leader, believe in the need for change, and be convinced that the new state will be better.

The first step in making any change is to identify, in a participative way, the discomfort, the "hurt factor" (Miller, 1986, pp. 357–385). Thus, if, after reading this chapter, you wish to use the concepts, you must first gain agreement that the failure of the organization to support continued learning, renewal, and vitality is a problem requiring management action in your organization. Both the managers who must make the changes in environmental design and those who must change their approach to job design must be convinced. In addition, the individual professionals who must gain increased capabilities must agree with the need. Without these agreements you will lack the basis for investing energy in change.

The single most difficult part of gaining this agreement is that obsolescence is almost always a potential *future* problem rather than a current situation. I can remember many times having to change the outlook of people at IBM who wanted to know how many people were obsolete. Only occasionally did we identify a group of currently obsolete workers. More often we were convincing people of the need to do things today to avoid problems tomorrow. This is the challenge of moving management from a short-term to a long-term view, from focus on cure to a strategy of prevention.

Once you get over this crucial hurdle, you can deal with integrating the various concepts presented here in a way that makes sense for your organization. Action and change plans require dealing with environmental design at the total organizational level. If this is done correctly, then what you have done will affect the actions of individual managers and individual professionals. It should motivate everyone to do those things that improve new learning and renewal. Everyone must come to believe that both individual and organizational survival depend on gaining today the capability to be successful tomorrow — vitality.

References

Davis, L. E., and Cherns, A. B. (eds.) *The Quality of Working Life.* Vols. 1 and 2. New York: Free Press, 1975.

Mastenbroek, W. "A Dynamic Concept of Revitalization." *Organization Dynamics*, 1988, *16*, 52–61.

Miller, D. B. *Changing Job Requirements: A Stimulant for Technical Vitality.* Continuing Engineering Studies Series, no. 7. Washington: American Society for Engineering Education, 1972.

Miller, D. B. *Personal Vitality.* Reading, Mass.: Addison-Wesley, 1977a.

Miller, D. B. "How to Improve the Performance and Productivity of the Knowledge Worker." *Organizational Dynamics*, 1977b, *5*, 62–80.

Miller, D. B. *Managing Professionals in Research and Development: A Guide for Improving Productivity and Organizational Effectiveness.* San Francisco: Jossey-Bass, 1986.

Thorsrud, E. In J. M. Rosow (ed.), *The Worker and the Job.* Englewood Cliffs, N.J.: Prentice-Hall, 1974. p. 6.

11

Harold G. Kaufman

Management Techniques for Maintaining a Competent Professional Work Force

It has long been recognized that obsolescence of knowledge or skills threatens highly educated professionals and managers (Dubin, 1972a, 1972b; Kaufman, 1974a, 1975, 1982b; Roney, 1966). Obsolescence has been defined as "the degree to which organizational professionals lack the up-to-date knowledge or skills necessary to maintain effective performance in either their current or future work roles" (Kaufman, 1974a, p. 23). This definition has been widely adopted by a variety of concerned parties, including the National Science Foundation (1978), behavioral scientists (such as Steiner and Farr, 1986), and management specialists (such as Bracker and Pearson, 1986).

All indications are that the problem of maintaining professional competence has been exacerbated, most notably by rapidly changing technology and organizational restructuring on an unprecedented scale. Indeed, in a national survey of engineers in industry, almost all reported that opportunities to avoid obsolescence were extremely or very important to them but most perceived their employers as not responding adequately to their needs (Engineering Manpower Commission, 1986). To meet the challenges of the future, it is critical that

Figure 11.1. A Systems Model of Maintaining Professional Competence.

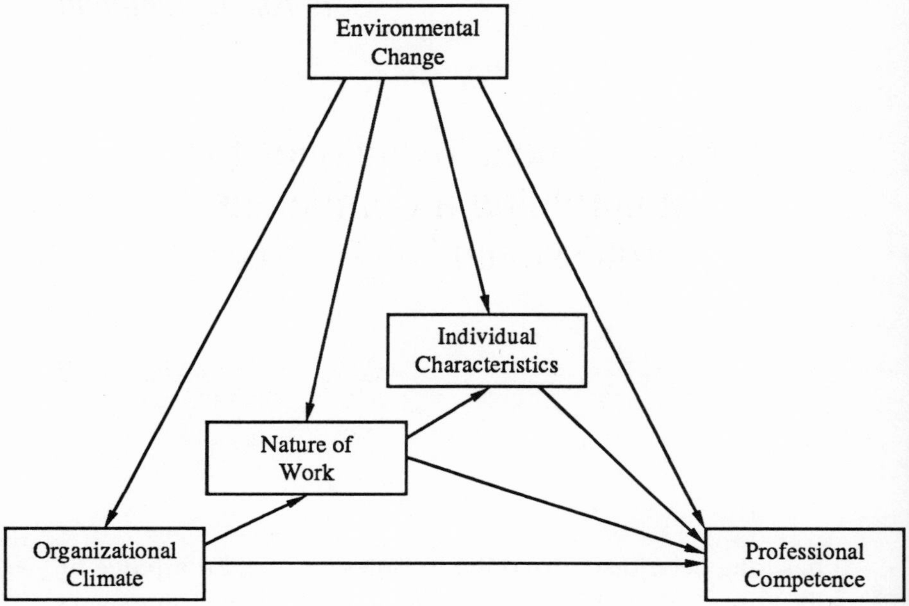

industry introduce effective management techniques for maintaining a professionally competent work force.

A Systems Model

A systems model approach to understanding the complex factors related to professional competence has long been advocated (for example, Dubin and Cohen, 1970). A more complete model uses an open system that recognizes the system's dynamic interaction with the external environment (Katz and Kahn, 1978). Such an open systems perspective has been used (Kaufman, 1978, 1979, 1989) in developing the model shown in Figure 11.1, which is applied here to the maintenance of professional competence. This model identifies four broad system components related to professional competence and the interrelationships among them:

1. Environmental change involving rapidly changing technology — the massive introduction of computers, the information explosion, and the exponential increase in technical knowledge — plus changes resulting from other external forces such as organizational restructuring, global competition, and demographic flux in the work force.
2. Organizational climate, determined largely by management policies and practices, especially those related to the organizational reward system.
3. Nature of the work as characterized by job assignments and the degree of challenge and growth they provide, especially through the use of knowledge and skills in one's position.
4. Individual characteristics, especially those that are psychological in nature involving cognitive, motivational, and personality factors (abilities, growth needs, rigidity).

The systems model takes into account the variety and complexity of the components contributing to professional competence. Somewhat similar causal factors have been identified by other researchers in models that focused on obsolescence or updating (Dubin and Cohen, 1970; Fossum, Arvey, Paradise, and Robbins, 1986; Kozlowski and Farr, 1988). A considerable body of evidence supports the validity of the systems model presented here (Kaufman, 1978, 1979, 1989). However, it should not preclude the development and testing of other models, especially to assess effects over time.

As we can see from Figure 11.1, environmental change is all-pervasive and affects every other component. However, since there is relatively little that the individual or organization can do to control the external environment, we will focus here on internal components that may be more amenable to manipulation and responsive to change. Nevertheless, management can still monitor changes in the external environment and use this information in its strategic planning. While technological change is widely recognized in strategic planning, most firms do not appear to incorporate the need for maintaining technical competence among professionals into such planning (National Research Council, 1985).

According to the systems model, organizational climate affects professional competence as well as the nature of the work carried out by professionals. The work, in turn, has a direct impact on their level of competence. The model also predicts that individual characteristics may be affected by the nature of the work, which has support from longitudinal research (Brousseau and Prince, 1981).

There are many ways an organization can develop and maintain a competent professional work force. Management's role can be addressed by focusing on each of the factors internal to the system — individual characteristics, the nature of the work, and organizational climate.

Individual Characteristics

Research indicates that individual characteristics may not be the most important factor contributing to professional competence (Kaufman, 1978, 1979, 1989; Kozlowski and Farr, 1988). Moreover, of all of the factors related to maintaining professional competence, individual differences may be the most difficult to control directly, particularly those that are psychological in nature (Kaufman, 1973, 1974a). Nevertheless, organizations attempting to monitor and control the individual characteristics of its professionals for the purpose of maintaining a competent work force have some techniques at their disposal, including the ones that follow.

First, monitor the degree to which professional competence is being maintained in the organization. In order for the organization to know that problems of obsolescence-related incompetence exist, some type of monitoring procedure is required (Kaufman, 1974a, 1975). Declining performance or productivity can be indirect indicators, but by the time such problems are detected it may be too late. Moreover, using performance as a measure of professional competence is not entirely appropriate since a low rating does not necessarily indicate that the individual is obsolescent (see Dalton and Thompson, 1971). Poor performance may stem from other causes. Conversely, high performance ratings do not necessarily signify that a person is up to date professionally.

Early-warning alerts can be obtained by monitoring data in human resource information systems (such as participation levels in training and education activities or skills inventories), but these too are, at best, indirect indicators of competence. More direct measures such as tests developed to measure levels of knowledge (see Mali, 1975) are difficult to construct and fail to account for effective performance. Professionals may lack the most up-to-date knowledge in their field but still perform effectively in the work role. However, obsolescence may become a problem if the job assignment changes and more up-to-date knowledge is required in the new job.

Surveys administered periodically to the professionals in an organization may provide the most accessible measures of their competence. A reliable and valid self-assessment, involving behaviors considered to be indicative of up-to-date individuals, can be used (Kaufman, 1978, 1979, 1989). This technique holds much promise in establishing controls to detect the degree to which professional competence is being maintained.

Second, avoid a mismatch of professionals and position requirements through effective techniques of selection and placement. One of the best ways management can capitalize on individual differences to help maintain competence is to use good selection and placement techniques (Kaufman, 1974a). The selection process is an input control on the quality of human resources, and placing newly hired professionals in positions for which they lack the appropriate abilities, motivation, or personality practically assures a decline in their competence not too long into their careers. Indeed, the first job experience is critical to professionals' subsequent career development (Kaufman, 1974a, 1974b). Only by a proper matching of candidates with positions can competence be maintained from the very start.

Third, use periodic objective appraisals of future potential and career development. When professionals are placed in permanent positions, various techniques of assessment and career counseling can be applied for individual professional development. Competence can be facilitated by monitoring professionals' careers and helping them make appropriate career decisions. Estimates of potential can be made by applying the assessment-center approach to career development (Kaufman, 1974a). Additionally, management by objectives can be used as the basis for a performance appraisal system and to direct attention to future professional development (Horgan and Floyd, 1971).

Nature of the Work

There is considerable evidence that the nature of the work is the system component most important for professional competence (Kaufman, 1974b, 1978, 1979, 1989; Kozlowski and Farr, 1988). Work assignments appear to be more critical than individual characteristics, especially since the latter are likely affected by the nature of the work (Brousseau and Prince, 1981). Management can apply several work-related techniques to facilitate competence, including the following:

1. *Use job assignments to stimulate the learning of new professional knowledge and skills.* The effective utilization of professionals is a key factor affecting their motivation and technical competence. A lack of either motivation or competence reduces a professional's capability to be productive or innovative. Professionals have a strong need to use their overall technical competence, but many remain poorly utilized (Kaufman, 1986). This problem appears to affect at least one out of every three engineers, regardless of age (Engineering Manpower Commission, 1986). Moreover, most believe their employers do not have an adequate concern for enriching their assignments to make them more challenging. A high degree of specialization among professionals may result in short-term competence, but be dysfunctional to their career development in the long run. Organizations need to improve their use of job assignments to stimulate learning new knowledge and skills. This can be accomplished by paying closer attention to job design, and should begin with the very critical entry-level positions.

2. *Select supervisors of professionals primarily on the basis of knowledge and skills that are relevant to the type of work carried out by their subordinates.* Supervisors typically control how job assign-

ments are divided among subordinates, so they are in key positions to determine the degree of utilization of professionals. However, there is evidence that utilization is a problem among professionals who work for supervisors who are not up to date and who do not base rewards on technical performance (Farr and others, 1980). Supervisors apparently contribute to the poor utilization of their professionals when they lack technical expertise and thus cannot properly evaluate the work of their subordinates. Professionals are most responsive to leadership when it is backed up by technical expertise (Kaufman, 1974a). Supervisory techniques used to encourage subordinates' competence, such as management by objectives, career counseling, and participative management, can be effective if supervisors' influence is based on their own technical competence.

3. *Provide adequate resources to professionals, including support services and up-to-date equipment, to raise the level of competence in problem solving.* Technical and clerical support, as well as up-to-date computer and other equipment, are necessary for professionals to achieve higher levels of competence (Kaufman, 1986; forthcoming). Professionals recognize the importance of such resources, but what many receive appears to be inadequate, especially technical support. This lack of support is one of the major factors contributing to poor utilization of knowledge and skills, which in turn can lead to a decline in professional competence. The way work is divided between professionals and their support services should be addressed directly, through appropriate job redesign techniques. The objective of the redesign would be to transfer the clerical and technician-level tasks to support personnel, leaving the professionals with more challenging work.

Organizational Climate

There is some indication that organizational climate contributes to professional competence, but less so than the nature of the work. Indeed, the importance of organizational climate appears to stem from its strong relationship to the nature of the work (Kaufman, 1978, 1979, 1989; Steiner and Farr, 1986). Organizational policies and practices that can affect the work of professionals to keep them up to date include the following:

1. *Enhance access to new information by increasing opportunities for professionals to communicate with colleagues on new developments.* Access to new technical information is critical, and much of the technical information needed by professionals comes from interactions with colleagues (Allen, 1977; Kaufman, 1974a, 1983). Open communication, both inside and outside the organization, is critical to staying up to date. Many professionals report that access to new information is inadequate, as are opportunities to communicate with colleagues (Kaufman, 1986; Engineering Manpower Commission, 1986). Facilitating more open communication can go far to increase the amount and quality of new technical information available. Many practices can improve communication: paying closer attention to information dissemination systems, the structure and longevity of project groups, and enhancing the role of technological gatekeepers, both internally and externally (Allen, 1977; Katz, 1982).

2. *Provide opportunities and encouragement for continuing education and career development to stimulate professional competence.* The so-called half life of a professional education has become extremely short. For example, in 1960 the half life of an engineering education was about five years, compared to more than ten years a decade earlier (Zelikoff, 1969). It is probably even lower today, given the rapid changes in technical knowledge and skills in recent years. This helps explain industry's almost exclusive focus on continuing education as the solution to maintaining competence (Kaufman, 1974a, 1975; Rosen and Jerdee, 1985). Yet, while continuing education and career development activities are important to most professionals, relatively few perceive opportunities for participation or believe that their employers encourage such activities (Kaufman, 1974a; Engineering Manpower Commission, 1986). This is all the more surprising given the widespread availability of employer support for courses.

Research results indicate the professionals who enrolled in the most technical courses tend to be more up to date

(Kaufman, 1982a). The number of hours spent reading professional journals and technical magazines and attendance at professional meetings and seminars were also associated with being more up to date. Thus, both formal and informal professional development activities were related to the maintenance of professional competence. However, course taking, while important for keeping up to date, may contribute as little as 5 percent to overall professional development (Kaufman, 1982a; Ross, 1978). Therefore, continuing education apparently makes a small but significant contribution to the maintenance of professional competence.

Commitment by top management to continuing education and other professional development activities is the key to participation in them. This commitment can be effectively translated into policies and practices that require implementation by the professionals' immediate supervisors and reinforced through job assignments and performance reviews.

3. *Expand the professionals' responsibility and autonomy by increasing their influence in the decision-making process.* The growing complexity of decision making and the problem of time compression from idea generation through marketing require increasing the influence of professionals (Kaufman, 1978). Practically all professionals desire these practices but most report that they are not characteristic of their organizations (Kaufman, 1975; Engineering Manpower Commission, 1986). This is particularly true for participation in decisions affecting the professionals' own work. By giving greater responsibility and autonomy to professionals, management can create a climate more conducive to pursuing new ideas, a climate that will stimulate the development of a more competent professional work force. This may be achieved by restructuring professional groups and individual roles in the organization, with greater emphasis on practices such as autonomous work groups and entrepreneurship.

4. *Use meaningful reward systems to motivate professionals to maintain up-to-date knowledge and skills.* One of the most difficult management problems is the development of reward systems that can foster professional competence. While money is impor-

tant to professionals, nonmonetary rewards are at least as important (Kaufman, 1974a). However, it is clear that neither type of reward is adequately provided to many professionals (Kaufman, 1986; Engineering Manpower Commission, 1986). If updating and career development are to be encouraged, commitment from top management to this goal must be present. This commitment can be translated into an effective performance review system, meaningful ladders of career advancement, and individualized rewards that reinforce behaviors directed toward maintaining competence.

Conclusions

Maintenance of professional competence is a complex organizational problem that requires a concerted, multifaceted effort on the part of management. Any one approach, no matter how well intentioned, is not likely to be very effective. Many management approaches have been suggested here; to be effective, they must be implemented in a systematic and integrative fashion. Such a prescription may require significant changes in management policy and practices.

Given the rapid pace of technological and other changes, it is not too far-fetched to envision computerized professional competence systems. They would determine individual career needs and professional competencies relative to projected changes in knowledge and skill requirements and the strategic human resource management decisions. Many organizations are likely to pursue the maintenance of professional competence as a goal, largely as a result of enlightened self-interest.

The professional labor market can serve as a powerful impetus to change. Experience has shown that shortages of professionals can stimulate organizations to introduce and support practices designed to maintain competence. All indications are that the professional labor market will experience significant shortages in the future (Finney, 1989). It may not be entirely coincidental that, concurrent with this trend, the view has begun to emerge that professionals are important organizational assets to be treated as part of the management team. As such views become the norm, the effectiveness of management techniques for maintaining a competent professional work force will be enhanced.

References

Allen, T. J. *Managing the Flow of Technology*. Cambridge, Mass.: MIT Press, 1977.

Bracker, J. S., and Pearson, J. N. "Worker Obsolescence: The Human Resource Dilemma of the '80s." *Personnel Administrator*, 1986, *31* (12), 109–116.

Brousseau, K. R., and Prince, J. B. "Job–person Dynamics: An Extension of Longitudinal Research." *Journal of Applied Psychology*, 1981, *66*, 59–62.

Dalton, G. W., and Thompson, P. H. "Accelerating Obsolescence of Older Engineers." *Harvard Business Review*, 1971, *49* (5), 57–67.

Dubin, S. S. "Obsolescence or Lifelong Education: A Choice for the Professional." *American Psychologist*, 1972a, *27*, 486–498.

Dubin, S. S. (ed.). *Professional Obsolescence*, Lexington, Mass.: Heath, 1972b.

Dubin, S. S., and Cohen, D. M. "Motivation to Update from a Systems Approach." *Engineering Education*, 1970, *60* (5), 366–368.

Engineering Manpower Commission. *Toward the More Effective Utilization of American Engineers*. Washington: American Association of Engineering Societies, 1986.

Farr, J. L., and others. *Relationships Among Individual Motivation, Work Environment and Updating of Engineers*. University Park: Pennsylvania State University, 1980.

Finney, M. I. "The ASPA Labor Shortage Survey." *Personnel Administrator*, 1989, *34* (2), 35–42.

Fossum, J. A., Arvey, R. D., Paradise, C. A., and Robbins, N. E. "Modeling the Skills Obsolescence Process: A Psychological/ Economic Integration." *Academy of Management Review*, 1986, *11* (2), 362–374.

Horgan, N. J., and Floyd, R. P. "An MBO Approach to Prevent

Technical Obsolescence." *Personnel Journal*, 1971, *50* (9), 686–692.

Katz, D., and Kahn, R. *The Social Psychology of Organizations*. New York: Wiley, 1978.

Katz, R. *Career Issues in Human Resource Management*. Englewood Cliffs, N.J.: Prentice-Hall, 1982.

Kaufman, H. G. "A Critical Incident Study of Personal Characteristics Associated with Technical Obsolescence Among Engineers." *Studies in Personnel Psychology*, 1973, *5*, 63–67.

Kaufman, H. G. *Obsolescence and Professional Career Development*, New York: AMACOM, 1974a.

Kaufman, H. G. "Relationship of Early Work Challenge to Job Performance, Professional Contributions, and Competence of Engineers." *Journal of Applied Psychology*, 1974b, *59* (3), 377–379.

Kaufman, H. G. (ed.). *Career Management: A Guide to Combating Obsolescence*. New York: IEEE Press/Wiley-Interscience, 1975.

Kaufman, H. G. "Technical Obsolescence: An Empirical Analysis of Its Causes and How Engineers Cope with It." *Proceedings of the 86th Annual Conference of the American Society for Engineering Education*, Washington, D.C., 1978.

Kaufman, H. G. "Technical Obsolescence: Work and Organizations Are the Key." *Engineering Education*, 1979, *68*, 826–830.

Kaufman, H. G. "Continuing Professional Development at Mid-career." *Proceedings, 1982 College Industry Education Conference of the American Society for Engineering Education*, Washington, D.C., 1982a.

Kaufman, H. G. *Professionals in Search of Work: Coping with the Stress of Job Loss and Underemployment*. New York: Wiley-Interscience, 1982b.

Kaufman, H. G. "Factors Related to Use of Technical Information in Engineering Problem Solving." Report to National Science Foundation, 1983.

Kaufman, H. G. "A Review of Previous Studies Relating to Engineering Utilization." In Engineering Manpower Commission, *Toward the More Effective Utilization of American Engineers*. Washington: American Association of Engineering Societies, 1986.

Kaufman, H. G. "Obsolescence of Technical Professionals: A Measure and a Model." *Applied Psychology: An International Review*, 1989, *38* (1), 73–85.

Kaufman, H. G. "Managing the Effective Utilization of Engineers: A Systems Model Approach." In D. Kocaoglu (ed.), *Handbook of Engineering Management*. New York: Wiley-Interscience, forthcoming.

Kozlowski, S.W.J., and Farr, J. L. "An Integrative Model of Updating and Performance." *Human Performance*, 1988, *1*, 5–29.

Mali, P. "Measurement of Obsolescence in Engineering Practitioners." In H. G. Kaufman (ed.), *Career Management: A Guide to Combating Obsolescence*. New York: IEEE Press/Wiley-Interscience, 1975.

National Research Council. *Continuing Education of Engineers*, Washington: National Academy Press, 1985.

National Science Foundation. *Continuing Education in Science and Engineering*. Washington: U.S. Government Printing Office, 1978.

Roney, J. G. *Report on First Conference on Occupational Obsolescence*. Menlo Park, Calif.: Stanford Research Institute, 1966.

Rosen, B., and Jerdee, T. H. "A Model Program for Combating Employee Obsolescence." *Personnel Administrator*, 1985, *30* (3), 86–92.

Ross, S. S. "(Continuing Education) = (.05) (Career Management)." *New Engineer*, Aug./Sept. 1978, pp. 31–39.

Steiner, D. D., and Farr, J. L. "Career Goals, Organizational Reward Systems and Technical Updating in Engineers." *Journal of Occupational Psychology*, 1986, *59*, 13–24.

Zelikoff, S. B. "On the Obsolescence and Retraining of Engineering Personnel." *Training and Development Journal*, May 1969, pp. 3–15.

12

Robert P. Sprafkin
Arnold P. Goldstein

Using Behavioral Modeling to Enhance Professional Competence

The use of behavior modeling (also referred to as social skills training) to enhance professional competence is little over a decade old (Decker and Nathan, 1985). As the name implies, its emphasis has been on presenting, or modeling, specific behaviors, rather than teaching work-related attitudes or principles. Its appeal has been its efficiency and effectiveness. To understand the development of generic approaches to behavior modeling for the purpose of enhancing professional competence, it is useful to trace the evolution of one particular approach, which we call structured learning. This approach exemplifies the development of the field and embodies the most widely used procedures.

Development of the Structured Learning Approach

The training of professionals was not the initial focus of structured learning. However, it immediately became clear that to implement the goals of structured learning, people would need to be trained in its procedures.

Origins in Therapy Design. Structured learning began in the early 1970s in the United States with a concern for the apparent inadequacy of existing helping interventions, particularly psychotherapy, for low-income patients. We found that a patient's social class was a significant factor in determining the efficacy of various psychotherapeutic treatments.

The lower-social-class patient often fares poorly in psychotherapy because the type of therapy we were most prone to offer — traditional, verbal, insight-oriented psychotherapy — is almost singularly a middle-class enterprise. Middle-class patients come to therapy expecting to explore their inner world and to participate actively in seeking insight. They tend to form a favorable therapeutic relationship, remain in treatment for an extended period, and, about two-thirds of the time, derive benefit.

Our own clinical and research interests have been with another type of patient: lower or working class, often middle-aged or older, physically ordinary or unattractive, verbally reticent, intellectually unexceptional, and vocationally unsuccessful or marginal. This person seeks psychotherapy often not with full volition, and expects not introspective behavior but active guidance from the therapist. This patient often views the problem as physical in nature, and so expects physical or drug therapies. This person tends to remain in treatment very briefly, form a poor therapeutic relationship, and derives minimal benefit from psychotherapy.

Structured learning reflects an attempt to try to develop a therapy to fit this lower-class patient. To determine the nature of such an approach, we turned primarily to developmental psychology research on child rearing and sociological writing on social class and life-styles. These bodies of literature reveal consistently that lower-class child rearing and life-style, with their emphases on action, motor behavior, consequences rather than intentions, and their reliance on external example and authority and restricted verbal code, ill prepare people for successful involvement in traditional psychotherapy, but, we speculated

(Goldstein, 1973), might prepare them well for treatment geared to their life-style.

This new treatment would be brief, concrete, behavioral, actional, authoritatively administered; it would require imitation of specific overt examples, teach role-taking skills, and provide frequent reinforcement for seldom-used but adaptive skill behaviors. These are the defining characteristics of structured learning, whose major procedures are modeling, role playing, performance feedback, and transfer training. The patient (the trainee) is provided with specific, detailed, frequent, and vivid displays of adaptive behavior or of specific skills in which he or she is deficient (modeling); given considerable opportunity and encouragement to practice the modeled behaviors (role playing); provided with positive feedback, approval, or reward for successful enactments (performance feedback); and required to engage in activities that enhance the likelihood that the behaviors taught in the therapy room will be used effectively in real life (transfer training).

Deinstitutionalization and Skill Deficiency. At the very time we were developing structured learning, a major movement was underway in the United States — deinstitutionalization, moving chronic adult mental patients, 85 percent of whom were socioeconomically lower or working class, from public mental hospitals into the community. Many newly discharged individuals came into the community ill prepared to meet even the routine minor demands of daily living. Often they had been too schizoid, incompetent, or unskilled in adolescence and early adulthood to function effectively in the community, so they entered mental hospitals and remained there for ten, twenty, or thirty years. Their "training" during hospitalization involved socialization into the "good patient" role, what others have described as a colonization effect: they were not taught what one needs to function outside the hospital in the real and often demanding world. Rather, they learned apathy, withdrawal, dependency, and passivity.

This was the challenge we hoped to address in our initial implementation of structured learning. As we developed techniques for use with these patients, we also developed corresponding techniques for training staff. These initial attempts with chronic psychiatric patients and their trainers were repeated, with modifications, with several other trainer–trainee groups.

Structured Learning Procedures

Modeling

Structured learning requires first that trainees be exposed to expertly portrayed examples of specific skilled behaviors we wish them to learn. To accomplish this, we developed a library of modeling displays using audiocassettes. Each display depicts a different daily living skill, and each skill is broken down into four to six behavioral steps ("learning points"). Each modeling display consists of several vignettes in which actors expertly portray the steps of that skill in a variety of community, hospital, and transitional settings. Each structured learning group consists of six to twelve trainees, selected on the basis of their shared skill deficiencies.

Trainers describe the first skill to be taught and hand out skill cards that show the name of the skill and its behavioral steps. The first modeling tape is then played. Trainees are told to listen closely to the way the actors follow the behavioral steps. For example, the "learning points," or behavioral steps, of the skill labeled "starting a conversation" are:

1. Choose the right place and time.
2. Greet the other person.
3. Make small talk.
4. Judge if the other person is listening and wants to talk to you.
5. Open the main topic you want to talk about.

Role Playing

After the tape is played, a brief, spontaneous discussion almost invariably follows. Trainees comment on the steps, the actors, and very often on how the situation occurs in their own lives. Since the primary goal of role playing in structured learning is to encourage realistic rehearsal, trainees' statements about their problems using the skill can often develop into material for their first role play.

To enhance the realism of the portrayal, the structured learning trainer has the trainee (now the main actor) choose a second trainee (co-actor) to play the significant other person who is relevant to the skill problem. One of the group's two trainers is responsible for keeping a record of who has played which role, and for which skills, to be sure that all participate about equally. The essential procedure is that the main actor seeks to enact the steps that have just been modeled.

The main actor is asked to describe briefly the real problem situation and the real people involved in it. During the role play, the co-actor is called by the name of the main actor's significant other. One trainer instructs the role players to begin.

At this point, the trainers' main responsibility is to be sure the main actor keeps role playing and attempts to follow the behavioral steps while doing so. If the main actor "breaks role" and begins making comments or explaining the background events, the trainers firmly instruct him to resume his role. One trainer positions herself near the chalkboard and points to each step, in turn, as the role play unfolds, making sure none is either missed or enacted out of order. If the trainers or actors feel the role play is not progressing well and wish to start over, this is appropriate. Observers are instructed to hold their comments until the role play is completed.

The role playing continues until all trainees have had an opportunity to participate, even if all the same steps must be carried over to a second or third session. While the framework (behavioral steps) of each role play in the series remains the same, the actual content can and should change from role play to role play. It is the problem as it actually occurs, or could occur, in each trainee's real-life environment that forms the content of the given role play. When the role playing is completed, each trainee should be better armed to act appropriately in the given reality situation.

Performance Feedback

A brief feedback period follows each role play. The goals are to let the main actor know how well he or she followed the steps or departed from them, to explore the psychological impact of the enactment on the co-actor, and to provide the main actor with encouragement to try the skill in real life.

In these critiques, it is crucial that the behavioral focus of structured learning be maintained. Comments must point to the presence or absence of specific, concrete behaviors, and not take the form of general evaluative comments or broad generalities.

Transfer of Training

Several aspects of the training sessions described above had, as their primary purpose, transferring the learning in the therapy setting to the trainee's real-life environment.

Provision of General Principles. It has been demonstrated that transfer of training is facilitated when trainees are provided with general mediating principles that govern successful performance of the training tasks. This procedure has typically been accomplished in laboratory contexts by providing subjects with the concepts or rationales that explain the stimulus-response relationships that operate in both the training and application settings. Structured learning trainees are given general principles about the skills in oral, pictorial, and written form. An example of a general principle is the idea that certain situations require use of the skill called "starting a conversation."

Overlearning. Overlearning is a procedure by which learning is extended over more trials than are necessary, to produce initial changes in the trainee's behavior. In a typical structured learning session the overlearning, or repetition of successful skill enactment, is quite substantial. The given skill is taught and its behavioral steps are modeled several times, role-played one or more times by the trainee, observed by the trainee as all the

other group members role-play it, read by the trainee from a
chalkboard and the skill card, written by the trainee in the
trainee's notebook, practiced in vivo one or more times by the
trainee as part of the formal homework assignment, practiced in
vivo one or more times by the trainee in response to adult or
peer learner coaching, and practiced in vivo one or more times
by the trainee in response to skill-oriented, intrinsically interesting stimuli introduced into the real-life environment.

Identical Elements. In perhaps the earliest experimental concern
with transfer enhancement, Thorndike and Woodworth (1901)
concluded that when one habit had a facilitative effect on another, it was because they shared identical elements. More recently, Ellis (1965) and Osgood (1953) have emphasized the
importance of similarity between stimulus aspects of the training and application tasks. The greater the similarity of stimuli in
the structured learning setting and the setting where the skill is
to be applied, the more likely the transfer.

The "real-lifeness" of structured learning is expressed in a
number of ways: (1) the relevant and realistic portrayal of situations in the modeling displays, all designed to be highly similar
to what trainees face in their daily lives; (2) the physical props
used in the role-playing setting, similar to real-life settings;
(3) coaching the co-actors or protagonists to be similar to real-
life figures; (4) the way the role plays themselves are conducted,
as close as possible to real life; (5) role-play implementation,
which provides behavioral rehearsal of each skill as the trainee
actually plans to employ it; (6) the in vivo homework assignments, coached and practiced during training; and (7) the training as a group patients who live together (such as all the members of a department).

Real-life Reinforcement. Given successful implementation of
structured learning procedures and the transfer procedures,
positive transfer may still fail to occur. As Agras (1967), Gruber
(1971), Patterson and Anderson (1964), Tharp and Wetzel
(1969), and dozens of other investigators have shown, perfor-

mance of newly learned skills in application settings is very much at the mercy of real-life reinforcement contingencies.

We have found it useful to implement, outside the structured learning setting, several supplemental programs that can help provide the rewards trainees need so that their new behaviors are maintained. Those programs include both external social reward (provided by people in the trainee's real-life environment) and self-reward.

To train structured learning trainers who may work with a variety of populations, we have used the same procedures we use with trainees: modeling, role playing, performance feedback, and transfer training. Potential trainers are taught structured learning procedures by participating as trainees in a structured learning group, where they are instructed to adopt the characteristics of typical trainees. First, they are exposed to models of structured learning sessions (live or recorded), they role-play, taking turns in both trainer and trainee roles, they receive feedback on their performances, and they are given instructions that facilitate transfer of training (homework, continued practice, trial groups, and the like).

Applications: Trainer and Trainee Population

As mentioned, the development and most extensive application of structured learning was with mental health professionals and paraprofessionals who were updating their skills in order to work more appropriately with chronic psychiatric patients. Shortly after that work began, supervisors in industrial settings were targeted for structured learning training.

In 1974 Goldstein and Sorcher published *Changing Supervisor Behavior*, the first application of structured learning procedures (there called applied learning) to supervisory problems in industry. These problems included such challenges as improving worker morale, improving productivity, reducing absenteeism and turnover, and the like. Most important, these chronic supervisory problems were conceptualized as proficiencies that could be taught as concrete behaviors. Many previous efforts at supervisory training generally failed because they tended to focus on theoretical or attitudinal issues, rather than on how to apply specific supervisory skills. The implication for updating of supervisory skills in industry was clear: one needs to learn and apply appropriate supervisory behaviors primarily; attitude change may also occur secondarily.

As Figure 12.1 illustrates, supervisors are unlikely to change their behavior toward employees simply because someone convinces them that employees require considerate treatment. Other factors generally preclude behavior change, such as the lack of time to give recognition, lack of concern about the well-being of line employees, or lack of knowledge of how to actually behave differently. But systematically showing supervisors how to change their behavior, and giving them practice and encouragement for these changes, may bring about change in both behavior and attitude.

Some of the specific skills taught to supervisors include:

1. Orienting a new employee.
2. Teaching the job.
3. Motivating the poor performer.
4. Correcting inadequate work quantity.
5. Correcting inadequate work quality.
6. Reducing absenteeism among disadvantaged workers.
7. Reducing turnover among disadvantaged workers.
8. Handling the racial discrimination complaint.
9. Handling the reverse discrimination complaint.
10. Reducing resentment of the female supervisor.
11. Discussing personal work habits with an employee.
12. Discussing formal corrective action with an employee.
13. Giving recognition to the average employee.
14. Overcoming resistance to change.
15. Reducing evaluation resistance.
16. Delegating responsibility.
17. Conducting a performance review.

An example of a modeling display for industry foremen follows. The situation is "motivating the poor performer." The

Figure 12.1. Traditional and Revised Models of Behavior Change.

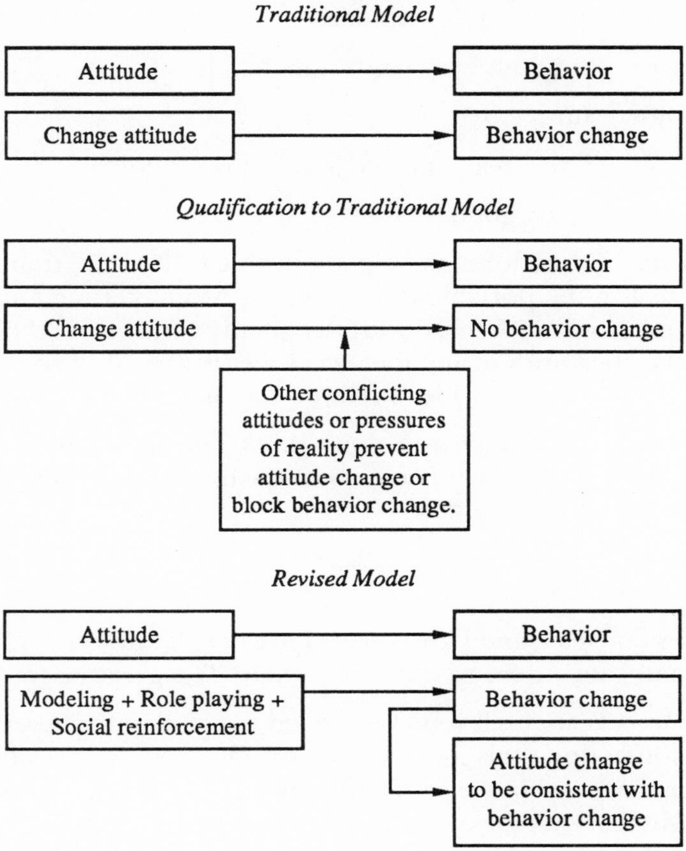

Traditional Model

Attitude	⟶	Behavior
Change attitude	⟶	Behavior change

Qualification to Traditional Model

Attitude	⟶	Behavior
Change attitude	⟶	No behavior change

Other conflicting attitudes or pressures of reality prevent attitude change or block behavior change.

Revised Model

Attitude	⟶	Behavior
Modeling + Role playing + Social reinforcement	⟶	Behavior change
		Attitude change to be consistent with behavior change

four learning points were portrayed in film vignettes using the following script.

Narrator: Hello, I'm Fred Harris, plant manager. In the film you are about to see you will find one of my very effective foremen talking to one of his workers about his performance. In their discussion the foreman will follow certain learning points:

1. Focus on the problem, not the employee.
2. Ask for his help and discuss his ideas on how to solve the problem.

3. Come to an agreement on steps to be taken by each of you.
4. Plan a specific follow-up date.

Foreman: John, can I see you a minute, please?

Employee: Sure.

Foreman: Have a seat will you, John? How's it going?

Employee: Pretty good.

Foreman: Great. John, we've got a problem. The, uh, transmission seal in the portable unit. . . we're just not getting enough vacuum. Now I've checked with our quality control and they say that the aperture size and the size of the seal are okay, so it's not that. Do you have any idea what it might be?

Employee: Uh, I hope you don't think I'm the problem. You know those, those parts come down the line so fast you're lucky to get 'em on there at all.

Foreman: Yeah. Uh, John, let's see, you've been with us about three years, haven't you?

Employee: Yeah, and I know what I'm doing. I know that it's not me that's causing the trouble down there. The parts are too fast.

Foreman: Yeah, I tell you I've noticed you in that three years—that you've done this job very well. In fact, you do it probably better than anybody else. That's why I called you in, John. I, I thought that with the two of us together we could get to the heart of this problem. And, I'd like. . . Now, the speed is the same. You're talking about speed—the speed is the same as it's been for the past couple of years. Now can you think of anything else we might do?

Employee: Well, possibly it could be the adhesive used to seal the rim. I. . .

Foreman: Oh yeah, what about the adhesive?

Employee: I think it's a little watery. I, I found it to be watery.

Foreman: All right. I didn't think about that. I'm gonna have, uh, I'm gonna have Jim Taylor check on that this week, some time.

Now is there anything else that you can think of that might be the problem?

Employee: Yeah, there's something that I would like to talk to you about. I think that, I think the bolts, the bolts coming down from section C, I don't think they're on tightly, and I think that's really affecting it.

Foreman: Uh-huh, section C is where the bolts are tightened, and if they're not tightened enough it would get loose on you.

Employee: Uh, I know.

Foreman: Well, I'm gonna check on that myself. I, I'm surprised at that. Now I'll check on that and I'll have Jim Taylor check on the adhesive. Now, is that it? Can you think of anything else?

Employee: I think, I think that's it. I think that's what he could do.

Foreman: I tell you what I'd like to do, John. I'd like to follow up with you, uh, let's say Thursday.

Employee: Thursday? All right.

Foreman: Okay now, I'm gonna come by your work area on Thursday about two o'clock and we'll take a look at this thing. In the meantime, John, I'd appreciate it if you'd check these units as they're coming through and take a look at the adhesive and the bolts and, uh, be sure that the quality on those is a little better. Well, I sure appreciate your doing that.

Each film was followed by a period of brief discussion and extended role playing, together lasting over an hour and a half. The discussions were largely concerned with fitting the learning points of each film to the realities of each trainee's work setting, to maximize both learning and transfer. During the first and second role-playing sessions, supervisors were at times awkward and tended to follow their own intuition instead of the specified behaviors shown in the modeling film and listed on the blackboard. However, rather rapidly, the foremen began to display the modeled behaviors for each situation and to adapt their own

style and ideas to them, perhaps partly to get a favorable response from their counterpart who was playing the role of an
employee, in addition to approval from the instructor and the
other foremen who were observing (Goldstein and Sorcher,
1974, pp. 75–77).

Although the basic structured learning procedures are
the same for different target populations, the specific trainer
techniques had to be modified somewhat to respond to their
characteristics. For example, trainers working with adolescents
often need to prepare more active, engaging modeling displays,
and facilitate faster group interactions than trainers working
with chronic psychiatric patients, who tend to be more passive.

Structured learning has been used with a variety of
groups, and its use as a tool for professional development has
been either direct or indirect. That is, it has been used directly to
teach the skills necessary for enhancing professional competence, and it has been used indirectly, as those who are learning
to be structured learning trainers are also enhancing their
professional skills.

To use structured learning techniques directly to affect
professional development assumes that trainees are deficient in
skills that, if learned, would enable them to function more
effectively in their job. It is not assumed that these trainees will
use structured learning procedures at work, but that they will
function more adequately because they learned certain skills via
structured learning. Some examples of this direct use of structured learning to update or enhance skills include teaching the
skill of empathy to nurses (Goldstein and Goedhart, 1973),
teaching counselors the skill of confrontation (Rosenthal, 1975),
teaching police officers skills in calming situations and gathering relevant information (Goldstein, Monti, Sardino, and Green,
1979), and hostage negotiation (Miron and Goldstein, 1979),
and teaching industrial supervisors relevant managerial skills
(Goldstein and Sorcher, 1974).

Direct teaching of skills for professional development is
illustrated with the following, taken from work with police cited
just above. Each skill is taught to police officers using structured
learning techniques. Here are four examples:

1. Observing and protecting against threats to your safety
   a. Consider your prior experience on similar calls.
   b. Anticipate that the unexpected may actually happen.
   c. Form a tentative plan of action.
2. Calming the situation
   a. Observe and neutralize threats to your safety.
   b. Create a first impression of nonhostile authority.
   c. Calm the emotional citizen.
3. Gathering relevant information
   a. Explain to the citizen what you want him to discuss with you and why.
   b. Interview the citizen so as to gain details of the crisis as clearly as possible.
   c. Show that you understand the citizen's statements and give accurate answers to his questions.
   d. Revise your plan of action if appropriate.
4. Taking appropriate action
   a. Carefully explain your plan of action to the citizen.
   b. Check that the citizen understands and agrees with your plan of action.
   c. Carry out your plan of action.

The indirect use of structured learning for professional development involves training trainers to use structured learning techniques with skill-deficient populations. Professional development occurs in the form of acquiring trainer skills, of becoming a structured learning trainer. And, as we saw earlier, one is taught these trainer skills by participating in a role-played structured learning group. The two most widely used indirect applications of structured learning have been to train trainers to work with psychiatric patients and to work with adolescents. Trainers have been taught to use structured learning techniques with elderly patients (Hoyer, Lopez, and Goldstein, 1981), mentally retarded children (Fleming, 1976), elementary school children (McGinnis and Goldstein, 1984), and child-abusing parents (Solomon, 1978), to mention a few.

Future Directions

What does the future hold for structured learning and other behavior-modeling techniques as vehicles for enhancing professional development? Structured learning will continue to be used to teach specific skills necessary to improve one's performance within an occupation. By defining effective work performance in terms of specific skills and then teaching those skills directly, we are able to upgrade workers' effectiveness. Also, there is impressive evidence that structured learning procedures are useful for teaching specific skills. Indirectly, structured learning may be employed with other groups, clinical and nonclinical. As this happens, additional trainers will have to be trained. Finally, structured learning is likely to be combined with other effective change techniques, as evidenced by recent work with aggressive adolescents (Goldstein and Glick, 1987). In this tailored or prescriptive application of structured learning, youth learn how to handle conflict situations skillfully, how to reduce the likelihood that they will respond aggressively (anger management training), and *why* to respond in the skilled rather than the aggressive manner (moral reasoning training). With such a goal-targeted, multi-modal strategy, the future use of structured learning appears quite promising.

References

Agras, W. S. "Transfer During Systematic Desensitization Therapy." *Behavior Research and Therapy*, 1967, 5, 193–199.

Decker, P. J., and Nathan, B. R. *Behavior Modeling Training: Principles and Application.* New York: Praeger, 1985.

Ellis, H. *The Transfer of Learning.* New York: Macmillan, 1965.

Fleming, E. R. "Training Passive and Aggressive Educable Mentally Retarded Children for Assertive Behaviors Using Three Types of Structured Learning Training." Unpublished doctoral dissertation, Syracuse University, 1976.

Goldstein, A. P. *Structure Learning Therapy: Toward a Psychotherapy for the Poor.* New York: Academic Press, 1973.

Goldstein, A. P., and Glick, B. *Aggression Replacement Training.* Champaign, Ill.: Research Press, 1987.

Goldstein, A. P., and Goedhart, A. "The Use of Structured Learning for Empathy Enhancement in Paraprofessional Psychotherapist Training." *Journal of Community Psychology,* 1973, *3,* 168–173.

Goldstein, A. P., Monti, P. J., Sardino, T. J., and Green, D. J. *Police Crisis Intervention.* Elmsford, N.Y.: Pergamon Press, 1979.

Goldstein, A. P., and Sorcher, M. *Changing Supervisor Behavior.* Elmsford, N.Y.: Pergamon Press, 1974.

Gruber, R. P. "Behavior Therapy: Problems in Generalization." *Behavior Therapy,* 1971, *2,* 361–368.

Hoyer, W. J., Lopez, M. A., and Goldstein, A. P. "Correlates of Social Skill Acquisition and Transfer by Elderly Patients." Unpublished manuscript, Syracuse University, 1981.

McGinnis, E., and Goldstein, A. P. *Skillstreaming the Elementary School Child.* Champaign, Ill.: Research Press, 1984.

Miron, H., and Goldstein, A. P. *Hostage.* Elmsford, N.Y.: Pergamon Press, 1979.

Osgood, C. E. *Method and Theory in Experimental Psychology.* New York: Oxford University Press, 1953.

Patterson, G. R., and Anderson, D. "Peers as Social Reinforcers." *Child Development,* 1964, *35,* 956–960.

Rosenthal, N. R. "Matching Trainees' Conceptual Level and Training Approaches: A Study in the Acquisition and Enhancement of Confrontation Skills." Unpublished doctoral dissertation, Syracuse University, 1975.

Solomon, E. J. "Structured Learning Therapy with Abusive Parents: Training in Self-control." Unpublished doctoral dissertation, Syracuse University, 1978.

Tharp, R. G., and Wetzel, R. J. *Behavior Modification in the Natural Environment.* New York: Academic Press, 1969.

Thorndike, E. L., and Woodworth, R. S. "The Influence of Improvement in One Mental Function upon the Efficiency of Other Functions." *Psychological Review,* 1901, *8,* 247–261.

13

Lois Granick
Alain Y. Dessaint
Gary R. VandenBos

How Information Systems
Can Help Build
Professional Competence

One hundred years ago the number of professionals in any particular field was but a tiny fraction of what it is today. Keeping abreast of developments in one's discipline consisted of attending an occasional meeting, regular perusal of four or five journals, and correspondence or conversation with a few colleagues. Even fifty years ago many professionals were successfully following this pattern in spite of the fact that the trends leading to today's "information explosion" were already quite apparent. More recent decades have seen the rapid growth of specialties and subspecialties within disciplines, an emerging internationalism in science and technology, and the appearance of entirely new disciplines burgeoning from the boundaries between formerly discrete knowledge bases. Today's professional enjoys a longer productive career, experiences more rapid change, is a part of a vastly expanded collegial peer group, and is both a participant in and heir to the ever-increasing amount of available information.

While the task of professional updating is more complex in today's environment, the same forces that fueled the information explosion have made possible the generation of the tools with which to manage and control it. An understanding of those tools and their appropriateness to a variety of applications is essential if today's professional expects to obtain timely and complete information.

The purpose of this chapter is to define some of the varying information needs a professional might identify; to discuss information systems, both printed and electronic, as mechanisms for professional updating; to describe these systems, particularly the electronic, in enough detail to permit a potential user to make informed choices; and to project from the current status to some future trends for use of information systems.

Information Needs

Interaction of Level of Expertise and Informational Needs Assessment. A professional in a given discipline has been trained in a body of knowledge that is composed of many interrelated subareas. As a result of professional (usually graduate) training, the individual achieves a mix of general understanding, competence, or expertise in these subareas that ultimately defines the level of specialization attained.

For example, the dentistry student will study and become knowledgeable about the prevention, diagnosis, and treatment of disorders of the teeth and adjacent tissues of the head, neck, and mouth. Some of the subareas that interrelate to form the total body of knowledge needed for the practice of dentistry include tooth preservation, alignment, rebuilding, and extraction; artificial teeth (bridge and dentures); treatment of gum disease; repair of bones and joints; oral surgery; diagnostic techniques, such as the use and interpretation of X-rays; and pain suppression. Even in this very incomplete list, it is apparent that the subareas represent potential specialty fields within dentistry and are themselves composed of many other interrelated sub-subareas of knowledge. After completing formal training, most professionals find that the balance among the many subareas begins to change. Meaningful specialization of knowledge and proficiency begins in a few core and subspecialty areas.

These usually increase in depth and breadth of knowledge and skills through the work experience, while through nonuse or nonexposure, expertise in other areas remains unchanged or deteriorates.

In terms of current knowledge and technical skill, a professional might be conceptualized within a four-category classification: (1) expert, (2) specialist, (3) generalist, and (4) underinformed or holding only noncurrent information. The appropriate classification of any given professional in a particular subarea will vary. No professional is an "expert" in all aspects of his or her profession. A typical pattern of competency might be: one or two subareas of expertise, four or five subareas of specialization, twenty to forty sub-subareas of general or average competency, and fifty-five to seventy-five sub-subareas of vague familiarity and under-informedness.

The nature of professional updating any individual may need will, therefore, vary by subarea and be related to current competency in that subarea. It is apparent, then, that there are also at least four types of updating needs. First, for an "expert" area, there is a requirement to have immediate involvement in the development of the latest scientific knowledge or technical applications, as well as prepublication knowledge of the current efforts of other experts in the primary area of subspecialization. Second, for a "specialist" area, there is a need to have immediate access to the five or six technical journals representing the subspecialty area, immediate access to the ten or twelve best highly technical books published each year in that subspecialty area, and regular attendance at the two or three specialized conferences held each year in the subspecialty area. Third, for a "generalist" area (representing typical or acceptable competency), information needs would include regular access to general overviews and advances and updates in a range of areas, most often obtained from general professional journals and conventions and with only occasional need for a specialty journal or a highly technical specialized book. Fourth, for those subareas in which knowledge is not current, the professional is, by definition, underinformed. Here, there is a need for access to general material that reintroduces the particular subspecialty area in which knowledge and skill levels have not been maintained, either because of nonuse or the lack of routine updating.

Professionals in all four levels are *already* using different methods and frequency of knowledge acquisition. They are *already* using a varied mix of knowledge acquisition means for different subareas, as their level of competency or involvement varies. The way computerized information systems can be used by a given professional will also vary with differing levels of competency or differing informational needs.

These comments do not, to a large extent, address the information needs of one who wishes to learn about completely new innovations, applications, and knowledge. A recent example of such a need can be found in the legal profession. A rapidly growing area, referred to as mental health law, has emerged as a result of landmark legal decisions handed down during the 1960s and 1970s (and the subsequent enactment of laws related to mental health issues by various legislative bodies). Changes such as these reflect the emergence of new nodes of information within a profession or a change in the boundary lines of a particular discipline. For the average professional who has not participated in carving out such a new subarea, updating actually constitutes new learning.

Beginning the Information Acquisition Process. Most professionals are familiar (or at least acquainted) with the abstracting and indexing services that report on the literature of their discipline. For some, that introduction occurred during their formal education. If the acquaintance was not pursued, today's professional may be unaware of the revolution in information dissemination that began in the late 1960s. Computerized versions of these indexes and collections of abstracts (bibliographic data bases) became available through remote terminal access to large mainframe computers. With the growth of telecommunications and data storage technology, the online information industry was well established by the mid 1970s.

As a new idea appears, it may be discussed locally at a colloquium and then nationally at a conference. It may then appear in a conference proceeding or a technical report. Eventually an article will be published in a scientific journal, and this may later be cited in an annual review of literature or similar state-of-the-art review. Finally, the concept may be extensively described in a book or summarized in standard textbooks. Bates (1984) has detailed this process, and has illustrated how "hard-copy" dissemination and computerized information systems parallel each other (see Figure 13.1). Schmittroth's directory (1982–83), while not exhaustive, lists more than 1,500 such "secondary" services, including abstracting journals, indexes, digests, bibliographies, and catalogs.

The Role of Computerized Information Systems

Professional updating needs can be served by systematic collections of information (abstracting and indexing services, printed or online), regardless of category. For the "expert," even when most of what is being published is known in advance, small bits of information may be missed because new work is being done by individuals not well known or in the current mainstream, or simply because a meeting was not attended. Secondary information systems can pull together references on the desired topic for the time period since the last such accumulation, permitting rapid identification of really new material. State-of-the-art literature reviews are facilitated by these systems as well.

While "specialists" regularly read the relevant journals in their specific subarea, abstracting systems can play a critical role in locating the 40 to 65 percent of material related to their specialty that was published in more general professional journals. For such specialists, computerized secondary information systems may be essential for gathering together all the references and material that are critical to the maintenance of truly comprehensive knowledge.

Professionals with "generalist" status in a given subarea regularly read a range of general professional books and journals. They do not need computerized abstracting systems to provide comprehensive bibliographic listings in a given area. They do need, however, a reasonably sized representative sampling of literature reviews, summaries, and commentaries of the given subarea. (Generalists can readily articulate the nature of problems and describe and use a range of varying but professionally acceptable solutions.) For them, review journals (such as *Psychological Bulletin*), annual edited volumes, and current-awareness publications (such as a PsycSCAN); and databases are frequent sources of information. A typical pattern would also include specialized conferences, continuing education workshops, on-the-job supervision, peer supervision, and information exchange.

Professionals who are no longer reasonably informed in a particular subarea need reeducation. They must move to more specialized summaries of targeted issues, to more detailed technical and research analyses. There is a need for conceptual "road maps" to begin the update process. Computerized information services can be particularly useful in identifying appropriate resources for specific needs. Information services help identify recent state-of-the-art literature reviews published in journals and current comprehensive handbooks to specific subareas. After such material is studied, computerized information services can again be used to obtain references to more selective, specialized, and focused material. These individuals also may use continuing education workshops, specialized instructional conferences, or even formal courses as vehicles for refamiliarizing and initially updating themselves in a particular area.

The Benefits of Computerized Information Systems. Though many databases are also available in hard copy (print), online information retrieval is generally considered much superior to manual searching. Powerful timesharing computers permit multiple users to carry on simultaneous searches through remote terminals. Interactive computer programs (software) allow the searcher and the computer to engage in two-way conversations. Online allows many more access points for searching; it is possible, for example, to search for author affiliation, document type, journal title, date of publication, language, and many other data points. Most databases permit free-text searching, where a meaningful word or phrase can be located in any part of the record including title and abstract. Searching with the use of

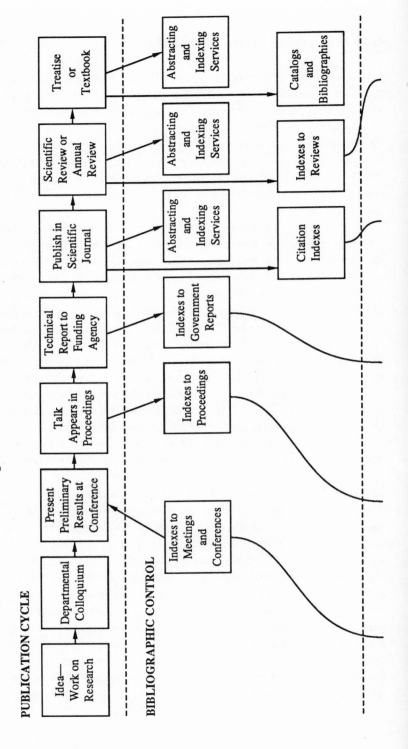

Figure 13.1. The Scientific Publication Cycle.

Figure 13.1. The Scientific Publication Cycle, Cont'd.

EXAMPLES

Scientific Meetings International Congress Calendar World Meetings: United States and Canada Forthcoming International Scientific and Technical Conferences	Index to Scientific and Technical Proceedings® (also online) Index to Social Science and Humanities Proceedings® Index of Conference Proceedings Received (British Library) Directory of Published Proceedings Proceedings in Print Conference Papers Index (also online)	Government Reports Announcement and Index (NTIS online) Scientific and Technical Aerospace Reports (NTIS online) Energy Research Abstracts (DOE or NTIS online) ERIC Resources in Education (ERIC online)	Science Citation Index® (also online) Social Sciences Citation Index® (also online)

Index to Scientific Reviews™

Note: Examples of abstracting and indexing services, catalogs, and bibliographies are not provided since these classes of resource are well known and very numerous.

From M. J. Bates, "Locating Elusive Science Information," *Special Libraries*, 1984, 75 (2), 116. Reprinted by permission.

Boolean operators ("and," "or," "not") and proximity (retrieve a record containing term A only if it occurs within *n* words of term B) allows the searcher to find connections between subject matters not only much more quickly but to a far greater level of complexity than manual searching. Rapid access storage devices continue to grow in capacity and reliability while decreasing in per-unit storage costs. Microcomputers and computer terminals (usually a typewriterlike keyboard and a CRT display similar to a domestic TV set) can transmit and receive almost instantaneously, and they are almost daily becoming more compact, portable, and inexpensive. Finally, telecommunications networks provide fast, round-the-clock access to remote computers at moderate cost.

The benefits of computerized databases have been quickly recognized by users. It is estimated that there were 1 million online searches in 1975; the annual number had grown to 18 million by 1985 (Williams, 1986b). The number of online users has also increased—from about 50,000 (mostly stockbrokers and librarians) in 1975 to more than 2 million in 1987 ("Selected Databases," 1987).

It is currently estimated that between 6,000 and 7,000 articles are published every day in more than 40,000 scholarly journals, and this number has been growing by an average of 13 percent a year over the past decade (Howarth, 1986). At this rate, it doubles every five years!

All professions have experienced the same information avalanche: there is an accumulated pool of more than 3.3 million American legal decisions growing at the rate of more than 30,000 a year (Knapp, Vandecreek, and Zirkel, 1985); 2 million U.S. patents with more than 70,000 new ones issued each year (U.S. Bureau of the Census, 1985, p. 539); more than 8 million chemical substance records, with 400,000 new substances added each year (CAS, 1987); 700,000 pages of working papers produced by the U.S. Congress every year—and the rest of the federal government easily topping that figure (Hoover, 1982); plus thousands of financial statements and reports produced every day by corporations and organizations.

The sheer volume of available information means that the

average professional needs help in finding relevant information for professional updating, even within increasingly narrow areas of specialization. The task of keeping up with this information overload, of identifying the few items that any single person will want to scan, cannot be effectively or efficiently done by manual methods such as card catalogues, printed indexes, or abstract journals. The speed with which new information is developed in some fields makes rapid updating imperative. Professionals cannot use information that they do not know exists and cannot therefore find.

Online Database Systems. The online information dissemination systems (or online retrieval systems) available to today's researcher have many things in common but enough unique characteristics that the first approach must be to learn something about each. Retrieval systems were developed to apply a single computer software logic to a variety of data collections. Some database producers try to ensure that their information is made available on as many systems as possible, while others have chosen to restrict themselves to one or two that offer software or other enhancements particularly compatible to the content of their data collections.

The choice of database is the first consideration for a user, followed by the choice of a specific retrieval system that offers access to the selected database. Many professionals may know of one (or even more than one) database that is relevant to their interests, but they may not realize that the number of online databases is increasing by about 30 percent each year. According to the January 1987 Cuadra directory there were 3,369 separate online databases available from 528 different services; in 1980, the numbers were 400 and 59, respectively (*Directory of Online Databases*, 1987). The Cuadra directory is updated quarterly; other directories include those by Williams (1985), Knowledge Industry (1984), and Hall and Brown (1983).

Databases may be classified as follows:

1. Reference databases (which point the user to a document, organization, or individual for additional information)

    a.   Bibliographic (citations, and sometimes abstracts, of journal articles, books, documents, reports, dissertations, patents, conference proceedings, newspaper items)

    b.   Referral (references, sometimes with abstracts, of unpublished information referring users to audiovisual or nonprint media, or to organizations and individuals)

2.   Source databases, sometimes called databanks (which contain original source material or specially prepared material)

    a.   Numeric (containing survey data or statistically manipulated representations of data, such as measurements over time for a given variable)

    b.   Text (complete news items, articles, books, specifications, court decisions, computer programs)

Academic researchers historically have used the bibliographic databases more than any other type. Legal researchers have shown an overwhelming preference for full-text databases, and this is reflected in the prominence of databases that cover the field, such as WESTLAW and LEXIS. But, increasingly, databases are developing into combinations of these types, combining handbook-type data, new developments, and bibliographic citations.

Databases may also be further classified according to subject matter:

1.   Discipline-specific databases (such as Sociological Abstracts, Historical Abstracts, Exceptional Child Education Abstracts, Language and Language Behavior Abstracts, America: History and Life, Psychological Abstracts/PsycINFO, MEDIS, LEXIS)

2.   Multidisciplinary databases (such as Biosis, Social Science Citation Index)

3.   Specialized databases (such as Comprehensive Dissertation Abstracts); one of the most successful is OCLC (Online Computer Library Center), which provides cataloging information in a manner that permits individual libraries to

draw the data directly from the system and automatically generate their catalog cards
4. Education databases (such as ERIC)
5. Mass-appeal databases (such as NEXIS)
6. Business and industry databases (such as Dow Jones News/ Retrieval, ABI/INFORM, PREDICASTS)

In 1982, *Online Review* surveyed 276 of the most frequently used databases and found that 150 were in science and technology, 67 in social sciences, 53 were general, and only 6 were in the humanities ("Databases Online," 1982).

Locating the Appropriate Databases. Databases are developed by publishers of printed index and abstract journals, publishers of reports and newsletters, consulting and advisory services, or government agencies. (Many are, in fact, computerized versions of printed abstracts and indexes.) Database producers have not put all their pre-1960s data online; therefore, retrospective searchers may need to use the printed versions as well as online services. However, because of the geometric rate of increase in the number of published articles and books after the 1960s, far more citations are available online than are available only in print. It is estimated that there are now more than 100 million bibliographic items available online (representing about 65 million unique items, because of overlap between databases) and 9 million new items (6 million unique) are being added every year (extrapolating from information in Hall and Brown, 1983).

Databases are accessed either directly from the producers (for example, Mead Data Central's LEXIS and NEXIS and West Publishing Company's WESTLAW) or through vendors, "database supermarkets," that load many databases on their computers, provide the retrieval software, bill the users directly, and pass on some part of the revenue in the form of royalties to the database producers.

The two largest vendors, DIALOG and Mead Data Central (MDC), account for 70 percent of database use and 80 percent of the revenues in the U.S. library and institutional market (see Simpson, 1984). DIALOG offers access to more than 270 databases; MDC provides access to over 200 information sources through the LEXIS and NEXIS services; BRS offers about 130 databases; the ORBIT Search Service offers more than 60.

Each online service vendor provides catalogs and descriptive information about the specific databases offered. In addition, there are compilations and indexes to the publicly available databases, both in print and electronic versions. The latter, databases of databases, may be most useful to the experienced user and knowledgeable librarian. For one who is making a first approach to this process, the printed versions should be consulted.

The decision of whether to use one database or many will depend on the user's degree of competency in a subject and the nature of the research topic. An expert who wants to retrieve every bit of information will typically search as many databases as possible to maximize recall; the "typical competent professional" may well be satisfied with using a core database to provide a representative sample. When both core and related databases are searched, coverage is increased and a variety of perspectives on the same topic are retrieved.

The nature of the research topic is also a consideration. A multidisciplinary topic will require the use of more databases than one that clearly falls within one academic discipline (see Tenopir, 1982). A specialist in health science, for example, will rely on Medline and Excerpta Medica as core databases, but if the topic is cancer, must also search CANCERLIT, CANCERPROJ, and CLINPROJ; if the subject is psychiatry or psychopharmacology, PsycINFO and Mental Health Abstracts (NIMH) must be consulted; if education or training is involved, ERIC will be rewarding; and both IPA (International Pharmaceutical Abstracts) and RINGDOC (Pharmaceutical Literature Documentation) would be necessary for a search involving drugs.

In this connection, an interesting study was conducted by librarians at the University of South Dakota (Evans, 1980). They found that 4 databases (ERIC, PsycINFO, Dissertation Abstracts Online, and Social Scisearch) were sufficient to answer almost half (49.5 percent) of all requests; adding seven more databases answered 75.5 percent of requests; and with 129 databases, 94.7

percent of requests were satisfied. On average, a search using only one database retrieved 61 percent of information; if a second database was added an additional 27.3 percent was captured (raising the total to 88 percent); and if three databases were used, 98 percent of information was retrieved.

The vast majority of use is concentrated in a relatively small number of databases. According to Advanced Technology Libraries (1983), the ten most frequently used databases among academic and public libraries are ERIC, ABI/INFORM, MED-LINE, PsycINFO, Chemical Abstracts, Management Contents, Compendex, NTIS, Magazine Index, and Predicasts.

Evaluating Databases. The proliferation of databases, their constantly changing forms, contents and services, and especially differences in indexing have made it increasingly difficult for a user to determine which database to search and which search strategy to employ. Often several databases must be searched for completeness. There are numerous chances for error and cost ineffectiveness. Vendors now offer cross-file services (such as DIALINDEX in DIALOG and CROS in BRS) that provide the searcher with information about the total number of postings for any particular subject term in each database distributed by the vendor. (When a record uses the selected term as a descriptor of subject matter, it is "posted" to the term. Using the ranked order of postings to a set of specific terms can help the user select one or a combination of databases for subsequent searching.)

In selecting databases, the searcher must consider a number of factors: (1) content coverage and time span, (2) time lapse between the item as it appears in the primary source and in the database, (3) indexing and coding practices, such as free-language keywords, controlled thesaurus, or hierarchical vocabularies, (4) size and growth rate (Williams, 1975), and (5) whether it provides citation only, citation and abstract, or full text. It is more difficult to evaluate database quality—the frequency and seriousness of errors such as misspellings, inconsistency in assigning index terms, incorrect dates and pages, updating delays. These quality factors can certainly affect results, however; one study of recall of journal titles in one database showed that only 21 of 256 items were recovered using the Journal Title search because of variant spellings and missing information (Keck, 1981; see also Norton, 1981).

Advantages and Disadvantages of Computerized Searching. Computerized searches are more exhaustive and more up to date than manual searches — and much, much faster. Many cost-benefit analyses comparing on-line databases and manual retrieval methods have been carried out (for example, Elcheson, 1978; Elman, 1975; Naber, 1985; Turner, 1983). They are *unanimous* in finding that the computer's speed, comprehensiveness, and currentness make computerized searching more cost effective and time efficient.

A few examples will suffice to illustrate the computer's greater speed and comprehensiveness. Hoover (1976) reports that 160 hours were spent on a manual search to retrieve 622 citations on six topics for NOAA's Environmental Research Laboratory, while online searching took only 15 hours to find 2,234 citations on the same six topics. In another comparison, he found that an online search (completed in 45 minutes with an offline print) cost $47, while a manual search required 22 hours (plus typing), and cost $250. Agricultural researchers at the University of Florida estimated they saved nearly 9,000 worker-hours a year by using the National Agricultural Library's CAIN (Cataloguing and Indexing, now called AGRICOLA [AGRI-Cultural On-Line Access]) database. When an exhaustive computerized patent search avoids a legal suit, or being alerted to a new medical procedure helps to save a life, the savings derived from such electronic searching are incalculable.

The cost of a well-planned search is quite reasonable, and it is generally considered to be within the economic reach of most professionals engaged in professional updating. The average search time is about ten minutes (producing an average of twenty-four printed citations) and costs about $30 (Sandy, 1982). This includes computer time, data communications and offline printing, but not terminal rental, telephone expenses, or personnel costs. Increasingly, professionals are budgeting for computer searches and libraries are including computer searching as a part of standard reference services.

However, there are some disadvantages. In addition to the increased cost of a computerized search over a manual search (if the time to pursue the latter is given a low value), the need to include an intermediary in the process is frequently deplored by the information seeker. The intermediary, usually a librarian, is familiar with the command languages used by the various system vendors, the characteristics of the available databases, and the best retrieval methods.

A successful search requires a balance of these skills with the user's knowledge of the specific discipline, its terminology, and the boundaries of the area to be investigated. In spite of this, it is sometimes both inconvenient and ineffective to rely on the interpretation of one's information need by another who may have little knowledge of the topic content. A poorly conceived or poorly executed search can result in many irrelevant references and unnecessary costs, so a successful outcome may depend on effective communication between intermediary and user.

Obtaining the original source document after securing references from a bibliographic search can introduce problems and delays regardless of whether printed or computerized secondary services are used. Unless the professional has convenient access to a major research library, interlibrary loans—a process that can take weeks—are necessary. This may be somewhat ameliorated in the future (but at unknown incremental cost), as more full-text documents become available online and as more online databases offer document delivery services. (Data Courier currently offers twenty-four-hour delivery of articles from some 600 business journals referenced in ABI/INFORM.)

Options: Intermediary or Direct? Presently, most end users conduct searches through intermediaries (usually a librarian), though there is a growing trend toward direct service as improved computer software makes some searching simpler. The intermediary will usually have a better idea of the different databases available, their costs, coverage, and which search strategy will work best considering the specific information requirement.

Hurt (1983) found that searches conducted with both end user and intermediary present provided the greatest amount of satisfaction. End users searching alone had difficulty with protocol, search logic, database user aids, and hardware. Although end users lack the training and experience of librarians or other intermediaries, they generally have few problems searching for specific information, for questions that are not complex, or in cases where comprehensiveness is not required. If the end user is only an occasional user of a database, it may be more time and cost efficient to use an intermediary.

Still, the trend is toward end-user searching. More and more individual information seekers are choosing to be trained to assume the intermediary role and search computerized information sources using home or office terminals (see Kolner, 1985; Stabler, 1984). The individual user of the retrieval systems need not learn to be proficient in more than one (or possibly two), and, since both the subject matter terminology and the applicable databases are already familiar, good results can be quickly obtained. (More discussion of the individual's role in online searching can be found later in this chapter.)

Very recent developments in software (known as gateways) provide users — novice and experienced searchers alike — with uncomplicated menu-driven access to almost all available systems and databases (see for examples Williams, 1986a). Gateways are software connections between discrete information vendors, each having very different retrieval systems and command languages. To access the unique databases residing on another system, the user can sign on to the home system and then be transferred via the gateway. Some gateways permit searching of the remote system databases through the home system command language, thus eliminating the requirement to learn more than one. Others simply open the telecommunications pathway, and searching on the remote system must be done using its specific protocols. Still others provide a menu-type interface that permits the user to exercise a multiple choice or yes/no set of options that are translated to a search strategy using the appropriate command language.

For instance, the National Federation of Abstracting and Information Services (NFAIS) has sponsored the development of EASYNET, which allows access to many different vendors without learning different search protocols and without signing contracts. EASYNET accepts access by either a terminal or a microcomputer, and the system has the capability of choosing the appropriate database for novice users. A valid credit card is required for billing purposes.

Another very recent development is the use of compact disc technology for data storage and retrieval. Known as CD-ROM (Compact Disc–Read Only Memory), this application, joining the power of the personal computer with the storage density of the compact disc, has produced a very user-friendly access to electronic databases. Intended for the personal computer user (an individual, or series of individuals), the software is specifically designed to accommodate the novice user and usually requires no specialized training.

Developing a Search Strategy. Whether the end user searches a database directly or through an intermediary, online or on compact disc, the first and most critical step is to define a search strategy. The professional who intends to use database searching for knowledge updating must be very clear about the specific focus of each strategy. It is easy to be distracted by related concepts, resulting in a very broad search that does not retrieve the desired material.

Since search requests and purposes vary so widely, it is difficult to develop general rules. However, there are some common features:

1. If using an intermediary, the searcher should write out a narrative statement of the problem or topic, and if at all possible should be present when the search is carried out. The interactive process works best when the search is dy-

namically modified to meet unanticipated needs for alternate terminology or synonym identification.

2. The search topic should be conceptualized, broken down into logically independent components, using Venn diagrams and Boolean logic if possible. Generally the search should start with the most specific aspect and only if sufficient information is not found should it be allowed to expand.

3. Database vocabulary aids should be used as much as possible: print or online thesauruses, classification codes, CA Search Registry numbers for chemical compounds, use of system functions such as EXPAND, NEIGHBOR, ROOT, EXPLODE, TREE.

4. Interactive capabilities should be used. Mapping out a complete search strategy, stacking commands, and requesting an offline printout are successful only if the subject, the database, and the search system are all very familiar. Usually results should be questioned, retrieved sets sampled, searches broadened, narrowed or reoriented, significant terms selected for incorporation into the strategy, and search strategy restructured or modified as it proceeds.

5. System capabilities should be used. Some systems allowed the searcher to copy index terms into search statements without retyping, or use truncation to allow for spelling variations (such as "behav" for behavior, behaviour, behave, behaviorism, behaviors).

Searching can usually be conducted using either controlled vocabulary or natural language (sometimes referred to as free text or uncontrolled). Controlled vocabulary encourages greater precision, and it is not necessary for the searcher to think of every synonym or every permutation of a phrase in order to retrieve relevant documents. Frequently an author may discuss a subject without using a subject category. This is especially true in case studies. For example, a story about new holiday destinations for young American couples might never make use of the term *life-style*, yet an indexer would probably apply the term and thereby make it retrievable to someone researching changing life-styles. Controlled vocabularies are frequently hierarchical in structure, incorporating the broader, narrower, and related terms. Some vendor systems display relevant portions of the vocabulary during search strategy formulation. Not all databases use thesauruses, but for most of those that do, printed versions are published and available for assistance in searching.

Natural-language searching of the words in the title and other text portions of the record (such as abstract, enriched title, key phrase, document text) can result in significantly greater recall as well as access to concepts too new or too rare to be incorporated into a controlled vocabulary. Free-text searching, as implemented by the online systems, is enhanced by commands that can select words adjacent to each other, within several words of each other, and spelled in a variety of ways. For many purposes, a search strategy that combines the precision of controlled-vocabulary indexing with the comprehensive recall of free-text retrieval produces optimum results.

Why Not Do It Yourself?

The greatest barriers to online or computer assisted literature searching by the individuals who actually plan to use the retrieved references are the lack of computer literacy and the resistance to acquiring it. Despite the enormous numbers of personal computers now in use, most are in office situations and many professionals have never considered using them themselves. Even word processing for correspondence and manuscripts is most often done by support staff from the professional's hand or typewritten drafts.

In professions where computers are routinely used during the educational process for calculation, problem solving, or display of graphic material, computer literacy may be relatively high and resistance relatively low. Research among practicing psychologists and psychiatrists indicates that even within the very small portion who own or lease microcomputers, use for purposes other than word processing is quite small (Levitan, Willis, and Vogelgesang, 1985; Levitan and Willis, 1985).

Still, those engaged in a structured approach to professional updating should work toward overcoming any resistance that may exist and learning the process of online searching. Most organizations that produce databases conduct training seminars and workshops for both new and experienced searchers. Such training may or may not require a fee. Information on this point, as well as on schedules and locations, can be obtained by contacting one or more of the databases known to be central to a particular discipline. Online system vendors also conduct training in the efficient use of their retrieval software. While vendor training may not deal with specific databases in any great detail, database training may not contain enough information on particular vendor systems. Users should make the choice between vendor and database training; both kinds of instruction should be a definite option.

On the other hand, there are a number of aids that make it easier for users to perform their own searches, including several good guides to the effective use of databases that walk the reader through the use of microcomputers, search procedures, command language on the major databases, logon and logoff procedures on the major vendors, the use of thesauruses, and so forth (for example, Borgman, Moghdam, and Corbett, 1984; Jones, 1987; Li, 1985; Meadow and Cochrane, 1981). The Institute for Scientific Information (ISI) has developed a menu-driven software package that performs automatic logon and logoff, uploads search strategies, and downloads search results from DIALOG, BRS, SDC, NLM and ISI Search Network (Stout and Marcinko, 1983). Computer-assisted instruction has been used successfully in several locations to train and assist users to conduct their own bibliographic searches (Marcus, 1982; Meadow, 1982). One of the major problems encountered by individuals doing their own searches is that more time is spent on the computer and therefore the costs are higher. Software packages such as Search Helper for use with Information Access databases on DIALOG can help lower cost (Ensor and Curtis, 1984; see also Shepherd and Watters, 1984; Stout and Marcinko, 1983).

As more and more individuals have begun to try online

searching for themselves, the system vendors have responded with specialized services. DIALOG offers Knowledge Index and BRS offers After Dark (see Ojala, 1983; Tenopir, 1983), both simplified versions of the regular retrieval software, available only during evening and weekend hours at greatly reduced rates. These services provide detailed manuals that encourage self-teaching and the very low rates encourage a trial-and-error, learn-it-by-doing approach.

What You Can Expect in the Future

Because of the rapidity of change in information technology, there have been frequent predictions of coming revolutions in the way information is processed and retrieved. More often than not, these revolutions fail to materialize. Current updating tools such as printed indexes and online bibliographic databases can be expected to be available for many years to come, but along with these there will also be new forms of presenting and retrieving information. The changes are likely to be incremental and gradual, however, rather than revolutionary.

The changes that are likely to take place within the next decade or two can be summarized:

1. Online services will provide full text of the selected documents electronically on request.
2. Professionals will conduct more of their own searches.
3. Databases will be queried in natural-language form.
4. More searches will provide direct answers to questions (rather than bibliographic references or raw data). (Much of this section is based on Howitt and Weinberger, 1984, and Lancaster and Smith, 1980).

Online Availability of the Full Text of Documents. The cost of converting printed text to electronic form, storage costs, and telecommunication costs will continue to decline. Soon, cost effectiveness will no longer favor the printed version (Tenopir, 1984). A vital prerequisite to a truly online document is the ability to mix text and graphics in the database and in the retrieved product.

Most information transmission employs the ASCII coding structure (American Standard Code for Information Interchange). One drawback to ASCII is that it is not now possible to mix text with graphics. Two developments should allow this to happen in the near future. One is the development of software packages that can translate ASCII into pictures. Another is the development of VIDEOTEX, a more elaborate code, that permits the mixing of text and graphics over telephone lines. (TELETEXT is a version that uses television signals, but does not allow two-way interaction). Already some business databases (such as MarketFax and Telichart) mix stock-market or economic statistics with color-coded charts and graphs.

The electronic journal, in which authors submit manuscripts via computer, editors and reviewers access the manuscripts through computers, and accepted manuscripts are sent by computer to photocomposers for computerized typesetting, will also increase in popularity. Prior to typesetting, the full text is available in machine-readable form, already accessible and needing only retrieval software to deliver selected items to the user. This movement of the information overload from print to electronic form will demand the development of new indexing tools, compilation schemes, and evaluative services designed to help users locate the most valuable sources.

Searches Conducted by Users Rather Than Intermediaries. Professionals will conduct more of their own searches, because it will be both cost effective and easy to do so. A number of technological developments, in addition to the continued decrease in access hardware costs, will contribute to the trend.

Transmission media are expected to become increasingly diverse and flexible, making access to databases possible from practically anywhere. Fiber-optic networks, cable, and FM sideband are all presently being explored as means of transmitting data. DATASPEED, for example, transmits stock quotes over an FM pocket-radio terminal.

Gateway services will make it increasingly easy for users to locate the information they want without needing to know either specific databases or systems. The searcher will perceive the world of information as one seamless source accessible by a single set of commands. For example, the Chemical Substance Information Network (CSIN) allows the user to access several databases using one set of menus.

Natural-Language Queries. It will soon be possible to communicate with the computer in written form but using everyday phrasing. This development is critical to mass acceptance of computerized information. When questions can be posed to the computer in the same manner as to a human expert, barriers will drop. Some software has already been developed, such as INTELLECT by Artificial Intelligence Corporation. There has also been some success in translating text to speech, but computer recognition of human speech is more difficult and is expected to require more time to develop.

Direct Answers to Questions. The next few years will see the development of intelligent screens, a software filter that can evaluate whether a given fact or document is the one sought. Current search strategies use proximity: retrieve a document if you find this term within n words of that term. Intelligent screens go beyond this to the semantics surrounding the word, and precision greatly increases.

A precursor of this development is Selective Dissemination of Information (SDI). SDI is essentially an electronic clipping service: customized computerized profiles of a researcher's interests are stored so that new items of information will be routed to him or her as soon as such information is added to a database. Future developments will introduce much more sophistication. Intelligence Report Generation, for example, will produce custom-tailored reports on any topic. Bell Labs has already developed ANA to produce natural-language stock-market reports from raw numeric data.

These technological developments will result in a restructuring of the way databases are organized. Not only will information become more complete and more timely, it will be more tailored to individual needs. Databases will make available more obscure and abstruse information that may be valuable only to a very small number of users.

They will also spur the development of knowledge bases, an unstructured set of facts along with rules of inference for determining new facts. Whereas databases store information in a uniform, structured way with, for example, a dictionary of individual terms and pointers to the records in which they are found, knowledge bases will be able to create their own paths between terms and records; they will be able to infer information from a few basic facts. Raw data loaded into a computer will become expert systems able to diagnose illness, custom-tailor investment strategies, produce hypotheses for historical correlations, and much more. Increasingly, databases will not only present data, but will make connections between data. Users may be able not only to identify experts in a given field, but through computer conferencing, they may be able to gather information directly from experts.

It is never wise, however, to postpone today's action for tomorrow's possible technological assist. Most of the future developments will be accessible, at least initially, only to those who are already in a position to take advantage of them. Learning to use today's tools effectively is still the best preparation for the even greater refinement and precision to come.

References

Advanced Technology Libraries. "Dialog Overwhelmingly Favorite On-line Services Vendor Among Libraries." *Advanced Technology Libraries*, 1983, *12* (2), 1–2.

Bates, M. J. "Locating Elusive Science Information." *Special Libraries*, 1984, *75* (2), 114–120.

Borgman, C. L., Moghdam, D., and Corbett, P. K. *Effective Online Searching: A Basic Text*. New York: Marcel Dekker, 1984.

CAS. *CAS—An international resource*. Columbus, Ohio: Chemical Abstracts Services, 1987.

"Databases Online." *Online Review*, 1982, *6*, 353–390.

Directory of Online Databases. New York: Cuadra/Elsevier, 1987.

Elcheson, D. R. "Cost Effectiveness Comparison of Online and Manual Retrospective Searching." *Journal of the American Society for Information Science*, 1978, *29*, 56–66.

Elman, S. A. "Cost Comparison of Manual and On-line computer Literature Searching." *Special Libraries*, 1975, *66* (1), 12–18.

Ensor, P., and Curtis, R. "Search Helper: Low Cost Online Searching in an Academic Library." *Reference Quarterly*, 1984, *23* (3), 327–331.

Evans, J. E. "Database Selection in an Academic Library: Are Those Big Multi-file Searches Really Necessary?" *Online*, 1980, *4* (2), 35–43.

Hall, J. L., and Brown, M. J. *Online Bibliographic Databases Directory and Sourcebook*. London: Aslib, 1983.

Hoover, R. E. (ed.) *Online Searching Strategies*. White Plains, N.Y.: Knowledge Industry Publications, 1982.

Hoover, R. E. "Patron Appraisal of Computer-aided Online Bibliographic Retrieval Services." *Journal of Library Automation*, 1976, *9*, 346–347.

Howarth, J. D. "New Technologies—How They Are Likely to Be Absorbed into the Economy and Culture over the Next Twenty Years." *Journal of the Market Research Society*, 1986, *28* (4), 355–362.

Howitt, D., and Weinberger, M. I. *Inc. Magazine's Databasics, Your Guide to Online Business Information*. New York: Garland Publishing, 1984.

Hurt, C. D. "Intermediaries, Self-searching and Satisfaction." Proceedings of the Fourth National Online Meeting. Medford, N.J.: Learned Information, 1983.

Jones, J. A. *Databases in Theory and Practice*. Blue Ridge Summit, Penn.: TAB Professional and Reference Books, 1987.

Keck, B. L. "An Investigation of Recall in the ABI/INFORM Database When Selecting by Journal." *Online Review*, 1981, *5*, 395–398.

Knapp, S. J., Vandecreek, L., and Zirkel, P. A. "Legal Research Techniques: What the Psychologist Needs to Know." *Professional Psychology: Research and Practice*, 1985, *16* (3), 363–372.

Knowledge Industry Publications. *Data Base Directory: 1984–*

1985. White Plains, N.Y.: Knowledge Industry Publications, 1984.

Kolner, S. J. "The IBM PC as an Online Search Machine, Part 1. Anatomy for Searchers." *Online*, 1985, *9* (1), 37–42.

Lancaster, F. W., and Smith, L. C. "On-line Systems in the Communications Process: Projections." *Journal of the American Society for Information Science*, 1980, *31* (3), 193–200.

Levitan, K. B., and Willis, E. A. "Barriers to Practitioners' Use of Information Technology Utilization: A Discussion and Results of a Study." *Journal of Psychotherapy and the Family*, 1985, *1* (1–2), 21–35.

Levitan, K. B., Willis, E. A., and Vogelgesang, J. "Microcomputers and the Individual Practitioner: A Review of the Literature in Psychology and Psychiatry." *Computers in Human Services*, 1985, *1* (2), 65–84.

Li, T. *An Introduction to Online Searching*. Westport, Conn.: Greenwood Press, 1985.

Marcus, R. S. *Investigations of Computer-aided Document Search Strategies*. Cambridge: Laboratory for Information and Decision Systems, Massachusetts Institute for Technology, 1982.

Meadow, C. "A Computer Intermediary for Interactive Database Searching, Evaluation." *Journal of the American Society for Information Science*, 1982, *33* (6), 357–364.

Meadow, C. T., and Cochrane, P. A. *Basics of Online Searching*. New York: Wiley, 1981.

Naber, G. "Online Versus Manual Literature Retrieval." *Database*, 1985, *8* (1), 20–24.

Norton, N. P. "'Dirty Data': A Call for Quality Control." *Online*, 1981, *5*, 40–41.

Ojala, M. "Knowledge Index: A Review," *Online*, 1983, *7* (5), 31–34.

Sandy, J. "Online Databases Vital for Scientific Research." *Science*, 1982, *216* (4553), 1367.

Schmittroth, J., Jr. *Abstracting and Indexing Services Directory*. Detroit: Gale Research Company, 1982–83.

"Selected Database Retrieval Services Ranked by Customer Count," *IDP Report*, July 16, 1987, p. 3.

Shepherd, M. A., and Watters, C. "PSI: A Portable Self-contained

Intermediary for Access to Bibliographic Database Systems." *Online Review*, 1984, *8* (5), 451–463.

Simpson, J. W. "Mead Data Central: Positioned for the Future," *Online Review*, 1984, *8* (5), 413–420.

Stabler, K. "The Continuation of Librarians as Intermediaries." Proceedings of the Fifth National Online Meeting. Medford, N.J.: Learned Information, 1984.

Stout, C., and Marcinko, T. "Sci-Mate: A Menu-Driven Universal Searcher and Personal Data Manager." *Online*, 1983, 7 (5), 112–116.

Tenopir, C. "Distribution of Citations in Databases in a Multi-disciplinary Field." *Online Review*, 1982, *6*, 399-419.

Tenopir, C. "Dialog's Knowledge Index and BRS/After Dark: Database Searching on Personal Computers." *Library Journal*, 1983, *108* (5), 471–474.

Tenopir, C. "Full-text Databases." *Annual Review of Information Science and Technology*, 1984, *19*, 215–246.

Turner, J. A. "Bibliographic Databases Help Researchers Gather Data More Efficiently." *Chronicle of Higher Education*, 1983, *27*, 27–28.

U.S. Bureau of the Census. *Statistical Abstract of the United States: 1986.* (106th ed.) Washington: U.S. Government Printing Office, 1985.

Williams, M. E. "Criteria for Evaluation and Selection of Data Bases and Data Base Services." *Special Libraries*, 1975, *66*, 561–569.

Williams, M. E., (ed.). *Computer-readable Databases. A Directory and Data Sourcebook.* Chicago: American Library Association, 1985.

Williams, M. E. "Transparent Information Systems Through Gateways, Front Ends, Intermediaries, and Interfaces." *Journal of the American Society for Information Science*, 1986a, *37* (4), 204–214.

Williams, M. E. "Who Uses Business Databases?" *Proceedings of the International Convention for Information Management, INFOBASE '86.* Herausgeber: Bertelsmann Datenbankdienste GmbH, 1986b.

14

Sherry L. Willis
Samuel S. Dubin

Maintaining
Professional Competence:
Directions and Possibilities

In this final chapter, we will attempt to integrate and synthesize issues raised in various chapters, and will suggest future directions in the study of professional competence.

This book was organized to focus on three issues related to maintenance of professional competence: (1) antecedents and moderators of professional competence; (2) definition, measurement, and assessment of competence for midcareer professionals; and (3) maintenance of professional competence across the work life. Models or approaches dealing with all three have been presented; here we will summarize these approaches.

Antecedents and Moderators of Professional Competence

Chapters One and Two present models dealing with the antecedents or moderators of professional competence. Both models assume that maintenance of professional competence involves an interaction between personal and environmental factors. However, the models differ in their level of analysis of environmental factors.

Fossum and Arvey (Chapter Two) focus at a meta-level on

the impact of market and organization factors that lead to a loss of competence as a result of skills obsolescence. They maintain that although loss of competence occurs at the individual level, the antecedents or mediators of loss of competence must be studied at the level of the marketplace and the organization. Skills obsolescence can occur as a result of changes in supply and demand in the marketplace and resulting organizational changes. Changes in the marketplace and ineffective responses by organizations can lead to a professional's current skills being rendered obsolete.

Dubin's model (Chapter One) also assumes that mainte- nance of professional competence involves an interaction of person and environment. However, Dubin is concerned with the factors in the *immediate* work environment that foster or inhibit the maintenance of competence.

Consideration of factors that influence professional com- petence at both the meta- and micro-level is useful. Further development of such models is needed to consider how changes at the macro-level (marketplace) influence the work climate at the micro-level (immediate work environment). For example, do downturns in the marketplace, leading to leaner organizations, reduce the layers of organizational hierarchy, thereby fostering communication and collaboration among professionals within the organization (see Chapter Ten)? Collegial collaboration has been shown to facilitate maintenance of professional competence.

At their current stage of development, both the Dubin and Fossum and Arvey models are *unidirectional*; person and environmental factors and their interaction are described as antecedents of competence or its loss. However, if these models were expanded to describe the process of maintaining compe- tence over the entire work life, then *reciprocal* relationships would need to be considered. For example, the individual's level of professional competence (or incompetence) at career entry has been shown to be related to the status of the position held at midcareer; higher-level positions held in midcareer, involving complex job demands and resource-rich work environments, foster the enhancement of professional competence at later career stages. Longitudinal research is required to examine these reciprocal relationships. In related research, the reciprocal relationship between intellectual ability and the complexity of the work environment has been studied longitudinally by Kohn and Schooler (1983).

While both the Dubin and Fossum and Arvey models identify personal and environmental factors that may serve as antecedents or mediators of professional competence, they do not describe the processes or mechanisms involved. That is, the models do not define the processes by which certain work-environment variables affect maintenance of competence. Expectancy theory, as described in Chapter Eight, is an example of a model that does specify mechanisms by which the work environment affects motivation to remain competent. Farr and Middlebrooks maintain that features of the work environment can foster or inhibit professional development efforts by influencing the professional's expectancies and beliefs about the efficacy and the rewards of remaining competent.

It is important to note that expectancy theory is a cognitive model: it is the professional's *beliefs* about the work environment, rather than its actual features, that affect motivation. While expectancy theory is useful in describing how the work environment affects motivation to update, it does not explain how these expectancies and beliefs develop. That is, the theory does not explain the personal characteristics (such as personality traits or IQ level) that influence the development of these expectancies, or individual variability in the types of rewards professionals value. Future research will need to focus on these issues.

Multidimensional Models of Competence

There has been much debate about whether professional competence is best defined and measured as a unidimensional construct (a unitary, global phenomenon), or a multidimensional construct, involving several distinct components or domains of competence. Chapters Four and Five illustrate that while both unidimensional and multidimensional models of competence are supported by empirical data, multidimensional models are particularly useful in assessing competence in midcareer professionals.

A multidimensional approach to competence is useful for at least three reasons. As individuals continue in their professions across the work life, their knowledge, skills, and abilities become increasingly differentiated and specialized. The wide variety of experiences accrued by midcareer results in development of competence in various domains. Second, a multidimensional approach is useful in identifying those components most in need of updating. It is likely that a midcareer professional's level of competence varies across different skill domains. Because of a supportive work environment or deliberate updating activities, a midcareer professional may remain competent in some dimensions but less competent in others.

Third, a multidimensional approach is useful in examining how specific factors in the work environment support or limit performance in particular competence domains. A number of work-environment factors have been identified as affecting competence (see Chapters One, Five, Eight, and Ten). However, there has been little research examining the relationships between particular dimensions of competence and specific environmental factors. For example, collaboration with peers may be particularly useful in maintaining an up-to-date knowledge base, while work assignments involving a variety of responsibilities may be more useful in maintaining clinical problem-solving skills.

Approaches to Maintaining Professional Competence

In Part Three, we considered three approaches to maintaining professional competence. The first focuses on features of the work environment that foster maintenance of competence. Some of these factors are discussed in Chapters One, Eight, Nine, Ten, and Eleven. The second approach emphasizes training in the skills identified as deficient; see Chapter Twelve. The third approach involves self-directed updating, requiring accessing the most current literature on a given topic. Given the current knowledge explosion, it is becoming increasingly imperative that professionals use electronic databases (see Chapter Thirteen).

The first approach, focusing on work environment factors, has received the most attention in the current literature. Four work environment factors were identified (see Chapters Eight, Nine, and Ten): challenging work assignments, communication and collaboration among peers and with management, organizational flexibility, and institutional commitment to professional development.

Challenging Work Assignments. A challenging work assignment is complex, and requires the professional to combine previously acquired knowledge and skills with newly developed information and proficiencies to solve the problem. Collaboration with peers in other disciplines or segments of the organization should be encouraged to foster the acquisition of the new information and skills required to complete the assignment successfully. The work environment should allow sufficient autonomy so that the professional has control over the scheduling and sequencing of task components. Some risk taking needs to be encouraged to permit exploration of alternative solutions and to foster creative thinking. Generation of a report on the completed assignment can be useful in summarizing and documenting the work process and the findings from the assignment.

Communication and Collaboration Among Peers and with Management. Exchange of information and ideas among peers not only facilitates the successful completion of complex work assignments, but also serves as a powerful mechanism for maintaining and enhancing professional competence (see Chapter Ten). Open communication and exchange between professionals and management can clarify each party's goals and expectations about work responsibilities and the level of competence required to carry them out. They also increase the likelihood that professionals will be involved in institutional decision making, thus enhancing their motivation and sense of control and autonomy. Control and autonomy are important features of challenging work environments, and are particularly valued by mid-career professionals (see Chapter Nine).

Organizational Flexibility. Flexible organizational structures and management policies permit reassigning personnel and work responsibilities so that a professional's current competencies are used well and new ones are developed through new and challenging work assignments. Organizational flexibility is needed to permit open career paths, which have been shown to be useful in maintaining and enhancing professional competence in mid-career (see Chapter Nine).

Institutional Commitment to Professional Development. The professional's intrinsic motivations about work have been shown to be particularly important in maintaining competence (see Chapter Eight). Organizations need to demonstrate awareness of and involvement in the individual's own particular professional goals and concerns.

Future Directions

The study of maintaining and enhancing competency in mid-career is in its infancy. As the chapters in this volume demonstrate, current theories and research on the topic are relatively narrow and discipline specific. However, we believe the time is ripe for a major thrust into this field. Given the aging of our society and work force in the next century, greater attention must be given to maintaining the competence of midcareer professionals. The chapters in this book suggest at least five areas in which further work is needed.

1. *Definition and measurement of professional competence.* Some professions have attempted to assess the competence of midcareer professionals (recertification exams, for example) and to develop continuing education activities *before* defining the nature of competence within the profession. However, each profession needs first to define the major tasks and responsibilities (such as role delineation) performed by a competent member of that profession. The knowledge base and skills necessary

to perform these basic tasks and responsibilities must be identified, and instruments must be developed that validly measure the knowledge base and skills.

2. *Development of interactive assessment procedures.* There is growing consensus that assessment of professional competence in midcareer requires evaluating what professionals can *do*, rather than solely what they know. Thus, assessment procedures will need to assess performance of critical tasks and skills. Maatsch (Chapter Four) emphasizes the importance of assessing the practicing professional's clinical problem-solving skills. Static, paper-and-pencil measures of substantive knowledge are considered insufficient. An interactive, simulation approach to assessment is being advocated. Melnick's description (Chapter Six) of the CBX model, a computer-based simulation procedure, highlights both the advantages and limitations of current assessment procedures. Further work is needed to develop assessment procedures that maintain the face validity and interactive nature of current simulation models, but circumvent their excessive cost and time requirements.

3. *Comprehensive approaches to professional competence.* There is need for integrating current approaches into more comprehensive models of professional competence. Current theory and research are fragmented. Some have focused on the antecedents and moderators of professional competence and its maintenance. Others have contributed valuable work on conceptual and measurement models. Innovative approaches to the maintenance of professional competence have also been examined. There is need now to examine linkages between these diverse perspectives and to move toward comprehensive models that examine the relationship between antecedents of competence, the assessment of competence, and approaches to its maintenance. In particular, there is need to relate measuring and assessing competence to approaches for maintaining it.

4. *Collaboration among groups within a profession.* Comprehensive approaches to the maintenance of professional competence will require greater collaboration and teamwork among diverse subgroups within a profession. The Practice Audit Model described in Chapter Seven highlights the utility of a

collaborative approach among academics, regulatory agencies, and professional organizations. There is need for further collaboration among academics involved in education and training and in the generation of new knowledge and technologies, regulatory agencies charged with formal assessment of competence via certification and recertification exams, and professional organizations and continuing education personnel involved in the delivery of professional development programs. In addition, management needs to remain informed about developments and activities in the professions of its people.

5. *Awareness of the impact of the nonwork environment.* While there has been considerable focus on the features of the work environment that foster or limit professional competence, little attention has been given to the impact of the nonwork environment. Some recent attention has focused on young professionals and issues such as maternity leave and child care. However, recent research in the social sciences indicates that there is significant spillover from family to work and vice versa for the midcareer professional (Crouter, 1984; Tosti-Vasey and Willis, 1988). Issues such as elder care, financing of children's college education, and dual-career marriages are of particular concern to senior and midcareer professionals. Future research on environmental factors that affect competence will need to consider the broader environmental context in which the professional functions.

These five issues represent only a limited subset of topics that need to be addressed as this new field continues to develop. Study has already begun in some professions. Since maintenance of competence is of concern in every profession, there is the potential for interdisciplinary contributions and collaboration. Part of the challenge lies in exchanging ideas and research findings across disciplines. It is our hope that this book has contributed to this exciting and vital venture.

References

Crouter, A. "Participative Work as an Influence on Human Development." *Journal of Applied Developmental Psychology*, 1984, *5*, 71–90.

Kohn, M., and Schooler, C. *Work and Personality: An Inquiry into the Impact of Social Stratification.* Norwood, N.J.: Ablex, 1983.

Tosti-Vasey, J., and Willis, S. L. "Issues of Professional Obsolescence and Updating Among Senior Faculty." Paper presented at the annual meeting of the Gerontological Society of America, San Francisco, Nov. 1988.

Index